'Over decades in broadcasting I've ¦
associations with many of the world's most courageous and insight-
ful foreign correspondents. In the case of Afghanistan it has been
an honour to have the contributions of Andrew Quilty. He sees
with clarity and uses words wonderfully, spoken or written, as this
heartbreaking book attests.'

Phillip Adams

'A compelling, thought provoking must-read about the days leading
up to the fall of Kabul and its aftermath from a photo-journalist
who spent almost a decade living in Afghanistan, capturing both
its sorrows and its joys.'

Yalda Hakim

'Raw, immediate, compassionately written and deeply sourced,
Andrew Quilty's unique account of the debacle in Kabul is essential
reading for anyone seeking to understand how a two-decade effort
collapsed in defeat, why it happened so quickly, and what the
resulting deadly chaos meant for ordinary Afghans.'

David Kilcullen

August
in Kabul

America's last days in Afghanistan

ANDREW QUILTY

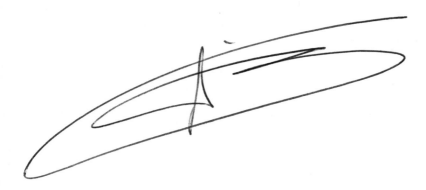

MELBOURNE
UNIVERSITY
PRESS

MELBOURNE UNIVERSITY PRESS
An imprint of Melbourne University Publishing Limited
Level 1, 715 Swanston Street, Carlton, Victoria 3053, Australia
mup-contact@unimelb.edu.au
www.mup.com.au

First published 2022
Text and images © Andrew Quilty, 2022
Design and typography © Melbourne University Publishing Limited, 2022

Text design and typesetting by Megan Ellis
Cover design by Philip Campbell Design
Cover image by Andrew Quilty
    Taliban fighters tour the tarmac inside Hamid Karzai International
    Airport the day the Taliban took full control of the facility after the final
    American military aircraft departed in the early hours of the morning,
    ending their 20-year presence in Afghanistan. 31 August 2021
Printed in Australia by McPherson's Printing Group

A catalogue record for this
book is available from the
National Library of Australia

9780522878769 (paperback)
9780522878776 (ebook)

Contents

Author's Note

Many of those whose stories are told in this book either held positions in the former Afghan Government administration and security forces or are viewed with hostility by the Taliban for other reasons. Many are still hiding from the Taliban.

I was initially sceptical of the risk posed to former government and security officials by the incoming Taliban. Promises of immunity came from the highest echelons of the Taliban administration and, despite the warnings almost every Afghan I spoke to gave me about distrusting the Taliban's conciliatory rhetoric, I wanted to believe them. I wanted to believe that an end to the war also meant peace for those who had suffered not only for the past 20 years but, as Afghans are quick to correct America-centric commentators, the past 42.

During the months spent researching and writing this book, I have come to realise the scepticism was well founded. The majority of those whose stories are featured have been actively searched for and threatened by the Taliban. Several continue to move houses regularly and have cut off contact with friends and relatives—effectively eliminating their own existence as Afghans—to lessen the chances of being found. In many cases it hasn't worked. Family members have been detained and threatened; homes and property have been seized. At the time of writing, several Afghans whose stories are told in this book continue to try to leave the country. They believe a failure to do so will result in their ultimate capture. At best, they believe that will mean the forfeiture of their freedom, and at worst, their lives. They are justifiable beliefs.

For that reason, the names of many who feature in this book have been changed, as have those of their family members and acquaintances. Using pseudonyms did not, however, limit the scrutiny under which I placed their accounting of events.

While I was in Kabul from 14 August until the final US evacuation aircraft departed in the early hours of 31 August, and had my own experience of those tumultuous days, the eight weeks of reporting I conducted on the ground thereafter revealed to me how different each individual's experience of that same period was.

This book could have comprised the extraordinary experiences of any number of the millions of Afghans who survived or perished during that month in high summer in the Afghan capital. Those whose stories I ultimately focused on were chosen because, to me, they represented a cross-section of experiences from within an infinite spectrum.

For those in positions of power who feature in the pages that follow, their actions and behaviour have necessarily been the subject of great scrutiny since long before August 2021 and will continue to be for years to come. The desire for senior officials who oversaw the collapse of the Afghan Republic to diminish their own culpability and launder their legacies after the fact poses a risk for a journalist trying to piece together events through those who shaped them.

While some scenes described in this book and the real motivations for the actions of individuals are difficult or impossible, respectively, to verify, I have tried to qualify those parts with language that indicates as much. That does not mean that anything a source told me, even with qualification or caveat, was considered worthy of inclusion; far from it. If I found an account implausible, I did not include it. Moreover, the deceit would factor into my assessment of everything else the source shared.

Some sources' accounts were so implausible, so self-eulogistic, that, despite their proximity to key events, their accounts were excluded altogether. On the other hand, understandable bitterness for the massive personal losses suffered as a result of the republic's collapse also tainted the credibility of some sources.

More forensic retellings of the last days of America in Afghanistan will be written as information is declassified and others who were involved come out of self-imposed public exile. This book represents the most accurate accounting of events—collected as they happened and in their immediate aftermath—that I can offer.

Maps

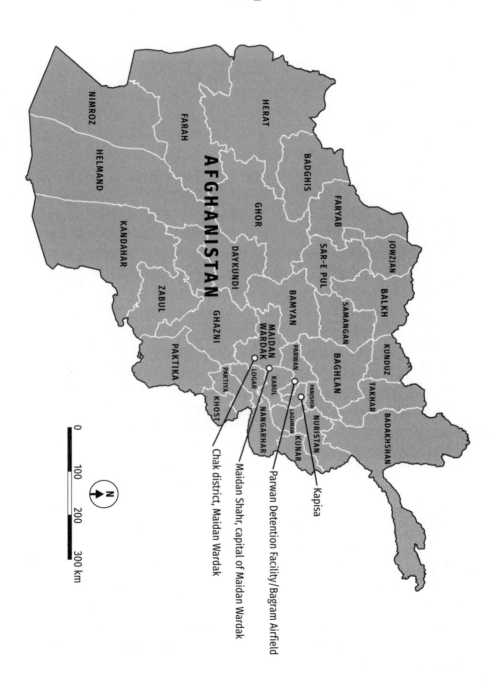

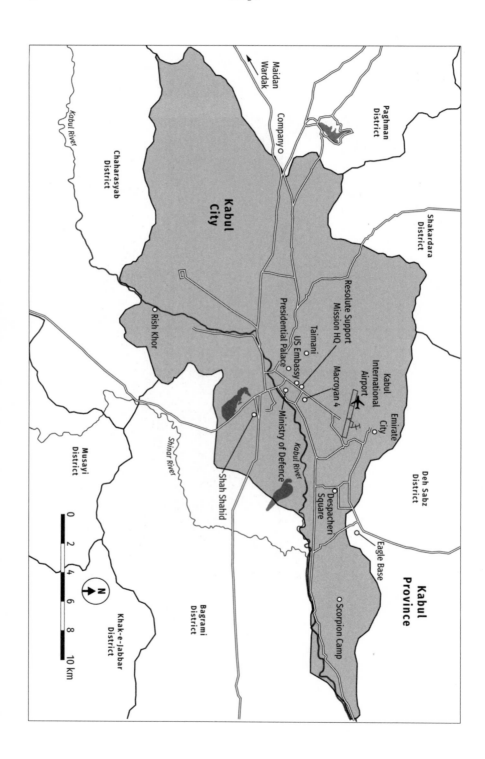

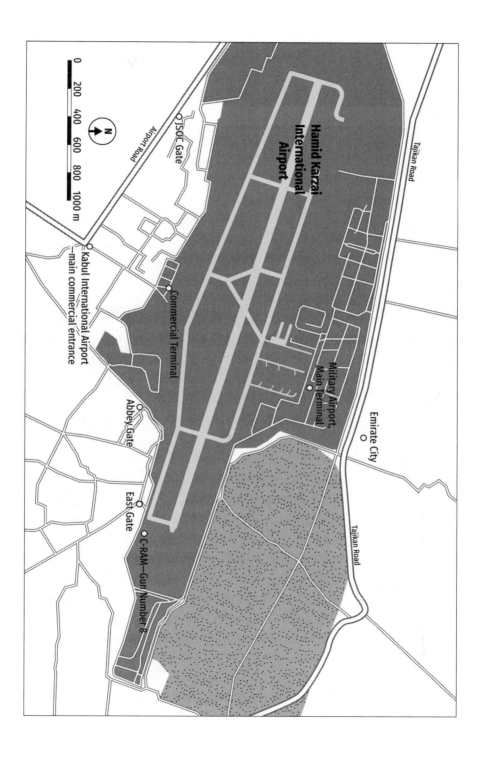

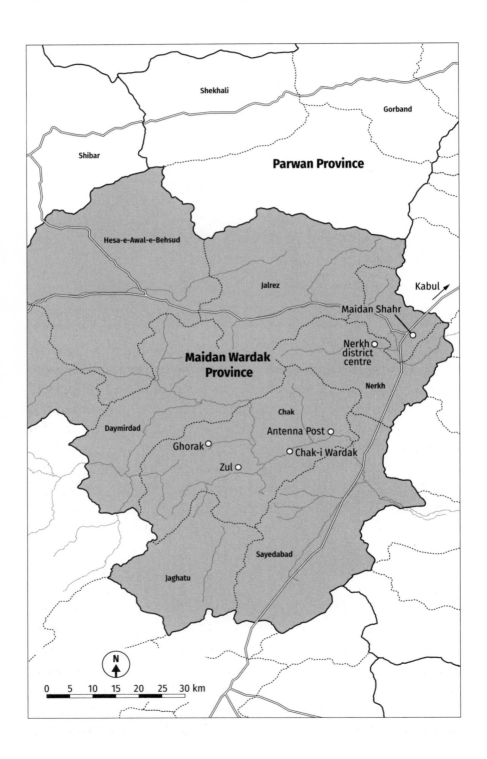

Prologue

The boarding of flight EK640 from Dubai to Kabul on Saturday 14 August 2021 was eerily routine. There were only 50 or so passengers—almost all Afghan—for a plane that seated around 400, but as anyone with the means was *leaving* Kabul, it was hard to understand why those already out would want to fly in. Yet passengers and cabin crew alike appeared unconcerned. An Afghan-American passenger told me he'd come from the United States for a wedding. The flight attendant packing an overhead storage bin told me the crew would stay in Kabul overnight and depart, as scheduled, on the return flight the next day. Had they not seen the news over the past week?

I'd been in France to attend the wedding of two friends, one French, the other British, who'd met in the Afghan capital a few years earlier while working for a UK development organisation. I was one of only two guests at Ed and Flore's nuptials who was still based in Kabul, the other being Ayesha Wolasmal, a Norwegian-Afghan friend. Having lived in Kabul for several years, summer weddings in the south of France of 'Kabul couples' like Ed and Flore—often multinational, multilingual pairings—had become an almost annual event. This was partly because southern France was brimming with idyllic wedding venues, but also because it was a relatively central destination for the kinds of peripatetic friends that couples who meet in a place like Kabul tend to collect.

For the dwindling number of foreigners who remained in Kabul—those of assorted vocations but similar ideals: aid and development workers, political advisors, analysts, human rights lawyers, journalists—these weddings enabled time, often overdue, well away from the low-frequency disquiet that distinguishes a city that, while not at war per se, hosts regular, isolated *acts* of war. The weddings also served as de-facto reunions for foreigners who had once lived in Kabul but had since dispersed. Some, like Ed and Flore, who'd built a business in London from the foundations they had laid in Afghanistan, or the journalists who continued to write about the country from afar, maintained meaningful, if somewhat dissatisfying, connections. They'd often describe being glad to be out of Kabul while lamenting an intangible deficit of purpose that tinged life in the Western capitals in which they'd resettled.

For any congregation of Kabulians, past or present, however, leaving Afghanistan the *land* was always easier than departing Afghanistan the *subject*. Like schoolmates or military veterans, conversation would invariably turn to the topic in which we had a great depth of shared experience. Afghanistan, it's fair to say, had shaped our identities in the way a school or a combat deployment might, but which a country itself rarely does. That was the way it felt to me, in any case, as I approached my ninth summer in the country.

‹ ›

Before I left Kabul for France in late July 2021, I spent a couple of mornings taking photographs and conducting interviews at Afghanistan's central passport office. That month, more than 5000 Afghans were being issued passports each day. It was an entirely manual process that required several hours-long visits to the office, in person, and a fee of 5500 Afghani[1]—roughly A$90, or half the starting monthly salary for an Afghan police officer. I'd arrive before sunrise to find a queue beginning at the entrance to the passport office and bending around several blocks of Karte 3, a residential neighbourhood in southern Kabul. Those at the front of the queue would tell me they'd been there since about 2 a.m.

The only other time passports had been in such high demand since the US-led war began in 2001 was in 2015. Then, facing deteriorating safety and economic hardship after the International Security Assistance Force had handed responsibility for Afghanistan's security over to the Ashraf Ghani government, hundreds of thousands made perilous bids for better lives in Europe. Of those, 180 000 Afghans made months-long journeys, enduring detention, persecution and poverty, and made it to Europe where they applied for asylum. They were the lucky ones. Untold numbers tried and were detained and deported back to Afghanistan, shot and killed by Iranian border guards, or perished in the Mediterranean while crossing from Turkey to Greece.

The difference, this time, was the kind of people leaving, or thinking about it. I asked Margo Baars, then the deputy country director for the International Organization for Migration in Afghanistan, about what their staff in the border provinces were seeing. 'Previously, it was mostly young men,' she said, suggesting that families would stay behind in Afghanistan and wait for the earnings a brother, son or father could send back via Western Union or *hawala* cash-transfer networks.

It was also the type of families that were thinking of leaving. While being escorted by a policeman into the passport office one morning, I heard my name called. At the door of a shop where applicants paid to have forms and passport photos printed was Alishah, an actor and film producer I'd last seen in 2019 when we were both working on *When Pomegranates Howl*, a film that Australia would nominate as its entry for Best International Feature Film in the 2021 Academy Awards. Alishah was carrying his physically disabled child, waiting to begin the next step in the convoluted process. Seeing him, one among the urban populace who had embraced and flourished with the opportunities on offer after the

Taliban were toppled in 2001, it struck me how much, and how quickly, things had changed.

For 20 years, a grinding conventional war had been fought by a highly skilled and equipped multinational force and an ad-hoc guerrilla army with small, improvised weapons almost entirely in rural Afghanistan. As a journalist, I was among a small group who tried to steer readers away from Kabul, from which, after international forces ceased all but the most covert of combat operations, the vast majority of reporting on the war was conducted. We tried to relate the experiences of Afghans in more remote areas who not only suffered the everyday depredations of life on the front line but saw few of the benefits promised by the international community and the government it supported in Kabul. While we never excused perfidious Taliban military tactics, such as the way they defined non-combatants in government and other sectors unrelated to security as legitimate targets, nor their authoritarian methods of control, to a small cadre of writers, this explained, to a large extent, why the group had not only been impossible to defeat but were now on the verge of total victory.

Now, however, for the first time in the war, it was the residents of Kabul and other provincial capitals for whom that war was coming. Most of them had encountered terror and violence and lost friends or family to bombings or more sophisticated attacks, but never before the constant fear of stray bullets, mortar or artillery shells, air strikes or homemade mines, that rural dwellers had experienced.

And, while the foreign journalists who lived in Kabul often travelled to rural areas for reporting purposes, it was mostly Afghans living in the capital, and to lesser extents the other provincial capitals—educated and multilingual—who we befriended and with whom we worked. The war was no longer just a series of stories to be told; it was life. The people affected weren't characters, but friends and colleagues.

In the days leading up to Ed and Flore's wedding, I tried to articulate my realisation, and the increasingly personal impact the changing battlefield dynamics in Afghanistan were beginning to have, in an article for *The Intercept*, an investigative American media outlet. I found myself writing in the first person, a point of view my early documentary photography mentors in Australia railed against. The unspoken mantra 'You are not the story' reverberated in my ears each time I typed 'I'. In this case, however, it was almost unavoidable. By July, friends, colleagues and complete strangers, for whom a Taliban takeover was now all but inevitable, were asking my foreign friends and me for help in leaving the country. Wahid, the long-time manager of the house where I lived; journalists and translators with whom I'd worked in a dozen provinces; even government soldiers—as the Taliban closed in, they were all looking for a way out. The imperatives of community were already beginning to take precedence over those of journalism. They would also contribute to my last-minute decision to return from France before the Taliban took control.

‹ ›

Thursday 5 August was the first day in a long weekend of celebrations planned for Ed and Flore in the village of Aups, halfway between Marseille and Nice, in Provence—in the 1850s, republican loyalists had mounted a failed resistance against Napoleon here. But conversation soon turned to Afghanistan. The vast majority of the country was in Taliban hands; the shock aroused by news of one rural district or another falling to the Taliban in May or June had long since become commonplace. Now, with several major cities surrounded by the Taliban, and government forces faltering, the dominant questions were which of Afghanistan's 34 provincial capitals would be the first to fall, how quickly would others follow, and how long could Kabul and the government hold out?

On 6 August, Taliban fighters moved into Zaranj, the capital of the remote south-western province of Nimroz. Scarcely a shot was fired. Having been routed in fighting to the north, government forces in Zaranj had either retreated to the district centre of neighbouring Chahar Burjak or shed their uniforms and escaped across the nearby border into Iran. The next day, before the wedding guests had congregated beneath the stone campanile of the church of Saint Pancrace, the Taliban claimed control of Sheberghan, the capital of the northern province of Jawzjan.

For Wolasmal and me, sharing a house in Aups with another former foreign Kabul resident, and being the only wedding guests who still lived in Kabul, the initial shock of the news was tempered by the fact that the two captured cities had limited strategic significance. The momentum that had aided the cascade of districts to fall to the Taliban had still not impacted the battle for the cities. But we were overlooking the impact that the fall of the two cities would have on the morale of government forces across the rest of the country. Jawzjan was the home of Abdul Rashid Dostum, one of Afghanistan's staunchest anti-Taliban military figures, and his fiercely loyal militia. If the Taliban could capture Jawzjan, what hope was there of stopping them anywhere else?

At the reception that night, as thunderheads threatened in the distance, the Kabul crowd was spared a night of ruminating over Afghanistan. At dinner, like all the family and social groups, the Kabulians were deliberately split up and scattered among the 250 guests seated on either side of dining tables joined end-to-end and arranged like the spokes of a wheel. Later, music and dancing pulsed through a circus tent until dawn.

The next day, Sunday 8 August, I was offered a ride back to Paris with Sune Engel Rasmussen and Danielle Moylan, a couple with whom I'd worked, travelled and shared a house, and some of my fondest memories, in Kabul before they left in 2017. As we drove north, over a string of Danielle's favourite 90s pop hits, I called out the names of each new province to fall as they appeared on my phone. We made it to Macon, halfway to Paris, for dinner, by which time the Taliban had taken three more provinces, all in the north. Reaching Paris on the Monday, I stayed with another Kabul journalist couple, Solene and Joris Fioriti, with whom I'd planned to spend a week while waiting for an important meeting in Amsterdam on 19 August.

Requests from Afghan friends for help in leaving the country were now becoming increasingly urgent. Afghan journalists were departing their home provinces for Kabul and being housed in hotels paid for by international media support organisations. Wahid had passports for his family, but no visas. After trying to get them at the Iranian, Uzbek, Tajik and Turkish embassies, he sent me a screenshot of a message he'd written in Dari and Google-translated. 'I am convinced that nothing can be done. I know that the Taliban [will not keep their] word and after a while they [will] start their investigation,' he said, inferring that his fate would be sealed once the Taliban discovered he had worked for foreigners. Sajjad Husseini, a friend who was at risk because of his public profile, and who had translated and guided Solene and me in July while working on a story in Bamiyan province, drove through a gauntlet of Taliban-controlled territory to collect his family's passports from Kabul. At the same time, several of his relatives were having their applications for Iranian visas rejected. Undeterred, the relatives travelled to the border and crossed illegally. Seconds after clambering over a wall into Iran, Husseini's mother-in-law was shot and killed by border guards.

I was in daily contact with Victor Blue, an American freelance photographer and friend who was staying in the house I shared with Nanna Muus Steffensen, a Danish journalist—she was seeing family in Copenhagen at the time—and a dog named Mushu. Vic had been working on and off in Afghanistan for more than a decade and had had enough close calls over the years to know if, or when, it was time to panic. 'I dread looking at my phone each morning nowadays,' I wrote to him on 9 August. 'Yeah,' he replied. 'It's grim. It's going down fast.'

The following day, I asked Vic whether things were as bad as they appeared from afar. 'Could be looking at weeks not months,' he said. I felt my chest constrict as I waited for more messages. 'If Mazar falls, the word is that some of the embassies are going to pull out,' he wrote. 'If that happens, so will some of the bureaus.' But he was also reassuring. He and I, like many foreign freelance journalists who had spent long periods in Kabul, trusted our own instincts more than those of the risk-averse embassies and media organisations, for whom decisions regarding security were based more on the erroneous protocols of consultants far away in London or New York City than on-the-ground realities. When I asked him how he was feeling, he replied, 'I'm all good. Just want to make some pictures. Staying open to the possibilities.' But he went on to say that 'today is the first day you can kind of feel it in Kabul. Taxis loaded with luggage. Small crowds outside the British Embassy trying to get in. I guess the hotels are completely full.'

I was beginning to doubt whether keeping my appointment in Amsterdam was prudent. The momentum of the Taliban advance on Kabul now seemed irreversible, and going to the Netherlands looked more and more as though it would preclude me, for better or worse, from being in the capital when they arrived at the gates. What happened after that was unknowable. American diplomats in Doha, Qatar, were frantically trying to avert a battle for the city, but in Kabul, as embassies burnt documents and made plans to evacuate, Taliban fighters and the Afghan Government's remaining security forces were preparing for war.

At midday on 12 August, I booked flights leaving Paris on the 14th and arriving in Kabul the following day. 'I think that's a good move,' said Vic. 'It's cracking up here.' By that afternoon, another three major provinces had fallen: Herat, Kandahar and Ghazni.

I'd barely slept the night before. My mind raced and my neck and shoulders had seized. A friend sent me a voucher for a massage. The masseuse pointed towards a small package on the table and left the room. After an unsuccessful attempt at fitting the face mask, I realised it was, in fact, a disposable G-string. I bought a pair of black Levi's to replace a pair whose seat had worn through, two portable hard drives and a stack of notebooks to take back to Kabul. During dinner at a Japanese restaurant in The Marais, Hanae Boughdad, a girlfriend with whom I'd lived in Kabul in 2018 and who had bought me the massage that morning, urged me to change my flight. Considering the rate at which government security forces were collapsing, she was worried airlines would stop flying into

Afghanistan or that the airport in Kabul would close altogether. Over sashimi and beer, I cancelled a meeting with my photo agency the following day and brought my flight forward 24 hours: I would leave the following night, 13 August.

I emptied my suitcase of all but the essentials, stuffing what I'd brought to France for those few weeks into another bag and leaving it at the Fioritis'. At this point, I figured there was a good chance that once I made it to Kabul I'd have to leave—or try to— soon after, and that when I did, anything I left behind would not be waiting for me once the violence and chaos—the unknowable that was to come—had faded.

Solene, who was close to completing a memoir on her time in Kabul, was anxious to get there as well. Joris, her husband, was dumbfounded. The two had spent years working in Afghanistan, developed a deep affinity for the region and the community-mindedness of Islamic culture, and raised their son, Ismail, in neighbouring Pakistan. But returning at such a volatile and unpredictable moment, as provinces continued to fall—five more that day, maybe six—Joris thought was reckless. In the end, circumstances in Kabul took the decision out of their hands: in 48 hours, Hamid Karzai International Airport would close to commercial flights.

News organisations were struggling to keep up with what was beginning to look like the imminent collapse of the Afghan Republic. Vanessa Gezari, my editor at *The Intercept*, and I had struggled in recent days to shape an article I'd compiled over the preceding month, in a way that would be relevant by the time it was published. 'No Exit: As the Taliban Seize Cities Afghans Are Trapped in an American-Made Fiasco' was online by the time I reached Charles De Gaulle Airport.

‹ ›

Because of Kabul's dramatic topography, pilots flying from Dubai skirt past the capital and head towards Jalalabad. Over the district of Surobi, they bank to the left above an expanse of barren ridges

and rivulets that, from a port-side window seat, looks like the
veins of a dead leaf. As you descend towards the runway from the
more gradual eastern approach, walled-off plots for unbuilt houses
appear at the foot of the mountains that fringe the capital. Pul-i
Charkhi Prison, shaped like the table arrangement at Ed and Flore's
wedding, can be seen to the south, then, to the north, Eagle Base, a
little-known Central Intelligence Agency facility that its operatives
would partially destroy with explosives in the weeks to come.

A Customs official stamped my visa with as little interest as
Customs officials stamp visas the world over. Through the X-ray
I took my carry-on and the two bottles of liquor I, as a foreigner
and a non-Muslim, was permitted, and which I suspected would
be important in the coming weeks, then walked out onto the concourse where an 'I ♥ Kabul' sign greeted arrivals. Aside from Rahmat
Gul, an Associated Press photographer who was taking pictures of
people departing, there was no portent of the chaos that would transpire there in 24 hours, and which would continue for the fortnight
that followed.

The traffic on my way in from the airport on the afternoon of
14 August was heavier than usual, but the taxi driver avoided the
usually bustling commercial areas, creating an illusion that Kabul
was running in the fitful, jerry-rigged way it had been before I'd
left. At home, I was greeted first by Mushu, then Wahid, who,
despite my travel updates, I suspect hadn't believed I would return.
I hugged Puk Damsgård, a Danish journalist who had stayed
with us previously and had arrived the day before. (Her bosses in
Copenhagen would demand her departure from the country within
24 hours.) Mushu barked and leapt. He was a street dog whose
temperament was manageable in our large compound in Kabul
but who wouldn't have gone a week in my home town, Sydney,
before sinking his teeth into the leg of a jogger or a child. If I left,
I knew I'd have to euthanise him. Puk knew it too, and it added to
the nervous ambience.

As journalists, we were in the middle of what would be the
biggest story in Afghanistan since the US invasion 20 years earlier.

There had never been so much 'news' to cover, nor so great a demand for it, yet we were all somehow paralysed, unable to divert attention away from the impending collapse of the city and the community we'd become emotionally invested in over the years, and towards our professional instincts. I resented the journalists who had flown into the capital on short-term assignments. They could shoot and report for 12 hours a day and elude any sense of responsibility towards the locals on whom they relied for transport, translation, meals and accommodation. Those of us who lived in Kabul, or who had put in time before the world's attention once again demanded it, were always going to fare better if circumstances necessitated an escape. Our status as foreigners—a term that, in Afghanistan, courts a discordant combination of derision and deference—would see us at the front of queues at embassies or first on the tail-ramps of aircraft. And, despite the fact that, as insurgents, the Taliban had coveted the capture of foreigners for propaganda or financial purposes, the dynamics of conquest and the dictates of the Pashtun moral code provided a measure of assurance that we would be at least relatively safe the moment the Taliban had total control of Afghanistan, if and when that came. And yet, despite the discomfiting privilege, as Afghan journalist friends and colleagues looked for ways out for themselves and their families, the 'story', as journalists refer to the lives and circumstances of those upon whom we report, was now almost too close to cover.

I rode my motorcycle to see for myself what Vic had described to me in the days before. I made a lap of Shahr-e Naw Park, a block of winding paths and pine trees only a few minutes from home. Hundreds of families had moved ahead of the Taliban's advance in the north and built flimsy shelters with scarves and blankets that kept out little more than prying eyes. Hundreds crowded around the entrances to banks, desperate to withdraw their savings. I wiggled my motorcycle through pedestrians on the footpaths to avoid the gridlocked roads. Jim Huylebroek, a Belgian photographer who had lived in Afghanistan for six years and was fluent in Dari, pulled up on an old racing bicycle and told me he was determined to stay through whatever was to come—he had acquired a couple of guns to protect his house and housemates from looters. Because of my own doubts, I craved the self-assurance of another long-time Kabulian. And despite my doubts, the same sense of solidarity that had compelled me to come back would, I knew, be crucial in the days and weeks ahead.

That night, Kate Clark, a former BBC correspondent and now one of the most respected foreign analysts on Afghanistan, invited me over for dinner. Over an omelette, she told me about the opportunistic raping and looting that had punctuated periods of security vacuum in Afghan cities in the past. She was booked to fly out in three days' time. At 2.30 a.m. the next morning, she received a call from the British Embassy: if she wanted to be evacuated, she had to be at the Baron Hotel, a heavily barricaded compound close to the airport, at 4 p.m. that day. Concerned about violence, chaos, crowds and her Afghan colleagues, whom she thought should be at home with their families rather than looking after her, she arrived at the airport at 7 a.m. It was 15 August.

PART I

Early August

'Everything Was out of Control'

1

Antenna Post, Chak District, Maidan Wardak Province

ntenna Post was one of four hilltop outposts manned by less than 100 soldiers from the Afghan National Army's (ANA) 203 'Thunder' Corps 5th Brigade, 2nd Battalion. The crest, 10 kilometres west of the turn-off from Highway One, and about two hours' drive south of Kabul in Maidan Wardak province's Chak district, caused its single road to bend before it continued deeper and deeper into Taliban territory. The Logar River, which guided the road, ran beneath it on the southern side. Locals called the area Dasht-e Langar—*dasht* meaning desert and *langar*, anchor—perhaps for the 90-degree hook in the river where it passed through the townships, but no-one knew for sure.

Of the four army bases in Dasht-e Langar, Antenna Post housed the highest-ranking soldier and the heaviest weapons, and, being on a hill overlooking the main arterial road through the district, it was of the greatest strategic importance to the combatants. The red-and-white mobile phone tower that gave Antenna Post its name stood inside a walled-off area. An engineer lived onsite and, as per Taliban orders, the disobeyal of which would result in the destruction of another tower in an area they controlled, turned the transponder on for a few hours each morning, then switched it off for the remainder of each day.

In May 2021, the 23 soldiers inside Antenna Post found themselves surrounded by Taliban fighters camped out in the two green, cultivated belts that met below in a three-way junction. They were being battered by high-explosive, rocket-propelled 'spears' from a tripod-mounted SPG-9 recoilless gun designed to disable tanks, by 82-millimetre mortar rounds, and by a DShK—a belt-fed, Soviet-era heavy machine gun. The only safe way in or out for the soldiers was by helicopter, at night. The only way they could be resupplied with food, water and ammunition: helicopter. But the air support provided by the Americans in years past had dried up because of political decisions made thousands of kilometres from Dasht-e Langar. The Afghan Air Force, whose fleet numbered 180 aircraft, was overstretched and unable to offer the fighters inside Antenna Post a reprieve from the daily Taliban assaults.

On 26 May, with supplies and hopes dwindling at Antenna Post, a young soldier named Amanullah walked to the base entrance, pulled aside a tangle of razor wire, and ran. The soldiers on guard fired as he skipped down the rocky hillside. Taliban fighters standing behind an abandoned home at the base of the hill stepped into the open and returned fire at the sentries from whom Amanullah was running.

For months, the Taliban had been trying to persuade the soldiers to surrender. On offer was not only amnesty but cash for any weapons they absconded with, and travel money with which to return home. Far from being a spontaneous decision on Amanullah's part, his family, from the northern province of Kunduz, had made contact with the Taliban's leadership in Maidan Wardak and orchestrated the escape.

Out of the line of fire from Antenna Post, Amanullah sat on the back of a fighter's motorcycle and rode towards a group of Taliban, who embraced him and hung garlands of colourful plastic flowers around his neck. A fighter filmed the scene, and by the next day the desertion had been shared across the country. It was a propaganda triumph for the Taliban and triggered doubt in the minds of yet more Afghan soldiers, whose determination to fight for their country was beginning to waver.

⟨ ⟩

Captain Jalal Sulaiman had been flown into Dasht-e Langar a week before Amanullah surrendered to the Taliban. He was to command the four bases there, and the Chak road that wove between them, from Antenna Post. Although he'd grown up in neighbouring Logar province, he wasn't familiar with the area or its people, but he had as much combat experience as any other Afghan of 33 years. After graduating from the Marshal Fahim Military Academy in Kabul in 2015, Sulaiman was sent directly to what had long been Afghanistan's most violent district, Sangin, in the country's most violent province, Helmand, where, he says, 'I was very happy fighting.'

Sulaiman had been stationed inside the ANA's 215th Corps 2nd Brigade headquarters in Sangin, a postage stamp of government control in a district, and a province, at the time otherwise largely controlled by the Taliban. Although bigger than Antenna Post, Camp Hamidullah—or Forward Operating Base Nolay, as it was known before the US Marines handed it over to the ANA in 2014[1]—was also virtually surrounded. 'The Taliban were firing mortars and rockets and we'd be hiding in our bunkers,' says Sulaiman. 'It was like this for a year.'

At the end of 2017, backed up by recently deployed American Marines and air support, Sulaiman was part of an operation to recapture the handful of smaller bases surrounding the brigade headquarters. As well as relieving pressure on its soldiers, it was hoped the operation, codenamed Maiwand Nine, would expand the government's territorial claim and, even more ambitiously, enable residents to vote in the country's parliamentary elections the following year.[2] 'For one year we tried to recapture the bases around the brigade headquarters in Sangin,' says a friend of Sulaiman's, and a commando himself. 'But we failed and decided just to focus on holding the headquarters.'

Nonetheless, Sulaiman had survived. And in the ANA, by 2020, as morale and recruitment sank, survival alone was ample criteria for promotion.

From Sangin, Sulaiman was first sent to the 5th Brigade headquarters of the ANA's 203 Corps, in Maidan Wardak's capital, Maidan Shahr. He spent less than a month there, familiarising himself with Chak district and formulating a plan to clear the surrounding area of Taliban and re-establish supply routes between the four bases soon to be under his command. Doing so, he thought, would enable supply convoys to not only reach his bases in Dasht-e Langar but also Chak-i Wardak, the Chak district centre, another 10 kilometres west, and the soldiers in the bases protecting it.

On 17 May 2021, Sulaiman boarded a helicopter in the head-quarters in Maidan Shahr and set off for Saqila Tolai, one of Antenna Post's three satellite outposts, and the one best suited to helicopter landings. Also onboard were rations: 100 kilograms of rice, 50 kilograms of flour, 25 kilograms of milk powder; bottled water, he was assured, would come later. The ammunition included crates of bullets for AK-47s and their larger PKM machine guns, and mortar rounds. The flight took only 10–15 minutes and, once the Black Hawk had landed inside Saqila Tolai, the supplies were hurriedly unloaded by the soldiers; the helicopter crew had become accustomed to coming under fire while supplying besieged outposts, and they wanted to spend as little time on the ground as possible. After two days at Saqila Tolai, Sulaiman stripped off his uniform, packed it in a duffel bag with some supplies, and, after the soldiers in the four outposts overlooking the road had confirmed the route was free of Taliban, sped 2 kilometres east to Antenna Post in a white Toyota station wagon the ANA kept in Dasht-e Langar for unexpected occasions.

There were several buildings inside Antenna Post's fortifications: family homes requisitioned by soldiers who had coveted the hill's strategic value years before. The walls in Sulaiman's room were painted turquoise and white. A layer of sandbags covered the roof to protect against mortar and rocket fire. His platoon of soldiers filled the remaining rooms. Another standalone structure, at the highest point in the outpost, had been converted into a mosque, complete with a head-high alcove—a *mihrab*—that faced west, in the direction of Mecca, and a shelf recessed into the same wall where a copy of the Qur'an was kept. Also inside Antenna Post were five *zarbati* commandos from one of the ANA's two Mobile Strike Force Vehicle Brigades. A month earlier, the commandos had fought their way through an ambush a few kilometres east, on the Chak road, and been separated from the vehicles behind them. With no guarantee of air support to shepherd them out of Chak, the commandos had been too afraid to leave once they reached Antenna Post. So they'd stayed, sleeping in converted shipping containers, or in the cramped confines of the heavily armoured Mobile Strike Force Vehicle—angled to deflect blasts and projectiles rather than absorb them—that gave the unit its name.

It didn't take one of the Taliban's daily attacks for Sulaiman to understand the precariousness of life in his new outpost. The soldiers he'd been sent to command were exhausted, dirty and, worst of all for a commander of troops, dispirited. After US President Joe Biden's April announcement of a final withdrawal date for international forces, the Taliban on the battlefield saw victory as all but assured. And while their leaders continued to placate American State Department officials in Doha, ensuring their counterparts in Defence and the White House carried out the troop extraction, the Taliban's fighters pushed harder and further in rural battlefields.

The neighbouring district of Nerkh had fallen to the Taliban in gruesome circumstances the previous week, and the reports the soldiers were receiving via social media were beginning to indicate a reality few among them had believed would ever eventuate: the Americans were leaving Afghanistan. Earlier in the week, US Central Command had announced that the withdrawal was 6–12 per cent complete. The day after Nerkh was lost, US troops flew their last equipment and personnel out of Kandahar Airfield, the international coalition's base of operations in southern Afghanistan.[3]

The besieged soldiers of Antenna Post were feeling more isolated and more vulnerable by the day.

Soon after arriving, Sulaiman reached out to elders in Dasht-e Langar. Although he assumed the locals had relationships with Taliban as well, building a local network from which he could glean intelligence and on whom he could rely to mediate if it became necessary, he had learned, was a crucial part of soldiering in Afghanistan.

Rahimullah, a 58-year-old farmer, maintained good relationships with most of Sulaiman's predecessors at Antenna Post. He grows apricots and apples in the village on the northern side of the Chak road, adjacent to the outpost. He also runs the local petrol station a kilometre further along the road, in the village of Alishahr. His house is 500 metres from Antenna Post and a kilometre from another outpost that lies to the west, and it is marked by bullets and by shrapnel from exploding mortars fired by the soldiers from both sides. 'Look what we've been living with for 20 years,' he tells me on a visit I make to the area, pointing at scarred walls and windows.

Having a decent rapport with the army was a basic survival tactic. 'I had a very good relationship with all the ANA commanders—they used to come to my petrol station,' says Rahimullah. 'Compared with others who didn't have relations, I suffered very little.' But his outward geniality was a facade for the resentment he held towards the soldiers. 'The ANA were always targeting civilians,' he says. 'They considered all of us as enemies. If a single bullet was fired toward them, all their posts would open fire on this green area even though they knew no Taliban were here. Many left the village because of it. Some joined the Taliban.'

Rahimullah sought permission from the local Taliban commander before agreeing to meet with Sulaiman. When he did, Sulaiman was deferential and acknowledged the wrongdoings of his predecessors in Dasht-e Langar. 'I know the soldiers committed many crimes here,' he said. Sulaiman offered to repay the debts his soldiers owed local shopkeepers and which the previous commander still owed for fuel. 'He was cultivating a relationship,' says Rahimullah, 'because they were under pressure.'

Sulaiman also started working his connections at the Ministry of Defence. If he and his men were to hold Antenna Post and the other outposts in Dasht-e Langar, he would need supplies for his men and aerial bombardments to shake the Taliban from their positions in the surrounding villages. They hadn't always been there, but the availability of American air support had fallen precipitously after the signing in early 2020 of the Agreement for Bringing Peace to Afghanistan, otherwise known as the Doha Agreement, which was allowing the Taliban to expand their territorial control not only in Dasht-e Langer and Maidan Wardak, but across Afghanistan.

On 19 May, Sulaiman received a voice message from Sayed Sayyaf, a friend from their time at the military academy in Kabul. After graduating, Sayyaf had undertaken further training and been posted to a commando battalion in Kandahar before, in 2021, being promoted to work as a bodyguard to the deputy minister of defence, and later as his assistant, in Kabul. 'Congratulations on your new position,' Sayyaf said to Sulaiman.

'This is a very difficult posting,' Sulaiman replied. 'I contacted [the ministry's head of operations] but he's not responding. I will tell you some of the problems which you can help me to fix.' Sulaiman explained the location of his outpost and its dire circumstances. 'There is a lot of fighting and there are six mortar positions targeting the base,' he said, exaggerating, in the hope it would spark a call to action. Sulaiman said he needed an attack helicopter to strike the locations where the Taliban had sunk mortar tubes into the earth. By bracketing their strikes over several days, the fighters had zeroed the weapons, ensuring direct hits on Antenna Post each time they dispatched their deadly payloads. 'We can't even go to the washroom,' said Sulaiman, for fear of being struck by mortar shrapnel. He also needed air support at night, when the Taliban mounted assaults on foot. On more than one occasion, he told Sayyaf, their fighters had come close to breaching the outpost's perimeter.

That same day, Sayyaf found the head of operations in the defence ministry and conveyed the desperate situation inside Antenna Post. The brigadier general was overwhelmed. He raised his palms to the sky and told Sayyaf: 'The whole of Afghanistan is in a bad situation. What should I do?'

Two days later, Sulaiman received welcome news over the radio. That night, he was told, a helicopter would be airdropping supplies, including drinking water. For months, the well and river water on which the soldiers inside Antenna Post had relied had been almost impossible to retrieve. The long-haul taxi drivers who ferried residents between Chak and Maidan Shahr, or beyond to Kabul, had for a long time loathed passing the ANA posts. The soldiers would fire bursts from their machine guns in front of the vehicles, forcing their drivers to stop, then call out to demand the drivers trudge up the hills, collect the empty containers up there, and return them, filled. But as the Taliban's grip on Dasht-e Langar tightened, they were able to find and punish those assisting the ANA, even if unwillingly, and the soldiers found they could no longer force motorists to help. And so they had begun rationing water and even forgoing ablutions before prayer.

On the night of 21 May, as it always did, Antenna Post stood out against the darkness of the Chak landscape like a beacon. Its soldiers had installed floodlights around the perimeter to thwart the telescopic sights equipped with night-vision sensors that some Talibs had mounted on their rifles and used to devastating effect in recent years—although several of the floodlights had been pilfered by Taliban fighters during attempts to overrun the base. The howl of a Black Hawk's rotor alerted Taliban fighters manning heavy machine guns nearby before its silhouette appeared. When it came into view against the refracted glow from the lights above the hilltop, streaks of red—tracer rounds—poured towards the shadow in the sky from Taliban PKM and DShK machine guns. The pilot, who had descended lower than he'd have liked to give the supplies the best chance of staying intact when they crashed to the ground, banked away and pulled on the collective lever to climb, as the crewmen struggled to push the supplies out the side door.

'The helicopter was hovering overhead and we began firing,' says Abdul Haq, a 21-year-old fighter from Chak who was on duty that night. 'The helicopter got scared and tried to avoid the bullets and, when the drop was made, it missed the target by 30 metres.' The Black Hawk disappeared into the darkness and, as its deafening roar withered, the soldiers inside Antenna Post came together to decide how to retrieve the precious supplies. They could see the piles of water bottles encased in plastic beside sacks of grains and flour within a stone's throw of the northern perimeter.

A soldier who had been complaining of thirst for several days bounded over the nearly 2-metre-high Hesco barrier and returned within a minute with two 12-packs of bottled water. By the time he returned to the scattered supplies with another soldier, the Taliban gunmen had repositioned themselves and opened up on the exposed soldiers with machine guns. 'They thought they could go and collect it,' Abdul Haq says. That first soldier was shot in the calf and was unable to climb the hill back to the outpost; a second had already retreated when the gunfire began. Three soldiers inside the outpost, their rifles slung over their shoulders, ran to an armoured humvee, drove through the gate and made a hairpin turn to the left, traversing the cone-shaped hillside without headlights and coming to a stop on the low side of the injured soldier and the spilled supplies, protecting them from the incoming Taliban fire. The two humvee passengers heaved their heavy, armoured doors open against the pitch of the hill and jumped out before the doors slammed behind them. The driver stayed behind the wheel. Rifle rounds pinged off the armour and ballistic windows as the soldiers loaded their injured man through the rear door, followed by the rest of the water, food and cooking oil. The driver, who knew the humvee wouldn't be able to make the turn on such a steep gradient, continued around the base of the outpost, eventually making another hairpin turn to the left, into the relative safety of Antenna Post.

Sulaiman calculated that, along with the supplies he already had, the food and water—two 20-litre jerry cans and 10 12-bottle packs—from the drop would sustain him and his men for a maximum of 20 days. The supply drop had resulted in two casualties, however. As well as the calf wound, a bullet from a DShK had grazed the flank of another soldier, shattering his ribs and leaving a messy wound. He was lucky: had a round from such a large weapon struck him more squarely, his chest would have exploded.

Sulaiman sent a voice message to his friend Sayyaf: 'I have two wounded. The situation is bad. We need a medivac helicopter.' He received no response.

⟨ ⟩

Abudajanah was 25 but had been fighting with the Taliban for 10 years when he joined the mission to capture Antenna Post. It was the first military target in a broader operation whose goal was for the Taliban of Chak to overrun the district administration centre in Chak-i Wardak. There, the government maintained a nominal presence with a single two-storey building surrounded by soldiers in guard towers and, beyond them, four hilltop outposts manned by ANA soldiers, similar to those in Dasht-e Langar. The building sat at the top of a cul-de-sac, along both sides of which war-ravaged shopfronts that had been abandoned a decade ago provided little more than a source of wood for government officials and soldiers, who salvaged timber rafters from their ceilings to burn for heat in the winter.

As with scores of district centres around Afghanistan after the majority of international troops departed the country at the end of 2014, the Ghani government was determined to maintain a presence in Chak. Although the district governor lived mostly in Kabul and his staff were unable to provide any actual governance to Chak's residents, preserving a notional footprint there allowed government propagandists to claim control of the entire district. To residents, it was a flimsy ruse. The only thing the government presence in Chak's district centre brought them was continued fighting. The soldiers defending the inoperative district administration centres, including those in Dasht-e Langar, were confined within the fortifications of their outposts, fighting and dying through the bitter winters and scorching summers, increasingly reliant on a dwindling supply of air support for their survival—all so Kabul could disguise its inability to secure rural Afghanistan.

In March 2021, Taliban military commanders from Maidan Wardak's nine districts convened in Nerkh, located between Chak and Maidan Shahr, further north. The Taliban controlled the vast majority of the province. The only pockets in which the government still maintained a token presence were the besieged district centres and the military outposts that protected them. The district centre of Jalrez, in northern Maidan Wardak, was considered the most vulnerable. It was also important, strategically, because it bordered Kabul province. Chak, on the western side of Highway One, Sayedabad on the eastern side, and Nerkh which abutted them both to the north, it was assessed, would be harder to capture because the government would likely expend more resources defending them.

Under Mullah Zubair, the Taliban's military commander in Chak, the insurgents came up with a plan to take control of Chak once and for all. 'We wanted to make our belt around the Chak district centre tighter,' says Abudajanah. 'And it was necessary for us to capture Antenna Post before we would be able to take the district centre.' He was one of between 15 and 17 fighters involved in the siege. Previously, he says, 'we couldn't surround their bases because of their air power'. But, he continues, 'after May, their air force was stretched because there was fighting all over Afghanistan', and so he and his fighters were able to dig in, emplacing heavy weapons and zeroing their mortars without fear of being targeted by warplanes. The aim, says Abudajanah, was to inflict the maximum amount of pressure on Antenna Post until the soldiers had no option but to surrender. When I ask Abudajanah whether he knows who was commanding the ANA inside Antenna Post at the time, he scrolls his smartphone and shows me a photo of captain Sulaiman.

Without air support, the ANA soldiers inside Antenna Post were forced to fire indiscriminately into the tree canopies, under which the Taliban could move freely without detection. But while the homes on the slopes immediately below the outpost had been abandoned two years prior, when shootouts became a daily occurrence, many of those living in the green areas beyond the Chak road and on the banks of the Logar River stayed. It was the ANA who were firing in their direction, but it was the Taliban's presence in the cultivated areas that attracted it, and although residents maintained relationships with both sides, it had little to do with affinity for either cause. The farmers and their families had little choice. Not only did they have to accept the fighters in their midst, but, when it came to the Taliban, they were compelled to feed them as well. It was a survival mechanism, a cultural obligation and, according to the Taliban, a religious duty, of which they took full advantage. As a consequence, in the village of Alishahr, beyond the Chak road, residents occasionally lost the cows that produced milk for their family to stray bullets. And the trunks of the various varieties of apricot trees—Biruti, Marlang, Shahi, Turkish, and the Amiri, prized for its sweetness—were scarred by bullets, as were the walls and windows of the homes of those who grew them.

The Taliban's siege of Antenna Post began around the same time as the supply drop on 21 May, the same day Jarez district was surrendered after the Afghanistan National Security Forces (ANSF) defending it ran out of ammunition.[4] The drop had been a minor setback for the Taliban, who knew the soldiers' supplies had been running low. Abudajanah thought the two soldiers the Taliban shot that night had been killed, but when no requests came to allow an ambulance from the International Committee for the Red Cross or the Ministry of Public Health into Dasht-e Langar to retrieve the bodies, as they often did, he figured wounded soldiers may be an even greater burden for his enemies. Perhaps, he thought, the ANA would send another Black Hawk to evacuate them, and he and his men would get another chance at taking down one of the multimillion-dollar machines.

Then, on 26 May, Amanullah, the soldier from Kunduz, fled Antenna Post. It was Abudajanah who filmed his surrender and was responsible for handing over the promised 80 000 Afghani (a little over A$1000) for his older-model, American-made M16 rifle. Just as valuable as the surrender clip for the Taliban's broader propaganda campaign were the phone numbers Abudajanah retrieved from Amrullah's mobile phone. It was with these that, as his fellow fighters pounded Antenna Post with ordnance, Abudajanah waged an information war—calling the soldiers within and offering amnesty and financial rewards—and undermined Sulaiman's efforts to rally his soldiers.

< >

Abudajanah was born in 1994 in the village of Ghorak at the farthest point on the road up the Nim Paikol Valley, 20 kilometres in a straight line but between two and three hours by road to Chak-i Wardak. Ghorak was built on the steep banks of a narrow rivulet which provided water for a few dozen farmers with small crops. Being the highest village in the valley, vehicles rarely came to Ghorak, and so, aside from the chatter of its residents, the cries and laughter of their children, and the five times daily call to prayer, the only sound came from leaves rustling in the wind and the trickle of snowmelt against the river stones. Abudajanah's father, Khairullah, named him after a companion of the Prophet Mohammed, Abu Dujana, who was known for his piety and bravery in jihad. After fighting the Soviets through the 1980s with Hezb-i Islami, one of the seven major factions that made up the mujahedin resistance—'mujahedin' is the term Taliban fighters use to refer to themselves—and the strongest in Maidan Wardak, Khairullah had returned to Islamic teaching in Ghorak.

When Abudajanah was two years old, a force of mainly southern Pashtuns, also born out of the anti-Soviet resistance, who called themselves Taliban, or students of Islam, moved north from Kandahar, deposed Hezb-i Islami in Chak and the eastern districts of Maidan Wardak, as well as another faction that controlled the two Hazara-majority districts in the north-west, and went on to take control of Kabul. Among the Taliban were a handful of fighters, originally from Chak, who had joined the group when it formed out of Kandahar's madrassas, and who took charge in Maidan Wardak.

The Taliban were initially welcomed there, and many young, uneducated male residents, enamoured by the group's piety, joined their ranks. But to Soviet-era communist officials, senior Hezb-i Islami figures and those with tertiary educations or financial means, the Taliban's devoutness foretold merciless intolerance, and they left the country, travelling to the West through costly smuggling networks or to neighbouring Pakistan or Iran, joining the millions who had moved there during the Soviet war, as refugees.

Despite his past with Hezb-i Islami, as a religious teacher, Khairullah was spared the Taliban's scrutiny and suspicion, and as a devout Muslim himself, he was happy living under a government whose ideals were no different to those he imposed in his own home. Khairullah commanded a large presence in his son's life. 'He was a very kind, educated man,' recalls Abudajanah. 'He encouraged me to study, to get an education.' But he was strict as well. 'I wasn't even able to eat without his permission,' says Abudajanah.

Although the Taliban's brutality was infamous in Kabul and other major cities that had seen pushes towards modernisation in the past, in rural areas like Chak, traditional village life had changed little over the decades. The Taliban's methods weren't exactly welcomed, but they were less of an affront to Chak's residents than they were to those in the cities. If anything, the new rulers' austerity mirrored local cultural norms. But the religious zeal the Taliban brought to Chak wasn't matched by a capacity to govern. Furthermore, the effects of a crippling drought on farmers were conflated with the Taliban's inability to run an economy, which was barely functioning in the wake of the civil war as it was, and to find solutions to counteract international sanctions.

Khairullah, who grew potatoes and wheat on small, tiered plots a short walk from home, relied mostly on his teaching salary. He moved according to where his services were required and was somewhat insulated from the economic insecurity that farmers experienced. The family's biggest move coincided with the American invasion of Afghanistan in late 2001. They rode motorbikes from Ghorak over White Mountain, which towers over the village and where locals say arrowheads from the Anglo-Afghan wars of the 19th century can still be found, and into the Araban Valley; their few household belongings were driven the long way around in a truck. Khairullah started teaching religious texts at a school near Lake Chak, which separates the start of the Araban Valley from the district centre. Being closer to Chak-i Wardak, Abudajanah saw more of the Americans than he ever would have in Ghorak, in which no foreign military forces have set foot in his lifetime. Like the Taliban before them, the Americans, who promised stability and prosperity, were initially welcomed. One of Abudajanah's closest friends, Rohullah, a Talib and a pharmacist, recalls the early years from his perspective as a boy, when the Americans would patrol the villages in large convoys, looking for weapons caches and former Taliban commanders—seemingly innocuous missions, if you weren't in their sights. 'The Americans were very nice at this time. Why should I lie? They gave us sweets and cakes,' says Rohullah.

But, as was the case across Afghanistan, in Maidan Wardak, those who allied with the Americans and the government they installed under president Hamid Karzai, many of whom had returned from exile after fleeing the Taliban, with grievances, now saw an opportunity—not only to gather wealth and power, but to exact revenge.

Wealth and power were garnered through nepotism and patronage in Kabul: government ministers could charge for allocating high positions in their districts; governors could demand commissions for permitting development projects in their provinces; district police chiefs could take a cut from opium profits; border guards could extort money from traders; and army officers could pocket the salaries of non-existent 'ghost soldiers'. Revenge, on the other hand, was meted out quietly, often under the guise of counterterrorism. Afghans with connections to credulous American intelligence gatherers would gain favour—and cash rewards—for identifying the 'al-Qaeda' fighters the foreigners had come to find. However, they didn't only proffer former Talibs to the Americans, but also business rivals, and families with whom they were embroiled in longstanding blood feuds or land-ownership disputes. Special forces operators would swoop into villages in the dead of night, blow the gates to family compounds off their hinges, burst into rooms full of sleeping men, women and children, and detain their target, shipping them off to be tortured and interrogated in Central Intelligence Agency (CIA) black sites, if they weren't shot and killed onsite.

Some of those who were taken, like Ustad Yasir, the influential Taliban ideologue from Maidan Wardak, were of legitimate concern. But, after years of degrading treatment in Guantanamo Bay, once released, they returned to the battlefield more determined than ever to rid the country of its invaders.[5] Some Wardakis simply resented the presence of outsiders, especially non-Muslims, who, after several years, started to be seen as occupiers rather than liberators. American rivals like Pakistan's Inter-Services Intelligence agency seized on the resentment. They rekindled relationships with guerrilla leaders from the 1980s and 1990s and began providing support for a Taliban insurgency. Others in Maidan Wardak were bitter about how little they, in rural areas, were benefiting from the post-2001 order in comparison to those in urban centres like Kabul.

In the mid-2000s, armed opposition to the Karzai government and its international sponsors was mostly ad hoc. Talibs from the former regime who had evaded the early wrath of the Americans and returned to their land or studies, reconnected with old colleagues and began to organise, arming small groups of disgruntled young men. They warned local elders against working with the new government and made examples of those who did. Abudajanah remembers the thatch of trees near a freshwater spring by the road in the Araban Valley where, in 2008, a nascent local Taliban group started to hang government collaborators and criminals, leaving their swinging corpses for motorists to ponder as they drove by.

When Barack Obama was elected president in 2008, he sent tens of thousands more soldiers to Afghanistan, determined to bring the US military's attention back to that country after its focus on the war in Iraq had allowed the Taliban insurgency to take hold. Within a year, the increased troop numbers and firepower in Maidan Wardak had only exacerbated the issues that had driven rearmament and insurgency in the mid-2000s. Taliban recruitment seemed to rise in proportion to American aggression.[6] 'At first there was no support for the Taliban,' a low-level commander from Maidan Wardak told me in 2020. 'It was when the Americans started killing civilians that people started supporting us, giving us food, bullets, and offering men.'

By 2011, violence in Maidan Wardak was surging. That summer, a US Chinook helicopter was shot down in Sayedabad district, killing 30 Americans and eight Afghans. It was the deadliest incident for US forces of the entire war.[7] Abudajanah was 17 at the time and had been studying at a madrassa after school. He donned a scrunchy black turban, as was customary for the religious students, and grew eager to join the jihad against the Americans. 'There was no military training,' he says of his time in the madrassa. 'Students just learned the Qur'an, which implored us to wage jihad against infidels.' He says he was taught that there were two sets of circumstances that made it obligatory, one of which applied in Chak: 'If a group of Muslims can't defend themselves, those in the surrounding area must come to their defence.'

Abudajanah was asleep at home early one morning in 2011 when his phone rang. Taliban fighters who slept in the madrassa had been encouraging him to participate in an ambush. 'The Americans are coming,' they told him. Abudajanah quietly left home wearing the clothes in which he'd slept and walked to a friend's house. In an undercover area where the family kept animals in winter were two Kalashnikovs they'd hidden. They slung the assault rifles over their shoulders, wrapped themselves in cotton shawls, and sped off on a motorcycle along a dusty path through wheatfields to the cluster of trees where they'd been instructed to meet. There, Abudajanah and his friend found at least 15 Taliban fighters standing around a mortar tube beneath a canopy that would shield them from the prying eyes of American surveillance aircraft.

Informants in Chak-i Wardak had notified fighters further along the road towards Araban that a convoy of Americans and ANA soldiers were heading for Sebak Bazaar, 3 kilometres west of where the fighters were now waiting. Before the convoy reached the spring where the Taliban had hung the bodies of traitors, two haphazardly aimed mortars were fired from trees about a kilometre away. Abudajanah and the others, who had raced up on motorcycles and concealed themselves behind a compound wall, opened fire when the mortar shells smashed into the ground well beyond the road. The air filled with dust from the backblasts of Taliban rocket-propelled grenades, and from the impact of the convoy's .50-calibre rounds slamming into the compound walls as it drove on, through the ambush, towards Sebak Bazaar.

The attack on the convoy was inconsequential, not even enough for the Americans to call for air support. But from then on, as Abudajanah explains, 'Whenever the Americans came, fighting was prioritised over school.'

The following year, Abudajanah graduated from the high school where his father taught and went on to study at a small teacher-training college in Sebak, near the site of his first firefight. His initial posting was to a madrassa where both his father and grandfather had taught in decades past, north of Chak-i Wardak in a valley so sparsely populated it doesn't feature on even the most detailed maps. Like many Taliban foot soldiers, Abudajanah lived a double life: teaching in the madrassa, where he would make a modest living from the funds that, despite his wish to portray the Taliban's resistance as home-grown, trickled into Chak from Taliban financiers like Pakistan, Iran and later Russia; and fighting. He was never paid to fight as such; residents of Maidan Wardak who opposed the government in Kabul and its American-led international backers saw fighters like Abudajanah as protectors—not only of them and their families, but of Islam itself—and paid them whatever they could afford in alms.

'Abudajanah was a good mujahid,' recalls Rohullah. 'He was always honest and never allowed me to play music in the car. He was a far better Muslim than I.' The two would drive to Kabul from time to time to buy new clothes or perfumes that weren't available in Chak. To avoid attracting the scrutiny of police and intelligence officers in the capital, they kept their hair and feathery beards short, more like the university students who modelled themselves on Western icons than the fighters in the districts who grew their hair long, parting it in the middle in the style of the prophet. 'We looked like school boys, not scruffy like Talibs from the village,' says Abudajanah.

In 2013, Abudajanah took his brother Saidullah, then 11, to the Kabul neighbourhood of Company, just past the city gates when coming in from Maidan Wardak. Saidullah was sick and the clinic in Chak didn't have the medicine he needed. After taking Saidullah for treatment and buying his medication from a pharmacy, Abudajanah put him in a shared taxi bound for Chak and returned to wander the bazaar. A rack of shoes he was sorting through suddenly disappeared behind a sack being pulled over his head. His arms were yanked behind his back and fastened with a scarf. Abudajanah was then wrestled into a vehicle and driven through stop–start traffic to the Department 40 prison in central Kabul, a notorious facility for terror suspects run by the government's intelligence service, the National Directorate of Security (NDS), and which had been the subject of numerous reports of torture and abuse.[8] 'I was accused of organising suicide attacks, planning attacks in Wardak and Kabul,' Abudajanah says, 'but they had no evidence against me. I was just a simple foot soldier.'

Abudajanah was permitted to continue his studies and teach Islamic texts to the other prisoners in his cell block. Even with a defence lawyer, however, 15 months passed, he says, with beatings and torture with 'electric shocks', before he was released. As was the case with American attempts to quell the insurgency on the battlefield, the abuse of prisoners in government facilities only helped to drive the insurgency. One report noted the practice was 'akin to trying to put out a fire with gasoline'.[9] Abudajanah's response to his treatment was a case in point, only hardening his resolve to bring down the government and rid Afghanistan of its occupiers.

In–between fighting missions, Abudajanah returned to the madrassa where he'd started teaching before his imprisonment, which sat alone on a gentle rise north of Chak-i Wardak in Upper Hewad. As well as teaching, during which, Abudajanah says, 'I encouraged my students toward jihad, first against the Americans and then against the government,' he worked as a manager of sorts, collecting donations and supplies, and dispersing students to preach in mosques in Chak upon, or even before, graduation. The work saw him travelling to all of Chak's valleys. He met mullahs and fellow fighters, and developed a strong, informal network throughout the district. He drew the attention of Mullah Zubair, who enlisted Abudajanah as a kind of propagandist for Chak. He would liaise with Zubair's sub-commanders around the district each day, reporting to senior Taliban officials outside the province on Taliban operations, captured enemy bases, vehicles and weapons, and the killing of enemy personnel. He would also collect allegations of war crimes carried out by government and American forces.

‹ ›

In late 2018, Abudajanah found himself at the nexus of a strange coincidence involving events that began to occur thousands of kilometres apart. In Doha, the first round of formal talks between the United States and the Taliban were being held. In Chak, and in the other districts in Maidan Wardak that the Taliban had dominated for years, stories of fearsome raids carried out by a mixture of American and Afghan paramilitaries, always at night, and always with an abundance of blunt force, began filtering through the valleys. It was no secret that the areas being targeted were crawling with Taliban fighters, but what terrified residents was, first, the terrifying frequency of the night raids, and second, that those being targeted were rarely fighters but rather old men, women and children.

The paramilitaries were from the 01 National Strike Unit, one of several established in the early days of the war, and trained, funded and commanded by the CIA. The shadowy unit was garrisoned in the heavily fortified Eagle Base on the northern outskirts of Kabul, and little was known of its operations until 2019, when it began to draw scrutiny from journalists, human rights groups and even a Swedish humanitarian organisation whose health clinics it targeted repeatedly. The paramilitaries would arrive in groups of as many as 100 or more aboard Chinooks around 9 p.m. Circling above them were drones, attack helicopters, fighter jets and, occasionally, the most feared of all US warplanes, the AC-130, a transport plane converted into a tri-cannoned beast designed specifically to assist American special forces from close range. The paramilitaries were almost always supported by American special operators loaned out by the Pentagon to the CIA, and they spent several hours on the ground, raiding one or more target locations within walking distance, several nights each week. The raids were often accompanied by air strikes, and around one in four targeted madrassa students—some as young as nine—sleeping in adjoining dormitories.

These secretive operations were never acknowledged by the CIA. At the time, even Afghanistan's most senior security official, Hamdullah Mohib, the then 38-year-old national security advisor, was at a loss to explain them. But the timing suggested that the campaign in Maidan Wardak was part of the military element of president Donald Trump's South Asia Strategy—essentially, his plan for ending the war in Afghanistan. In carrying out the plan, which he unveiled in August 2017, Trump vowed to unleash 'all instruments of American power—diplomatic, economic, and military—toward a successful outcome'.[10]

Two months later, without specifying where or with whom, the then director of the CIA, Mike Pompeo, indicated that the agency, too, would be ramping up its operations with 'partner services throughout the world'. The CIA, he said, 'must be aggressive, vicious, unforgiving, relentless'.[11] According to a report by *The New York Times* soon after, the CIA was 'expanding its covert operations in Afghanistan, sending small teams of highly experienced officers and contractors alongside Afghan forces to hunt and kill Taliban militants across the country'.[12]

The 01 unit and its American advisors first came in winter, to the village of Wala Khail, then to Mohammad Khail, near Chak-i

Wardak, where a school principal on a government salary was executed inside his home. Then, in spring, in Azad Khail, a mentally disabled man who slept in the village mosque was shot in the head at close range and killed. Similar incidents took place in the villages of Goda and Sufi Khail. The worst, however, came in late summer, in Abudajanah's home valley of Nim Paikol. Nine madrassa students were massacred in Sar Posh, more in his friend Rohullah's village of Chonai, and, on the night of 4 September 2019, in Zul, in the Araban Valley.

Prior to the attack in Zul, drones had been roving the skies above the Araban all day. 'We knew to expect a night raid,' a resident told me later that month. Around 9 p.m., the aircraft arrived, firing flares that, as they floated to the ground, lit up the valley and the two Chinooks hovering above it. The Chinooks deposited soldiers in separate locations, who joined up on foot a kilometre south of Zul, long after the helicopters had disappeared back towards Kabul.

Although the 01 unit hadn't previously come to Zul itself, stories of their raids in adjoining valleys had. Families prepared by digging out identity papers or documents that pointed to their work with government schools or clinics. The villagers hoped the files would placate the raiding soldiers if they came to their home. The sound of gunfire combined with shouts and screams could then be heard across the village. It was coming from the direction of the madrassa, the outer wall of which sat flush against the single dirt road that ran through the valley. A sign prohibiting entry with weapons, which, it was hoped, would prevent raids by government forces, had been posted on the door.

In the early hours of the following morning, 5 September, the Chinooks returned, departing minutes later with the 01 para-militaries and their American advisors. At around 3 a.m., once the faint sounds of drones had completely faded, men from the village, many of them Taliban fighters, hurried to the madrassa. Twitching beams of light from mobile phone torches illuminated the bodies of five of the madrassa's older students in the fields between the school and a stream down the hill. One had several bullet wounds across his back. Another had been shot in the back of the head and, because of the force of the round on exiting, his face was unrecognisable. Yet another had had his cheek sliced with a blade from the corner of his mouth to the base of his ear. One young man who had been taken from a nearby home had, according to a witness, been 'shot in the back so many times his left arm had almost separated from his body'.

When Abudajanah and I drove through Araban in 2021, he refused to stop at the madrassa in Zul. 'The teachers themselves may have suffered at the hands of infidels,' he said, inferring that they might not take kindly to another non-Muslim visitor. Abudajanah may have been shielding me from the fact that the victims of the September 2019 raid were both students *and* Talibs, but under the circumstances described, there is little distinction in the eyes of international humanitarian law between the extrajudicial killing of an unarmed combatant and a non-combatant civilian. And regardless, the effect in Chak, and in Maidan Wardak more broadly, was, like Abudajanah's experience in prison, akin to fuelling the fire rather than putting it out.

Maidan Wardak's residents, including members of the Taliban, were surprisingly forgiving of military operations targeting the insurgent fighters themselves. Although the Taliban feared and despised the virtually invisible armed drones, it was war, and both sides used whatever means they had to the most devastating effect possible, often with little care for civilians in the vicinity. The Taliban, after all, had a weapon that put just as much fear into the sleepless minds of Afghan and international soldiers, and young boys and girls into prostheses or early graves: the improvised explosive device (IED).

Rohullah and I were driving through Nim Paikol Valley late in 2021 when we passed a memorial of coloured flags for a man killed in an American drone strike. 'Most of those killed by drones were Taliban,' said Rohullah, matter-of-factly. 'Unlike those killed during the night raids,' he added, before pausing. 'The recklessness of them, even for those who were completely against the Taliban, it could turn you against the government and the US.'

In late 2019, as the talks between US and Taliban representatives in Doha gathered momentum, the incidence of the 01 raids eased. And after the Doha Agreement was signed on 29 February the following year, the raids all but stopped. If it wasn't for a single 01 operation in May 2020, a security analyst based in Kabul told me, she'd have thought 'the earth had swallowed them whole'.[13]

It wasn't only the 01 unit whose operations were curtailed by the obligations imposed on the Afghan Government under the Doha Agreement. Notwithstanding the 01's counterproductive campaign of night raids, the ANSF had limited success in other parts of the country in 2019. While it was far from what would have been required to turn countrywide military momentum in the government's favour, ANSF operations stemmed the Taliban's impetus in some areas, even retaking control of several districts, including in Ghazni, neighbouring Maidan Wardak to the south, which had previously been under the Taliban. 'This was because the South Asia Strategy provided good air cover,' says Hamdullah Mohib. That winter, the Ministry of Defence drew up plans for major offensives, building on the successes of 2019, in the north and east of Afghanistan. The operations would merge together in the south the following summer. 'That's when we stopped receiving air support,' says Mohib, in a tone typical of his belief in US culpability. Or at least, he added: 'Not the kind of air support that would have made those operations doable.'

The Doha Agreement was celebrated by the Taliban in Chak and across Afghanistan. It signalled the end of their war with the Americans, who, as part of the agreement, vowed not to conduct offensive operations against the Taliban so long as they ceased attacking American targets and their international allies; it was also the beginning of the end of the government they supported.

Civilians in Chak, too, were relieved after the signing of the agreement. The victim of a 01 night raid in a neighbouring district confirmed this to me at the time. 'There's no bombardments or night raids. People are happy; it's like Eid,' he said, referring to the holiday atmosphere during the religious festival. 'The Taliban,' he added, 'are more relaxed, too.'[14] In the Nim Paikol and Araban valleys, some families who had feared becoming victims of 01's campaign of terror and left for Kabul, returned. Residents joked about the joy of driving through Chak's district centre and its ANSF checkpoints without having to hide their SIM cards for fear of incriminating themselves.

For Mawlawi Mushfeq, one of Abudajanah's Taliban superiors in Chak, the signing of the Doha Agreement had a huge impact. 'I was very happy with the agreement,' he says. 'Not only for the mujahedin—mujahedin are here to fight and to die—but for the civilians. They were the ones suffering the most. For them, it was a message of happiness because, since then, the night raids and drone attacks have ceased. Now they can live in peace.'

Mushfeq headed the Taliban's Invitation and Guidance Commission—the Taliban's shadow government equivalent of a ministry—in Chak, which, by his own admission, was relatively ineffectual before the Doha Agreement. Mushfeq's job then was to facilitate defections and surrenders of ANSF members to the Taliban. 'Very few ANSF used to come and join us,' he says. After the agreement was signed, however, Mushfeq was instructed by the Taliban's provincial leadership that pardons were now to be granted to any member of the ANSF who wished to surrender. 'After the order from the leader of the faithful came,' says Mushfeq, referring to Taliban leader Haibatullah Akhundzada, 'suddenly, the number of ANSF [surrendering] really increased. Because they have been pardoned, surrendering soldiers thought, they will not be prosecuted—not punished for what they did.'

If a member of the ANSF posted to Chak surrendered, Mushfeq would provide a letter on Taliban letterhead with his phone number. Once that soldier returned to their home province, it was his responsibility to introduce himself to Mushfeq's counterpart, who would contact Mushfeq, verify the letter and provide another, thus ratifying the amnesty. The same would occasionally happen in reverse, when ANSF members originally from Chak would return from distant provinces with a letter requiring his certification.

Pardons, Mushfeq says, were only guaranteed if the applicant possessed both letters.

Mushfeq was also in charge of coordinating efforts to entice surrenders. The offer of pardon was broadcast by Taliban AM radio networks and over the military radios both they and the ANSF used, and whose frequencies were easily attained. Getting out of their own bases and outposts was the responsibility of the ANSF members themselves. But once they got out, says Mushfeq, 'we guaranteed their safety'. Some, he said, would accost passers-by in bazaars close to their outposts and ask them to notify the Taliban of their intention to surrender. 'We didn't trust them enough to allow them to join the Taliban,' says Mushfeq, 'so we only sought surrender, not defection.' After the order to offer pardons was handed down in early 2020, in Chak alone, he says, 'we issued about 200 letters for *taslim* [surrender]'.

'It was a very good strategy,' says Captain Sulaiman, the commander of Antenna Post. 'Morale went down. Soldiers started handing in their weapons and surrendering.'

It wasn't only Taliban strategy that undermined the ANSF's capacity to wage a war after the Doha Agreement. On the first page of the agreement, the Taliban and the United States agreed that the Afghan Government and the Taliban would 'start intra-Afghan negotiations ... on 10 March 2020'.[15] But the Afghan Government claimed it wasn't consulted by the US about participating in negotiations with the Taliban—nor whether it would agree to another facet of the agreement whereby it would release 5000 Taliban prisoners in exchange for 1000 of its own. President Ghani, affronted by the Taliban's unwillingness to recognise his legitimacy, and believing he should be leading the negotiations himself, pushed back against the preconditions for 'intra-Afghan negotiations'. Ghani had advocated for the release of prisoners while campaigning for president in 2014, but since then, circumstances had changed dramatically. Plans for the commencement of negotiations stalled and the United States pressured Kabul to make further gestures of goodwill to coax the process along.

President Ghani ordered his armed forces into a defensive footing, largely suspending offensive operations. In April, he amended the order from 'defensive' to 'active defensive', but the semantics changed little for ANA commanders on the ground. 'We were handcuffed,' says Sulaiman. 'We weren't allowed to fight.'

The government was under pressure from the Americans to implement the revised military posture. 'We had no choice,' says Mohib. 'Of course we agreed with it.' But, he adds: 'Once the agreement was signed, the general understanding was that the Taliban will now choose a path of peace.' Mohib says that, months later, the prevarication on the battlefield—the ambiguous language of 'active defence'—played 'a big part' in the demise of the security forces. But Mohib had no military training or experience of his own—he's studied computer systems engineering in the UK—and his assessment of battlefield realities had always been open to question. In mid-2019, he said in an interview with TOLONews that the ANSF would 'break the Taliban's backbone in four months'.[16] When he made a similar comment to Afghan and foreign journalists at an off-the-record dinner gathering at his residence later that year, the room was stunned into silence by Mohib's hawkish delusion.

By late 2020, after six months spent falling in line around the idea of peace talks, with the Taliban pressing their advantage on the battlefield, and with the Afghan Government's grip on power beginning to loosen, Mohib's tone again turned bellicose. 'I think war and peace go together,' he told the BBC's Lyse Doucet in October 2020. 'The Taliban will never make peace with us in earnest if they don't believe we can defeat them in war.' In early 2021, with the United States' backing looking increasingly shaky, Mohib travelled to Azerbaijan and other allied countries in the region in search of a new military patron. While declining to disclose the patron he found, Mohib says that 'a new technology' was acquired, but that the changing circumstances didn't allow for its implementation. And, as the US continued to withdraw its remaining forces through mid-2021, withering morale within ANSF ranks meant there was little existing means or capacity with which to enact the leadership's warring words. Peace, as Mohib and Ghani saw it, appeared to be contingent on the retention of their own power, regardless of how many lives were 'sacrificed', as Mohib often put it, in the process.[17]

Confined to their bases, and with the United States only offering air support in the most dire of circumstances, the commanders in outposts across Afghanistan simply waited to be attacked, while watching the Taliban gloat over their new-found—seemingly protected—status. Without the constant fear of airstrikes, Taliban fighters were able to set up checkpoints on highways to search for government and security officials, and to extract taxes from motorists, plant IEDs at will, host foreign journalists, and both manoeuvre and amass forces with a freedom the likes of which they hadn't known the entire war.

Rahimullah, the elder who lives between two of the four ANA outposts in Dasht-e Langar, says that before Doha, 'we had no Taliban in our village. But this year, as the posts became weaker, the Taliban were able to infiltrate our village and even come on the main road. Previously, all the Taliban could do was come secretly, plant IEDs and leave'.

In Kabul and the provincial capitals, on the other hand, the Taliban were winning plaudits for ceasing large-scale attacks and bombings, as per their commitment in Doha, and speaking the rhetoric of peace in general. Far from taking the pressure off the government, however, the Taliban simply changed tactics, adopting an approach that would not provoke serious repercussions from the United States. They eschewed spectacular violence for a more discreet, less headline-grabbing, but equally effective, campaign of targeted killings.

The assassination of scores of security officials, journalists, religious figures, activists and judges by the Taliban also provided cover for government intelligence operatives to eliminate non-Taliban rivals. The crimes were almost impossible to trace, let alone prove, and doing so was scarcely worth the risk. But segments of society began to fear being targeted by government operatives as much as by the Taliban, and many fled the country. Mohib says that even the Americans suspected senior government security officials and the NDS were responsible for some of the killings. 'It was very frustrating,' he says. 'They talked to us as if it was a sure thing that it was the government'.

< >

By the end of May, holding Antenna Post and the three satellite bases in Dasht-e Langar was becoming more improbable by the day. After Amanullah's desertion, and with Sulaiman's requests for air support going unanswered, morale among the soldiers continued to deteriorate. The two soldiers wounded in the aftermath of the resupply effort were languishing in the outpost. There was an army medic at Antenna Post, but no supplies with which he could attend to the injured men's wounds. Furthermore, after the bungled delivery of the water, grains and flour, Sulaiman knew the strained pilots of the Afghan Air Force would be reluctant to return to such a vulnerable drop zone in the future. And the supplies from the drop on 21 May were disappearing more quickly than he'd anticipated.

Further eroding the morale of Sulaiman's men were the stories coming from Maidan Wardak's districts. In May, two of the province's nine district centres had fallen to the Taliban. The circumstances that precipitated the collapse of Nerkh on the 12th, in particular, gave the soldiers inside Antenna Post yet more reason to consider their options.

In April, Taliban fighters in Nerkh had been ordered to dig a tunnel. The excavation began in an abandoned house at the base of a hill and ran more than 100 metres into its core, stopping underneath a compound that housed the government's district administration centre. Within the compound were three buildings: one contained the governor's office, the second Nerkh's police chief, and the third a unit of Afghan Local Police (ALP). 'It took 50 days,' says Sabir, the Taliban shadow governor who ordered the digging of the tunnel. Once it had penetrated the ground beneath the building closest to the abandoned house, the ALP base, Sabir ordered it filled with explosives.

Torakai, a veteran local police commander, says, 'Many times, the Taliban said, "You should surrender or we will kill you. We have the whole place filled with explosives."' Torakai scoffed at the claim. How could they have explosives inside, he thought.

On 12 May, Mohammad Jan Mohammadi, an assistant to Sabir, phoned Torakai. Torakai made out that he was inside the ALP headquarters. In fact, he was several kilometres away in the provincial capital, Maidan Shahr, while a handful of his local police had remained in Nerkh.

'Okay, what do you want me to do?' asked Torakai when he answered the call. 'Surrender?'

'Yes,' replied Mohammadi.

'This is our country. These are the lines of our country.'

'We're doing you a favour. We don't want you to get hurt. If you surrender, we'll accept whatever you say.'

'Okay.'

'Do you understand?' pressed Mohammadi, unsure whether Torakai had grasped the severity of the situation.

'Yes,' said Torakai. 'One of us can fight 30 of you. We will fight until we have no more breath in our lungs.'

With that, in a voice that betrayed no consequence, Mohammadi said, 'Okay, that's good.' And from a cluster of shops 150 metres down the road, he instructed Sabir's bombmaker to detonate the charge.

Torakai heard the explosion over the phone. The local policemen inside the base, unaware of the conversation that had decided their fate, disappeared into flames and a cloud of dust and shattered concrete. Talibs watching the spectacle from the shops and the abandoned house cried, 'God is great!' The blast left a 20-metre-wide crater where the ALP base had been and broke the will of the remaining government forces in Nerkh, who surrendered the same day. Afghan Air Force pilots were ordered to bomb the seized government buildings and barracks.

In Dasht-e Langar, Taliban foot soldiers under Mullah Zubair were rotated in and out for one or two weeks at a time. Abdul Haq arrived for duty on a motorcycle, having folded two thick blankets on the seat to cushion the ride there on bumpy roads. He came with nothing more than the clothes he was wearing and a Kalashnikov rifle, and he slept beneath a blanket in the mosque 300 metres west of Antenna Post. Haq and the other fighters were forbidden from entering houses that were still inhabited, so villagers were asked to bring them food.

When he wasn't sleeping, Haq moved forward to the edge of the cultivated green zone at the base of the hill below Antenna Post. He worked with a three-man team operating a PKM machine gun. They moved around beneath the canopy and through holes smashed in the walls of abandoned compounds, the closest of which were only 100 metres from the outpost's perimeter. The team would man the machine gun for four hours before handing off to one of two other teams. 'We would always have a finger on the trigger,' says Haq. 'As soon as they raised their heads, we would open fire. If they fired, we would return fire.' The teams repeated the cycle constantly, 24 hours per day—the soldiers were given no reprieve.

Behind Abdul Haq's hide-out, Abudajanah was with another group of fighters who were firing either *shotaki*—conventional rockets laid on the ground, which were haphazardly aimed at a target by manoeuvring a rock or tree branch under their bellies, and ignited using a jerry-rigged fuse—or *jahanum* (meaning 'Hell'): improvised rockets built from scratch by Taliban bombmakers using gas canisters, or the pipe and tin sheeting commonly used in wood-burning heaters in Afghan homes. *Jahanum* looked more like homemade car mufflers than weapons, but nonetheless, Abudajanah had an almost unlimited supply of them. 'We had a laboratory and a stockpile of explosives and materials in Paktiya,' he says, referring to a province to the south-east. In Chak, the Taliban had a shipping container filled with around 20 *jahanum*, all freshly spray-painted green with white squiggles. 'We had a technical group who developed them from the internet,' says Abudajanah. 'Most of the designers were killed by their own experiments.'

Several *jahanum* had been fired at Antenna Post in the few weeks since Captain Sulaiman had arrived disguised as a civilian in a white station wagon, but with no targeting technology beyond trial and error, they had all strayed wildly and exploded or fizzled out in the hills and plains of Dasht-e Langar. Abudajanah often filmed the missile attacks, as capturing one of the Taliban's homemade missiles striking its target would be of huge propaganda value. In the first week of June, he perched a digital camera on top of a low wall and zoomed in until Antenna Post and its phone tower filled half the camera's screen. Twenty seconds or more passed before, to Abudajanah's surprise and delight, a burst of dirt and rubble erupted behind the outpost's Hesco barrier, towards the northern side, closest to the Chak road. There were 22 soldiers stationed inside Antenna Post, which was around the size of half a football field, but miraculously, only one was injured in the strike, struck in the shoulder by shrapnel.

By 9 June, the Taliban had gotten hold of Sulaiman's phone number. Abudajanah called him several times each day, at once taunting him and coaxing him towards surrender. 'They were telling us they were well equipped and never thought they'd be captured,' says Abudajanah. 'He was saying "Fuck your mother, fuck your sister, go back to Pakistan" and these things.' But it was a bluff. The wounds of the two men struck on the night of the supply drop more than two weeks prior were now rotting. The soldiers had finished the last of their drinking water and had started draining what was left in the radiators of the armoured vehicles. Once that was gone, they began urinating into empty water bottles and consuming the murky amber liquid.

The heaviest fighting came at night, when the Taliban had the advantage of darkness under skies that were now almost entirely bereft of warplanes. 'Two years ago we had nowhere to hide,' says Abdul Haq. 'But now, at night, we would even get behind their walls.' The sense of encirclement felt by Sulaiman and his soldiers was

becoming more acute by the day, and as the Taliban's siege intensified, so, too, did the soldiers' careless attempts to protect themselves.

On 11 June, Rahimullah called Sulaiman. 'The Taliban are
here,' he said. 'Do you want to fight or surrender? Because if you
want to fight, we civilians have to leave.' Sulaiman told Rahimullah
to give him five days to decide. 'It's too long,' said Rahimullah.
'Okay,' Sulaiman replied. 'Three days.'

When those three days were up, Sulaiman invited Rahimullah
up to Antenna Post. Rahimullah first consulted with Abudajanah,
who suggested that he take two other elders with him, 'so there
isn't any trouble'. 'I could see they were in a bad situation,' says
Rahimullah. 'They had no food, no water, and four soldiers
were wounded.' When Rahimullah and the elders reported back,
Abudajanah gave them a message to relay to Sulaiman: 'You are
from Afghanistan. If you're killed, your widows will be our widows,
so surrender and we'll give you safe passage.'

Surrender was something Sulaiman had never considered. He
had always imagined fighting until his last magazine was empty.
But the helplessness of besiegement, and the growing realisation
that the government for which he was fighting was losing the
capacity to fight for him, changed the calculus. Dying for a dying
cause felt absurd. However, Sulaiman still had his pride, and he told
Rahimullah that he'd only surrender as long as he didn't have to
hand over any war matériel: 'Not even a single bullet.' 'Impossible,'
Abudajanah responded through Rahimullah, before agreeing to
permit the soldiers to keep their own personal weapons.

Sulaiman called Rahimullah at midnight, informing him that
he and his men would surrender the following morning. The next
call he made was to his brigade commander in Maidan Shahr.

At 7 a.m. on 15 June, Sulaiman, dressed in full uniform, with
ammunition magazines in the pouches across his chest and an M16
over his shoulder, and delirious with thirst and hunger, staggered
down the hill from Antenna Post with half his men in tow. The
others, including the five *zarbati* commandos and the four wounded,
were still gathering their belongings when Abudajanah and several

other fighters made their way inside. The Taliban fighters greeted the surrendering soldiers courteously, without pity or pride, shaking hands and placing their hands over their hearts. 'Peace be with you,' they said.

Before the last soldiers had left Antenna Post, as Taliban fighters still wandered about, admiring their spoils, the sound of aircraft could be heard in the distance. The wounded soldiers were lifted from their beds and hurriedly carried down the hill by the remaining soldiers and Taliban fighters. The air support that Sulaiman had pleaded for had finally come. High above, the pilot inside the Afghan Air Force MD-530 helicopter fired rockets at the outpost's two humvees, destroying them. Next, two 250-pound bombs fell from an A-29 Super Tucano propeller plane, destroying the commandos' Mobile Strike Force Vehicle and a D-30 artillery piece. The ANA soldiers and Taliban fighters stood and watched from the road as the aircraft returned to Kabul while the dust settled over Antenna Post.

2

Presidential Palace, Kabul

It was as if Hamed Safi was living in two different worlds: one, where he worked inside the Arg, as the presidential palace was known locally, where it was business as usual; and another, outside the palace's fortifications, where panic was beginning to spread among his friends and family as the Taliban rounded on Kabul.

Hamed, who was 38, had begun working in the Office of Strategic and Public Affairs in 2013 during then president Hamid Karzai's twilight years in the palace. He was a passionate public servant who eschewed the partisan politics occupying the minds of many with whom he worked. As an Afghan of Tajik heritage, he was instinctively suspicious of the country's Pashtun hegemony, but he worked first and foremost for the republic, not the government who led it. After Ashraf Ghani assumed the presidency in 2014, Hamed was promoted and began managing the president's media schedule. In 2017, he was awarded the Mir Masjidi Khan Medal by president Ghani for his 10 years of service to the media. From 2018, he headed the media relations department, one of the four sub-branches that made up the Office of Strategic and Public Affairs.

In the palace, where staff were routinely sidelined for working against the interests of the government, keeping the nation informed—without misleading it—required a deft touch. By the beginning of August 2021, Hamed was seriously questioning his part in a desperate palace strategy to divert the nation's attention from its faltering war effort. Although promoting the government's dull bureaucratic accomplishments and playing down its failings was hardly a novel approach to public relations, with the Taliban now controlling three times as many districts as the government,[1] it was beginning to seem farcical.

Two weeks earlier, during a prayer ceremony attended by senior government officials to mark the beginning of the Eid holiday, the threat beyond the palace walls made a rare incursion. Hamed arrived at the venue two hours prior to brief the media covering the event. He also chatted with a member of the Presidential Protection Service (PPS), in which his older brother Mahmoud was a senior officer. It turned out the PPS weren't happy that the event was being held outdoors. 'Security reports,' said the PPS, 'indicate that the missile attack will happen probably during Eid prayer or during the president's speech.'

Sure enough, as president Ghani knelt for the prayer's first *rakat*, flanked in the first of a dozen rows by Hamid Karzai, vice-president Amrullah Saleh, the republic's chief executive Dr Abdullah Abdullah, and national security advisor Hamdullah Mohib, a rocket whizzed overhead and crashed a couple of hundred metres behind the congregation, near the palace cafeteria. Three maintenance staff who had been enjoying the sun during a break in their work were wounded; one lost a leg. Saleh, who had survived several bomb attacks in the past year alone, flinched before regaining his composure and dropping to his knees in prayer. A second rocket then fizzed over the palace treetops, prompting one worshipper, who had remained on his feet, to spin around, looking for a place to run—another crash. The worshippers went down for one more *rakat*. Another rocket tore across the sky and slammed into the ground near one of the palace's main entry gates. 'We heard that a woman with her baby daughter was wounded and the little kid lost her two legs,' says Hamed of the third rocket strike, adding that 'this information wasn't released to the media'.

By August, palace colleagues who lived in majority Pashtun neighbourhoods like Karte Naw, in south-eastern Kabul, were telling Hamed that Taliban fighters had begun quietly moving in: 'They have guns. They have everything.' Locals who had never previously voiced sympathies for the Taliban, said the colleagues, were either emboldened by the insurgents' battlefield momentum, or, seeing the political tide turning, were purporting affinity for the incoming regime—as Afghans had done for centuries—in order to survive the return of the Taliban. Others were from Taliban sleeper cells that had been secretly infiltrating the capital and its institutions for years, reporting on government workers, recruiting fighters, and feeding intelligence to commanders who were planning attacks.[2] The more the government teetered, the more brazen the Taliban sleepers and sympathisers became. 'We were hearing this every day,' says Hamed.

On 6 August, the Taliban assassinated Dawa Khan Menapal, who headed one of the Office of Strategic and Public Affairs' four departments. He was a direct counterpart of Hamed's and well known among Kabul's press corps. Menapal's murder was the first in a recent spate of assassinations for which the Taliban claimed responsibility, with a spokesperson stating that the government official had been 'punished for his deeds', and threatening further killings.[3]

The next day, Hamed and his colleagues approached Wahid Omar, the director of the Office of Strategic and Public Affairs. 'What's happening?' Hamed asked. 'You're demanding that we denounce the Taliban on Facebook but you can't guarantee our safety.' The palace, Hamed pointed out, had provided Menapal with an armoured vehicle and a bodyguard, and still he was killed. 'But we don't have these things,' he continued. 'How can we be expected to write against the Taliban?'

The following day, gunmen shot Toofan Omar, the manager of a private radio station, on the outskirts of Kabul. The next day, television journalist Nematullah Hemat was kidnapped from his home in Helmand province (he was later released). Twelve Afghan journalists and media workers had been killed since the Doha Agreement was signed 18 months earlier.[4] Understandably, their colleagues were also coming to Wahid Omar with concerns. 'The media had a lot of questions,' says Hamed. 'For a long time the president hadn't appeared at a press conference and the media weren't happy, so we arranged an off-the-record meeting.'

On 10 August, in the presidential palace, Ashraf Ghani sat in a high-backed chair at the head of a long, oval-shaped table, beneath a 5-metre-wide mural depicting Bala Hissar, the ancient fort in Kabul's south that was occupied by British forces during the second Anglo–Afghan war in the late 1870s. Fifteen media representatives sat on either side of the table. A framed photo of Dawa Khan Menapal stood in a bed of palace roses in front of his empty chair. 'The president did all the talking as usual,' says Hamed. He recalls Ghani saying: 'I'm ready to die in the palace, but I'll never leave the country like Amanullah Khan and other kings of Afghanistan.' Hamed adds: 'Everyone was happy after the meeting.' He says they felt that 'if the president will stay in Afghanistan, is so full of energy and determined to defeat the Taliban, it's our responsibility, as media, to stay, too'.

Hamed had always found president Ghani's 'lectures', as he called them, invigorating. Even then, with a quarter of the country's provinces in Taliban hands and more on the brink of collapse, Ghani's words were reassuring. But two days later, government forces collapsed in the provinces of Kandahar, Ghazni and Herat. On 13 August, video footage of the capture of Herat's most senior military commanders, including the famous mujahedin leader Ismael Khan, spread quickly. Hamed decided it was time to leave Afghanistan. He searched for flights and booked a ticket for 23 August.

'He lied,' says Hamed of Ghani's earlier reassuring words to the media. 'It's very difficult to know when he's lying.'

Hamed Safi was born in Kabul in 1983, four years into the Soviet occupation of Afghanistan. His mother, Sahar, worked as a typist at a co-op which sold discounted goods to workers from the communist government. His father, Mujib, was a shopkeeper in the same store. The Soviets departed in 1989 and three years later the Afghan communist government collapsed, after which Mujib was offered a job with the new mujahedin government, through a friend from their native Badakhshan province in the Tajik-majority north-east of the country.

Hamed, the second of five children, was 13 and in grade six when the Taliban took charge of Kabul in September 1996. 'After the seven groups of mujahedin had been fighting over Kabul,' he says, referring to the factions who had fought ruthlessly for control of the capital for four years, 'everyone was positive about the coming of the Taliban.' But the peace the Taliban brought to Kabul's streets was soon usurped by a new set of problems for the city's residents. 'Day by day, they began to show their real faces,' says Hamed.

Mujib didn't stay in Kabul long enough to experience the Taliban's brutality. Expecting reprisals for his work with the communists, he escaped to Pakistan with a friend days after the Taliban took control. Hamed and the rest of the family didn't hear news from their father until, two months later, the friend with whom he'd fled returned to Kabul with a letter. 'I'm alive,' his father had written. 'Come to Pakistan. We'll start a new life.'

At the time, the highway between Kabul and the Pakistani border, explains a friend of mine who made the same journey, was 'more like a series of ditches—most from war—that the vehicles ebbed and flowed in an out of, with dust blocking sight'. The Safis left Kabul at 4 a.m., arrived at the Torkham crossing 14 hours later, and spent the night on the floor of a hotel, waiting for the border gate to open the following morning. At dawn, along with hundreds of others hoping to leave Afghanistan, they fought their way through Taliban fighters who were striking the crowd with electric cables. The Safis didn't have passports, but by paying bribes to the Pakistani soldiers, they were allowed to cross.

Mujib had rented an apartment with a single large room in Peshawar. 'You rented an entire mosque for us,' Sahar joked, 'not a room.' Mujib opened a small shop where he served ice cream, burgers, or chicken and corn soup, depending on the season. Over time, he saw how dependent Afghan refugees were on the help of others and encouraged his children to eschew handouts and strive for independence. Their first opportunity arose close to home when the Safis became friendly with a neighbouring family, also Afghan refugees, who were carpet weavers. Soon, Hamed and Mahmoud were taken on as apprentices. After three months spent learning to weave, the Safi brothers built a loom in their apartment. The neighbours provided wool as well as patterns to replicate, and, outside school hours, Hamed and Mahmoud knotted dyed wool over the warps that stretched in hundreds of rows from the top to the bottom of the loom. It would take the brothers two months to complete an entire carpet, which the neighbours would then sell to a wholesaler on their behalf.

Early on in Pakistan, the Safis registered as asylum seekers through the United Nations' refugee agency, and just before the Taliban was toppled in late 2001, the family was offered resettlement in the United States. Sahar, who had recurring health problems, took the three youngest children with her to the US, while Mujib stayed in Pakistan with Hamed and Mahmoud until the boys could finish high school. When the United States invaded Afghanistan, Mujib received an invitation to return to work with his former boss, leaving Hamed and Mahmoud to finish the school year in Peshawar before they, too, returned home in the spring of 2002.

Hamed studied German literature at Kabul University, graduating in 2008. He undertook a scholarship in Germany and upon his return took a job teaching German in the evening at the Goethe Institute in Kabul. During the day, Hamed worked in the media-monitoring department at the presidential palace under Karzai. He then rotated through several jobs in the administration, including at the Government Media and Information Centre. There, he worked alongside advisors from the US military, collating security reports from the provinces and producing a daily briefing for the president. In 2012, he joined the Office of the Spokesperson to the President, which was later reconfigured and renamed the Office of Strategic and Public Affairs.

Through his father's connections with the old communist regime, Mahmoud went from high school into the 10th Directorate of the NDS, which was charged with providing security for government ministers, before joining the PPS in 2005. There, Mahmoud Safi was assigned to the counter-assault team before being promoted to the president's close protection team, which, he explains, involved 'protecting the president everywhere but the bathroom and bedroom'. He accompanied presidents Karzai and Ghani on a total of 14 international trips. He likes to show photos of himself standing beside—or behind—foreign leaders such as Barack Obama, French president Nicolas Sarkozy and British prime minister Gordon Brown, and a ream of American generals.

Sahar, meanwhile, returned to Kabul with her daughter Samira after they were issued with American passports. Samira was enrolled in grade seven where she struggled initially, having forgotten much of her native Dari in the United States. Her younger brothers remained in America to study at university there, while making annual visits to see the family in Kabul.

In early 2020, the COVID-19 pandemic prompted Sahar and Samira, who was by then married and looking to secure a visa for her husband, to return to the United States. It was around this time that the Doha Agreement was signed. While the Taliban refused to negotiate with the Afghan Government, who they regarded as illegitimate puppets of the US and thus sidelined from the talks, Hamed felt positive about the agreement at first. If the Taliban were no longer fighting the US, he thought, America would pressure them to negotiate with the government. He thought they could 'send educated people' to 'explain that Afghanistan is not the Afghanistan of the 1990s—there is a government, a military and an election system—and we'll have the upper hand'. Hamed envisaged members of the Taliban joining the government just as one former enemy, the mujahedin leader Gulbuddin Hekmatyar, had in 2017. 'I didn't have a problem with this,' he says.

Most of the promises the Taliban made in the Doha Agreement were vague and the United States wasn't willing to enforce them. The Taliban were nonetheless granted significant concessions on the battlefield. First, within a matter of months, the US and other international militaries would begin withdrawing forces from Afghanistan, and they would be entirely gone by 1 May 2021. Second, the US would cease offensive operations and air strikes against the insurgents. Furthermore, while supposedly pressuring the Taliban to talk peace with the Afghan Government, the US also insisted that the government make goodwill gestures to create momentum for this. When Ghani duly ordered the ANSF into a defensive posture, the Taliban capitalised and started overrunning rural areas. From the Americans, beyond public pronouncements of disappointment at the Taliban's lack of commitment to peace, there came no substantive repercussions. Hamed says that it was at this point that 'whispers' of secret deals between the government and the Taliban started swirling inside the palace.

In fact, Ghani's government was in no position to be making deals with the Taliban. What little leverage it believed it had was being whittled away by the day. As a senior Taliban military commander told me in 2020, the only deal the Taliban would accept from the government was surrender. And America's lack of resolve, brought on by its waning patience for the war itself, as well as Kabul's political infighting, wasn't helping.

According to Hamdullah Mohib, in 2019, while US–Taliban talks were proceeding in Doha, Dr Abdullah Abdullah told him that a large proportion of former Northern Alliance commanders—long-sworn enemies of the Taliban—had begun making contact with Taliban commanders. 'The Americans' move to negotiate directly with the Taliban without the presence of the Afghan Government,' says Mohib, 'was perceived as a signal by society—a signal that the Americans were handing over to the Taliban,' even if he didn't believe it himself. 'These people have to think about their survival,' he continues, about 'what happens when the Taliban are in charge of the government tomorrow'.

Nor was the Afghan Government making a genuine effort. It was a widely held view, says Ross Wilson, the US chargé d'affaires at the time, that 'one of Ghani's principal motivations was retaining his position as president. A second priority of president Ghani's was preserving the Islamic Republic, preserving the gains of the past 20 years, which we also sought, and he was quite difficult when it came to making concessions that he felt would call that into any serious question … it is pretty clear that in the period from 29 February [2020] to the fall [of the government], there was foot-dragging on the Afghan Government's part'. One Afghan political analyst told me it was less 'foot-dragging' and 'more placing IEDs on the path to peace'.

This was in part due to the bitter divisions between president Ghani and Dr Abdullah Abdullah, the titular head of the government-led negotiation efforts, who, Wilson says, were overwhelmingly united in their negotiation goals with the Taliban, but bitterly divided—personally and politically—in the wake of disputed presidential elections in 2014 and 2019. Furthermore, Wilson says, there was a well-founded belief that the Ghani government was 'trying to run out the clock to our presidential election and see if there's a change in the predilection to depart' Afghanistan. In other words, Ghani, a famed technocrat, was resorting to finger-crossing. If Biden won, Ghani hoped he would tear up the Doha Agreement and halt the troop withdrawal—a negligent miscalculation based on Biden's historical views on the Afghan war in and of itself. As Kabul stalled, however, the number of foreign troops dropped in accordance with the terms of the agreement. American forces alone went from 13 000 at the time it was signed in February 2020 to 8600 in July, months before talks between the Afghan Government and the Taliban had even commenced. 'The leverage the presence of US forces should have provided to the Afghan side in the talks started to wither away,' says Wilson, without crediting the Taliban's own deft hand in affecting the circumstances. 'We believed that the

Afghan side would have been better [placed] if they'd gotten to the table earlier and at a time when our leverage was greater.'

By the time President Joe Biden took office in early 2021, the US had only 2500 military personnel in Afghanistan, and the closer the 1 May deadline for the withdrawal of all troops drew, the more assured of victory the Taliban became.[5] On 14 April, Biden addressed the media in the White House briefing room. 'I'm now the fourth United States president to preside over [an] American troop presence in Afghanistan,' he said. 'Two Republicans, two Democrats. I will not pass this responsibility on to a fifth.'

The withdrawal wouldn't be complete by 1 May, as set out in the Doha Agreement, but it would continue nonetheless. 'We will not conduct a hasty rush to the exit,' said Biden. 'We'll do it responsibly, deliberately and safely.' A four-month extension, it was thought, would give the ANSF time to halt the Taliban advance.[6] 'The plan has long been "In together, out together,"' Biden added. 'US troops, as well as forces deployed by our NATO [North Atlantic Treaty Organization] allies and operational partners, will be out of Afghanistan before we mark the 20th anniversary of that heinous attack on September 11th.'[7]

I met Hamed Safi soon after Biden's briefing. In May 2021, I was at the presidential palace to photograph president Ghani for the German magazine *Der Spiegel*. Hamed, clean shaven, his hair carefully combed, wore a dark-blue tailored suit. It was almost a uniform for the young palace functionaries who modelled themselves on the foreign diplomats and Western advisors who had been common fixtures in the palace over the years, but Hamed wore it well. His work wardrobe was free of the small but noticeable sartorial slip-ups—branded white sports socks or clip-on neck-ties—made by some of his colleagues. By this time, Hamed had made more than 30 trips overseas with the media relations department. He was softly spoken but confident and genial—he also spoke several languages, including English and German. He showed me around the presidential library in the Haram Sarai Palace, one of several within the sprawling citadel of the Arg. Ghani, a famous reader and a co-author himself, was known to spend several hours each day reading from its collection.

I photographed Ghani while he was being interviewed by Susanne Koelbl, the *Der Spiegel* reporter, during which, in response to a question about how long his government could resist the Taliban's attacks without US support, Ghani replied: 'Forever.'[8] A few days later, after the story had been published under the headline 'I Know I Am Only One Bullet away from Death', one of Hamed's colleagues contacted me and asked whether I would spend two weeks mentoring the palace's in-house photo/video production department. As a journalist, I questioned the ethics of working for the government on the side, not to mention the prudence of casting doubt on my impartiality if the Taliban were to come to power. As it happened, with the war escalating quickly, and hopping from one province to the next as I was, with little time in Kabul, the proposal never eventuated. But Hamed and I kept in touch nonetheless.

On 8 July, Biden announced that he'd revised the withdrawal date. The symbolism of ending a war on the 20th anniversary of the attack that triggered it was poor. Instead, it was to be completed by 31 August.[9] Only two weeks before that announcement, Hamed had been in Washington, DC for president Ghani's two-day US official visit. He'd travelled with a small advance party: the president's deputy chief of protocol, two members of the PPS, and two US State Department advisors who worked with the Afghan Ministry of Foreign Affairs. Before the group had set off, the president's chief of protocol had emphasised the importance of the trip. 'The purpose was clear,' says Hamed. 'To get the support of the US administration and military and for [support] regarding the peace process' with the Taliban. The advance team arrived on 20 June and checked into the Willard Hotel, beside the White House. President Ghani, vice-president Saleh, Dr Abdullah, foreign minister Hanif Atmar, Hamdullah Mohib and a delegation of nearly 50 others arrived four days later.

The final meeting of the visit, on the afternoon of 25 June, which besides Ghani had Dr Abdullah and Mohib in attendance, was with Biden in the Oval Office. Ghani looked uncomfortable. He had forgone Afghan garb in favour of a black suit plus a grey tie that hung well below his belt. He sat awkwardly, both elbows on the armrests of an oversized chair, like a child sitting on a throne. Biden was breezy and informal, and his message was one of tough love. 'Afghans are going to have to decide … what they want,' he said. 'But we're going to stick with you. And we're going to do our best to see to it you have the tools you need.'

In the private meeting that followed, Ghani was more pointed. He had two requests regarding American involvement in Afghanistan in the near future. First, he asked about the level of military support his government could expect. Would Biden provide more helicopters? Would logistical and maintenance support continue to be supplied by defence contractors after the military withdrawal?[10]

Asked whether the delegation felt reassured by Biden's response, Mohib responds, 'Not really.' He says that, since he began dealing with the Americans in 2015 as ambassador to the United States, 'we were always in an uncertain state'—support was never assured for more than a few months at a time. Mohib says that 'we didn't have clarity whether we would have American support beyond September 11', the withdrawal deadline before it was brought forward to 31 August.

Ghani's second request was that the Americans refrain from evacuating Afghans in the lead-up to their withdrawal deadline. Word had made it to the palace that serving ANSF officers were among the US Special Immigrant Visa applicants awaiting resettlement; it was a similar situation with other countries. The prospect of thousands of citizens being flown to safety, undermining the president and heightening the growing sense of panic in Kabul, was bad enough. But if active-duty ANSF officers left, the blow to morale within the armed forces would be devastating. Further rankling Ghani and his cabinet were the contradictory messages being sent by the Americans as they publicly professed support for the Afghan Government while simultaneously evacuating Afghans with whom they had affiliations.

Afghan politicians had been criticised for years for housing their families in foreign countries, but Ghani seemed oblivious of the hypocrisy in his demand of Biden. The darkening reality, however, wasn't entirely lost on the Afghan delegation. Two of Mohib's children, eight-year-old Mariam and five-year-old Karlan, were aboard the charter from Kabul to Dulles International Airport, but not the return flight after the official visit. 'I hitched a ride on the delegation plane' with the children, says Lael Mohib, Hamdullah's wife. 'And from DC flew with my kids commercial to Florida to drop [them] with my mom.'

At Dulles International Airport, before boarding his flight back to Kabul, Hamed ran into his boss, Wahid Omar, who was booked on the same flight. Rumours that delegates were using the opportunity to flee Afghanistan were circulating on social media. 'He was shocked,' says Hamed. Omar had fully expected him to stay and apply for asylum. 'You're going back to Kabul?' he asked in disbelief.

< >

Being the head of the palace's media relations department, Hamed Safi brushed shoulders with the president and his most senior advisors on an almost daily basis. The palace, to and from which he was driven each day by a personal driver, was the centre of a republic that had been built from scratch over the previous two decades. Not since Hamed had begun working as a public servant in 2008, however, could he recall a time when his interactions inside the palace were as at odds with those outside, among ordinary citizens, as they were now.

Hamed lived in an enormous apartment complex on the narrow sliver of land between the northern side of Hamid Karzai International Airport and a mountain that marked the edge of the city limits. The Sheikh Khalifa Bin Zayed City Housing Complex, better known as Emirate City, was inaugurated in 2018 at a cost of US$190 million.[11] It comprises more than 3000 apartments in a total of 111 blocks. A large proportion of the homes, built by the Abu Dhabi Fund for Development, were offered at heavily discounted rates to government workers and the ANSF.

In the same year that the complex opened, Hamed moved there with his wife, Zarifa, who was 31 and taught at a private school in Kabul. Hamed and Zarifa's marriage was arranged by their families in 2011, 'then we fell in love with each other', he says. By 2021 they had two children—Heela, who was nine, and Yasin, two—and Zarifa was then six months' pregnant with their third. Hamed's father lived in another block in Emirate City, five minutes away by foot.

Hamed's mother, brothers and sisters all lived in the US, but that August, much of the family had reunited in Kabul for the first time since the COVID-19 pandemic had shut down global travel in early 2020. 'I'd already emphasised to my sister that they shouldn't come to Kabul,' says Hamed. 'The situation in Kabul wasn't good and I wasn't feeling good about the future. But my mother is her own boss.' Sahar had indeed already made up her mind. She missed Hamed, Mahmoud and her husband, who had raised the two boys alone in Kabul and had a case pending for residency in the US. Her health had been declining in recent years as well. In addition, Hamed's sister Samira had already taken leave from her work in the US and wanted to come to Kabul to work on a visa application for her husband.

As a senior member of the PPS, Mahmoud Safi knew that the safety of his family was his responsibility. He hadn't initially objected to their Kabul trip and took turns with Hamed in hosting the family members for dinner. In any case, Sahar would have come whether he had assented or not. 'In Islam,' says Hamed, 'we say we don't know our good days from our bad days. In the end, it will be God's way.' So they had come, and the Safi men had welcomed them. But, Hamed says, 'day by day, things got worse'.

When provincial capitals started collapsing after 6 August—the day Hamed's colleague Dawa Khan Menapal was shot dead—concern among the family mounted. However, for the Afghan adults, some of whom had been through several violent changes of government before, the primary concern wasn't for women and children, as on a sinking boat or in a burning house, but rather for anyone who had worked with the falling government. Having several years of combat experience with special forces units, Mahmoud talked down the risk to himself, even boasting that provinces falling to the Taliban didn't worry him. 'We were inside the palace,' he says. 'We thought we'd be safe there—we could fight and defend.' It was his brother Hamed he was most worried about.

Zarifa wanted Hamed to leave. 'We'll be okay,' she'd tell him, 'but without you, our lives aren't worth living.' But Hamed knew his wife, who had grown up in Pakistan, hadn't fully considered what might happen if she and their children remained in Kabul. 'Those who haven't lived under the Taliban,' he says, 'they don't know what life under their control will be like.'

Hamed's mother-in-law felt as his wife did. 'Every day she'd call,' he says, promising 'she'd come to stay with my wife and children while I go to the US'. But Hamed told her he couldn't leave his wife, especially while she was pregnant. 'Of course the security situation isn't good,' he told her, 'but I expect it to improve. I was hearing good news from the office—that the government forces will resist, that they will fight against the Taliban, and that even if the Taliban took all of Afghanistan, they can't enter Kabul. There is a negotiation process ongoing. They will negotiate a new government and there will be no fighting.'

When his mother begged him to leave, Hamed asked why he should go while she stayed behind. 'I'm an old woman,' she told him. 'I don't have a future ahead of me. You should get out of the country, build your future. You have kids and a young wife—you guys should not be here.' Besides, she said, there would always be a way for herself and the family to leave as they were US residents. 'We can leave anytime,' she said, 'but it's a very bad situation for *you*. You're working for the government and you're a target.'

Sahar was still haunted by the day in July 2014 when Afghanistan's largest television network, TOLONews, broadcast footage of the aftermath of the bombing of a vehicle with government plates. The white minivan was dotted with shrapnel holes, and a stream of blood ran from the frame of a shattered window. The victims had been taken from the vehicle, but journalists at the scene believed that one had been Hamed, the name repeated several times as the camera panned across the scene. Sahar and Mujib had been watching TOLONews at the time. 'I was on my way to the office when he called,' says Hamed of his father. 'They're reporting you're dead!' his father had exclaimed.

Even as the political elite inside the palace reassured their workers, the PPS warned in a weekly meeting that its intelligence channels were reporting a huge increase in threats to government staff, particularly in Emirate City. A member of the PPS intelligence office told palace staff: 'The Taliban are in the city and aiming to assassinate Arg staff. You should change your location. We can't protect you.'

That evening, Hamed relayed the warnings to Zarifa, and they decided to go and stay with Zarifa's sister, who lived closer to the palace—they left everything in their apartment. Zarifa and their daughter Heela would stay home from their respective schools until things improved. Hamed would continue travelling to the palace for work, but he would instruct his driver to use his private car instead of his government-issued vehicle, with its government plates.

Mahmoud, who had seen palace staff burning documents, was also growing tense. He had shared his concerns with his boss, Qahar Kochai, who tried to allay Mahmoud's fears: 'There's no cause for concern. Everything is normal.' Mahmoud wasn't convinced and insisted not only that Hamed should leave, but the rest of the family as well. 'I was yelling at them,' says Mahmoud. 'They became angry that I was using such strong language. My sister was so upset— they'd come to visit us and now I was demanding that they leave.'

He wasn't as forceful with his younger brother, but Mahmoud's message to Hamed was the same. Like his mother and sister, Hamed also had a visa for the US, from his June visit to Washington, DC. Mahmoud says he told his brother: 'The situation isn't going to improve. You should go. I will take care of your family.' Hamed's instincts as a husband and father, however, won out. 'I thought it was my responsibility to stay with my family,' he says.

At her sister's home, Zarifa taught their daughter while Hamed worked at the palace. Having no intention of returning to work at her school, she called the principal and told him that she was staying home because of complications with her pregnancy. But by 12 August, after more than a week with Zarifa's sister, Hamed was feeling frustrated with living away from home. Even as he watched the provinces tumble one after another, and continued to receive warnings about Taliban assassinations, the idea of being in his home, with his family, was one of the few thoughts that brought him comfort. Returning to their apartment would also give him a chance to water the small garden he'd grown, which would be withering in the summer heat, and to gather his family's documents in case they needed to leave in a hurry. Having witnessed the lawlessness that previous chaotic transitions of government in Afghanistan had brought, Hamed also wanted to be at home so he could defend it, if necessary with a Soviet-era Makarov pistol that Mahmoud had given him when he'd first moved to Emirate City. 'Every time Kabul has collapsed in the past,' he says, 'even your neighbours will enter your home when you're not there and steal everything.'

While Hamed could make decisions based on what he himself knew, and his experiences in the past, the mixed messages he and his brother were getting from inside the palace provoked only doubt and indecision. He didn't know who or what to believe.

< >

President Ghani and his war cabinet were overwhelmed by the Taliban's rapid advances, but they still believed they had options— to fight or negotiate—for Kabul. It was a delusion.

On the night of 11 August, Ross Wilson met with Hamdullah Mohib at his residence on the palace grounds, where Mohib told him that Ghani was willing to relinquish power on the condition that his successor was chosen in an election. Wilson told Mohib that, under the circumstances, it was an unrealistic expectation.

The pressure on Ghani continued to mount. Less than two weeks earlier, he had declared in a special joint parliamentary session that 'a clear plan is prepared for reaching stability in six months and the implementation of the plan has started'. Details of the supposed plan were never made public. If they existed at all, they were by now in tatters. Still, the government pounded major cities with desperate and merciless aerial bombardments even after any realistic hope of salvaging control over them was gone. In Kandahar, Afghan Air Force warplanes—re-arming inside the city's airfield, which remained in government hands—ran constant bombing sorties over the city even after it had been forfeited. Dozens of Afghan special forces soldiers were sent to their deaths from Kabul in a futile effort to stop Lashkar Gah from falling as Afghan and American aircraft obliterated the city from above. Despite the bravado of lieutenant-general Sami Sadat, the ANA's commanding officer in Helmand, and his empowerment by the likes of Mohib in Kabul, the reckless defence only delayed the city's inevitable fall and in the meantime cost an untold number of lives—many of them among Afghanistan's most elite soldiers.

The following day, news had come in that Herat, Afghanistan's third-largest city, had fallen. In the wake of Wilson's cool response to his suggestion of an election the night before, Ghani told Mohib that, instead, with the consent of key political leaders, he would be willing to hold a Loya Jirga—an extraordinary assembly of representatives from across the country. 'We didn't understand this to be a negotiated surrender,' says Mohib, of himself and Ghani. 'This was something we saw the Taliban having to agree with.' If they did, Mohib and Ghani reasoned, the fighting could stop and the country's future could be decided by consensus in Kabul's Loya Jirga hall rather than by bloodletting in the streets of Kabul. 'The idea was that the Loya Jirga would endorse a transfer of power,' says Mohib. 'We still thought we had enough leverage to negotiate.'

Mohib arranged to once again meet with Wilson to update him on the latest developments. He brought with him Fazel Mahmood Fazly, head of the Administrative Office of the President. During such a critical period, Mohib thought, Fazly would serve as an alibi in the event of rumours of secret deals surfacing. At the meeting, which was held at the National Security Council's (NSC) guesthouse in the palace grounds, five minutes by car from the US Embassy, Mohib informed Wilson of the president's Loya Jirga compromise proposal. He also outlined the government's preconditions: 'No persecution or prosecution of former ANSF officials or government officials, including attorneys from the Attorney-General's Office, former judges, which we thought would be an especially vulnerable group, civil society, media—that these protections should be agreed to first, then we would enter into negotiations, followed by a Loya Jirga.' Wilson says, 'I took on board what he had to say and reported it to Washington.'

That night, Ghani spoke via conference call with US Secretary of State Antony Blinken and Secretary of Defense Lloyd Austin. He was expecting his Loya Jirga proposal to be the main item on the agenda. More important to the Americans, however, were their own immediate interests in Kabul. Blinken told Ghani that the US Embassy was moving from its site beside the international military mission's headquarters to the airport. Mohib said that wasn't 'in line with the ideas that were being discussed', and that it was yet another indication of the lack of confidence the Americans had in a peaceful transfer of power. Austin said he was bringing in additional troops to assist in the final two weeks of the withdrawal. It now appeared that it was not only America's troops who were leaving but its diplomats as well.

'Leaving with the military by [31 August] was one outcome,' says Wilson, 'perhaps the likely one, but this decision had not been made by that time.' Nonetheless, there was no mention of the Loya Jirga idea. By the time the desperate, last-ditch proposal was directly raised two days later, in another call between Ghani and Blinken, the circumstances in Kabul had deteriorated dramatically. It was, says Mohib, 'a missed opportunity'.

At a security meeting in the palace on the morning of 13 August, Dr Abdullah, who had recently returned from Doha, was invited to address Ghani and his war cabinet. Abdullah and his team didn't believe the Taliban were interested in negotiating for the kind of peace they were seeking. Peace in the republic's view would see the Taliban brought into the existing system: the Islamic Republic of Afghanistan, with its leaders, still seemingly oblivious to on-the-ground realities, remaining in power. Peace as the Taliban saw it was nothing less than the unconditional return of the Islamic Emirate of Afghanistan, as they referred to their administration, and they would achieve it militarily if they could. Once briefings had been given by the ministers of defence and the interior, as well as vice-president Saleh and the director of intelligence, Zia Seraj, a recommendation was made to the president: 'Since the Taliban don't want to see peace, we must resist.' Such a resolution, it was agreed, would require an equally strong message, a video recording, from the president and the minister of defence, 'a message of full-on war with the Taliban'.

There was fervour in the room. Saleh, who had pushed for the mobilisation of militias, tweeted that 'it was decided with conviction & resolve that WE STAND FIRM AGAINST TALIBAN TERRORISTS & DO EVERTYHING TO STRENGTHEN THE NATIONAL RESISTANCE BY ALL MEANS AND WAYS. PERIOD. We are proud of our ANDSF'.[12]

The briefings that morning had allayed some of Mohib's fears, in particular that the Taliban could threaten Kabul within the week. But despite the passion aroused, Wilson's pragmatic tone over the past two days rang in Mohib's ears: after the security meeting, Mohib says he conferred with the president and suggested toning down the bellicose rhetoric in case the resistance failed. Mohib later told Fazly that 'the message of war that was recommended to the president is the wrong recommendation. I am following security updates across the country more intimately these days than anytime in the past, and I find that there is hardly any resistance wherever the Taliban attack now. People are not fighting back'.

There was truth to Mohib's analysis, but going against the cabinet's recommendation and making a unilateral decision with the president was exactly the kind of behaviour for which Mohib had been drawing criticism from palace staff like Hamed Safi in recent months. 'Dr Mohib was always trying to handle everything himself,' says Hamed. His office had even begun asserting control over independent government departments inside the palace, like the PPS and protocol. It deepened both the confusion among palace staff and the belief that the republic was now a two-man show.

That afternoon, Hamed was informed that president Ghani would make an impromptu trip outside the palace that evening. In accordance with security protocols, he wasn't told where the president would visit, only that he needed to arrange for his video and photographer colleagues to travel with the advance party. The president was apparently going to deliver an important message that would need to be sent to the media immediately for broadcast.

Mahmoud Safi was dispatched with the advance party in a road convoy. PPS teams usually arrived several hours in advance of the president to reconnoitre the location: they would sweep for bombs, make emergency evacuation plans, emplace snipers and generally secure the area. On this occasion, president Ghani would be arriving by helicopter, but Mahmoud called the palace to inform the pilots that conditions at the site's helicopter landing zone, the Bala Hissar, were poor and would send plumes of dust into the sky, and potentially into the president's aircraft. The PPS would need time to water down the landing zone. However, it transpired that the helicopters—a second one carried Bismillah Khan Mohammadi, the minister of defence—were already in the air and would be landing soon. There was an air of impatience that was unfamiliar to Mahmoud and the PPS, which always demanded thorough planning and adherence to protocol.

At Bala Hissar, a palace videographer attached a lavalier microphone to the president's collar and filmed a piece to camera.

A photographer then composed a handful of frames with the president and the defence minister pointing into the distance, as if surveying a front line. Later that night, Hamed would watch the edited footage inside the palace media office and discuss it with Wahid Omar. 'This is a clear message in support of fighting,' Omar would say. But he had already been told by Mohib, who by then didn't believe the security forces would be able to muster a defence of the capital, to hold off broadcasting the piece to camera, and he would instead order Hamed to ensure it wasn't circulated.

‹ ›

On the same afternoon that Ghani filmed his video message, 13 August, Mohib invited two nephews with whom he had grown up and their wives to his residence. Esmat, who ran Zawia, an online media outlet in Kabul, and Sebghat were similar in age to Mohib, and they had always referred to one another as brothers. Mohib had told the pair a week or two prior that they should think about leaving the country; now he was adamant. The men agreed and booked flights for 15 August.

Before they left his home, Mohib handed Esmat and Sebghat a bag he'd filled with personal belongings: notebooks, the Frederique Constant watch he and his wife Lael had bought when he was named ambassador to the US, a silver pen given to him by CIA Director William Burns, and another pen (a Montblanc) that Dr Abdullah had used during negotiations with Ghani to form a government after the disputed 2019 election, subsequently gifted to Mohib. He asked his nephews to take the bag with them and give it to Lael, who had lived in Kabul since 2009 but had left for Abu Dhabi in the United Arab Emirates with Sara, Mohib's daughter from a previous marriage, a month earlier, on 12 July, after several rocket attacks on the palace led her to conclude that 'it wasn't worth the kids' lives'; she was also pregnant with their fourth child.

Later, when it was past midnight, Mohib would text Lael to explain which item was for which of the children; the notebooks

were for her. 'When the story's written,' he would say, 'I want
you to know what happened.' At the time, he didn't believe he
would survive.

After his nephews had left, Mohib says he called the director
of intelligence and the ministers of the interior and defence for
a heart-to-heart. Based on his own doubts, Mohib wanted to
reassess with the security chiefs whether continuing to stand up
to the Taliban was something for which they still had the capacity.
Perhaps, away from the cabinet, where any stance other than all-
out war was liable to be perceived as weak, the security heads
would provide a more sober assessment. He also thought that the
Americans in Doha would soon begin negotiating with the Taliban
over his and Ghani's Loya Jirga solution, and he says he didn't
want to contradict that with a public war cry, especially if what
remained of the government's forces couldn't back it up—he still
believed both options were on the table. Mohib deliberately kept
the army chief of staff out of the meeting, concerned, he says, that
talk of a possible negotiated settlement might distract him from the
foundering resistance he was trying to lead.

Mohib says he grilled the others about whether the decision the
war cabinet had come to that morning, the one recommended to
the president and almost made public with the recorded message—
to fight—was still tenable. Herat had fallen since then, and all the
reports the security chiefs were receiving from their commanders
outside Kabul indicated that their men weren't fighting. 'The
unanimous view,' Mohib says, in complete contradiction of their
pugnacious appraisal only hours earlier, 'was, "It's not possible."'
According to Mohib, Mohammadi said 'his forces weren't fighting
and that he had never seen a situation like this before in his life'.
The defence minister also discounted the possibility of mounting
a resistance from the Panjshir Valley, where anti-Soviet and anti-
Taliban movements, of which he himself had been a part, had arisen
in the 1980s, 1990s and early 2000s; the supply routes they'd relied
on in the past were now in Taliban hands, and there was little
support from the civilian population. Even the families of Afghan

Air Force pilots were urging them to abandon their positions because of the danger it placed them in.

Abdul Satar Mirzakwal, the minister of the interior, discounted the possibility of the president retreating to the province of Khost, where his tribal support was strongest, and relying on Pashtunwali, the Pashtun tribal code that would obligate the Tanai tribe to protect him. The majority of the Khost Protection Force, a notorious CIA proxy group from the area dominated by the tribe, was fighting its way towards Kabul while tribal elders were busy trying to negotiate their safe passage.

According to Mohib, intelligence director Zia Seraj, who was supporting uprising forces in several provinces, said the militias were defending in some cases, but that ultimately they weren't able to halt the Taliban's momentum. Ismael Khan and several senior security officials had been captured in Herat, in the west, and the former mujahedin commanders in the north, Ata Mohammad Noor and Abdul Rashid Dostum, had both fled across the border into Uzbekistan. 'The only way forward,' says Mohib, 'was a negotiated settlement.'

Mohib relayed the message to Ghani, who asked Mohib to inform his vice-president and Dr Abdullah of the reversal. The Taliban were yet to agree to the arrangement—they never did—but Abdullah was nonetheless charged with assembling a team to travel to Doha to negotiate the presumed settlement and, along with it, the fate of Afghanistan. With that decision, Ghani told Mohib, who would be part of the delegation, that he felt he no longer held the authority of the leader of the republic.

Antony Blinken wasn't informed of the decision until the following evening, 14 August, when he spoke with Ghani by phone, insisting he send the delegation to Doha as quickly as possible.

Earlier that day, Mohib had met with Amrullah Saleh, who was the most aggressively anti-Taliban official in the government, and who had become renowned for his antagonistic public pronouncements against the insurgents. The vice-president still believed in fighting and was upset that the message agreed to the previous day had not been broadcast. Mohib explained what the security chiefs had told him, in private, the night before. The pair also spoke about what they each planned to do in the event that resistance and negotiations both failed and the Taliban took Kabul by force. Saleh fully expected to die. Mohib said that if the Taliban came to the palace, 'I would sit in my office and let them do it there—let them kill me there.'

In the Office of Strategic and Public Affairs, meanwhile, Hamed Safi once again asked Wahid Omar what to do with the video clip of the president and the minister of defence from the previous day. 'We are not publishing it,' maintained Omar. Mohib, by this point, was convinced that mounting a military defence of Kabul was futile. Broadcasting a message of aggression would only rile the Taliban, with whom the director of the Afghan intelligence agency was also in the middle of negotiating for the release of the captured security officials in Herat. Instead, a handful of photos of Ghani and Mohammadi, purporting to have been taken that day, were released and published accordingly by several international media outlets. The photos, Mohib thought, would at least dispel mounting rumours that the president had fled.[13] (That same day, the officials in Herat would be released, escorted to Herat airport by Taliban fighters, and flown to Kabul on a chartered aircraft.)

Hamed thought Mohib was looking for a quiet escape and had undermined the president, who was more inclined to defend Kabul militarily. 'My plan was to stay beside the president,' says Hamed. 'It would have been a matter of great pride to die fighting by the president.' According to Mohib, he had no such escape plan. When a member of the NSC staff told him that American officials had put the staffer's name on a list guaranteeing him a seat on an evacuation flight, a bolt of panic shot through Mohib. 'I realised then,' he says, 'that our allies were making plans to cut their cord with Afghanistan by completely withdrawing all their civilian presence and every person they considered an ally.'

Mohib spoke to Tom West, then America's deputy special representative for Afghanistan reconciliation, who was in Doha at the time, telling him: 'I found out about this list. Am I and the president included on your list?'

West asked whether that was a request. 'If it needs to be a request,' Mohib replied, 'I'll make it one.'

West asked Mohib to send him something in writing. After doing so, Mohib received a curt, written response: 'Received.'

It was a far cry from the guarantee Mohib had expected. It also triggered the realisation that an escape plan may in fact become necessary.

That evening, Wilson received an unusual request: both he and Admiral Peter Vasely, the commander of US forces in Afghanistan, were asked to meet with president Ghani and Mohib. Before that, Wilson had only been requested by Ghani to meet once or twice in his 18 months as the top US diplomat in Afghanistan. Also present was the CIA's Kabul chief of station and lieutenant-general Haibatullah Alizai, newly appointed as army chief of staff. Alizai, who had been omitted from the meeting with Mohib the previous night so he could focus on tactical and strategic matters rather than policy, surprised the others with an 'upbeat' plan—not only to defend Kabul, but to push the Taliban back. By now, only Jalalabad—the capital of the eastern province of Nangarhar—along with Mazar-i Sharif, Khost, Kabul and parts of the provinces neighbouring Kabul, remained under government control. Alizai would, he said, deploy around the capital existing special forces battalions based in Kabul and others that had recently retreated there, as well as those awaiting transportation from outlying provinces that had already collapsed. He told the meeting that it would take 'at least three days to a week' to emplace the troops in preparation 'for securing Kabul until the end of August and beyond that'.

Lieutenant-general Sami Sadat, a brash young soldier with years of military training abroad, and a reputation for braggadocio, would be brought in as chief of security for Kabul. A presidential decree was written up and signed to formalise the appointment. Major Behzad Behnam, the commanding officer of the Afghan Reconnaissance Unit, the ANA's most elite fighting force, said the appointment should have come weeks before, at least. 'The appointment of Sami at that moment,' says Behnam, 'was like a prayer.'

After the meeting, president Ghani approached Alizai and thanked him. Mohib was also impressed, not least because in the past it had been extremely difficult to get the Ministry of Defence to explain its plans. To Alizai, Mohib said, 'I'll admit one thing: I wish that we had brought you in way before this.'

'Yes, it's already too late,' said Alizai, 'but let's cross our fingers and do our best.'

The Americans were even less convinced of the chances of success. At the beginning of the meeting, Wilson was taken aback when a group of journalists and photographers was ushered into the room, which he took as an indication that the meeting was a photo-op called primarily to reassure the Afghan public that the US Government was continuing to support Kabul. It would also show the Americans that Ghani was still united with his senior defence leadership. The plan, says Wilson, 'wasn't a bad plan'. But many of the soldiers on whom Alizai would rely to secure Kabul were stuck in Kandahar or in Helmand or other provinces from which 'the government had no means, really, to get them back to Kabul, because the air force, at that point, was not able to do that'. Wilson says of himself and Admiral Vasely: 'Both of us had the same reaction.' The meeting was 'a signal to his [Ghani's] people and to us that they got it, they're united, they have a plan, and also, I think, a sense that it wasn't very realistic'.

The decline of the Afghanistan Government's diplomatic and military standing had been precipitous. Wilson says that in the middle of July, the Americans still believed that, with a combination of political unity and a plan for the consolidation of the ANSF, Kabul could buy enough time to ensure that 'some kind of a power-sharing arrangement could be obtained in which the Taliban would have a very large and significant role, but not the only role, [and] that there was a reasonable chance to try to get some guarantees or provisions about future elections, about at least a few of the basic human rights issues and maybe most importantly some kind of orderly transfer of power as opposed to [a] collapse'. With the government's failure to secure either, says Wilson, it became clear 'that the best one could hope for was … by early August, defending a rough area around Kabul to try to help to secure a reasonable negotiation'. But as the days passed and the Taliban moved closer to the capital, Wilson says 'the imaginable terms became worse and worse for the Afghan [Government] side'.

Wilson continued: 'We had been drawing down our staff since late April, in the run-up to May 1st [the original withdrawal deadline] and [amid] concerns about what might happen then. We carried out a further substantial reduction in the latter part of July or early August—about 400. We decided on maybe the 12th [of August] on another draw-down of another 400-plus people … and we began preparations for potential evacuations—taking down stuff that didn't need to be around the embassy, packing things up, preparing to ship out material, drawing down our holdings of weaponry and ammunition, armoured vehicles … That really accelerated on the 13th and 14th.'

Wilson says that, a week into August, he and other US officials expected the fighting would continue outside the capital into September and that the Taliban would not seriously threaten Kabul until after the American forces had completed their withdrawal. But when 'the capitals in the south-east started to fall, especially Ghazni [on 12 August] … an armed invasion of Kabul started to look a lot more likely'. By 14 August, Wilson says, 'the game was up'. He adds: 'What accelerated our planning and especially our execution [of the evacuation] was the [Taliban's] push up through the provinces in the south-east, Ghazni and then Logar and Wardak, increasingly putting a kind of noose around Kabul.'

Mohib was waiting for Ghani after his call to Blinken informing the Secretary of State about the plan for the Loya Jirga. The two had been close for more than a decade, ever since Mohib had hosted Ghani, during a speaking tour for *Fixing Failed States*, the book he co-authored, at the Afghan Students Association U.K. in London in 2008. Mohib found Ghani to be unlike other high-profile visiting

Afghans, who 'just talked about themselves'. 'He was very humble,' says Mohib. 'He was on his own, carrying his own laptop bag without an entourage, and when he sat down and started talking he talked about the country ... he had ideas, for dams and water management and how to build the economy, and I was very taken by that'. When Ghani had invited Mohib, then only 26, to join his presidential campaign team in 2009, Mohib says he accepted because he wanted to see the ideas Ghani had spoken about realised, 'to create the Afghanistan we had envisioned'. But following the call with Blinken, Ghani was exhausted. Mohib walked him to his residence and then, accompanied as always by a bodyguard, continued on to his own residence to work.

Later that night, Haibatullah Alizai called Mohib to tell him Sami Sadat couldn't accept the role of Kabul security chief. Sadat had been injured by shrapnel during fighting in Helmand and wanted to travel to India for treatment. Mohib continued communicating with security officials until 4 a.m. the next morning, 15 August. Just before he lay down to try to sleep, he received news that Jalalabad had surrendered. He knew this meant the Taliban would be at Kabul's eastern gate within a matter of hours.

‹ ›

After finishing his work at the presidential palace on 14 August, Hamed Safi returned to his family in Emirate City to find that Zarifa was upset with him. The Taliban had seized Mazar-i Sharif that day, and now only six or seven provincial capitals remained in government hands. Kabul was almost completely surrounded. Zarifa had believed that, because her husband worked in the palace, he had access to all the best information, and that he would know, before almost anyone, when the situation began to spin out of control. 'It's too late,' she said. 'You should have already left like I told you.'

Hamed doesn't remember eating that night. His daughter Heela pleaded with him not to go to the palace the next day. He felt as though he was being torn apart by his obligations to his family. Having experienced the fall of the mujahedin government to the Taliban in the 1990s, he knew the coming weeks might well become violent and chaotic, but as a husband and father he didn't want to show the fear he felt. Above all, he needed to work out how to keep his family safe.

After dinner, Hamed packed the documents he'd gathered into a case and placed it inside the front door. He then sat on the floor with his laptop and phone and began contacting the Americans he'd worked with between 2010 and 2012 at the Government Media and Information Centre, individuals who had assisted Hamed by compiling security news from around the country for the president's office. Hamed told his American friends that he was the only member of the family with a visa. 'I can go to the airport by myself,' he said, 'but my family will be here. My biggest concern is my family.' He was asked to send scans of the most important documents he'd collected.

An American soldier who'd remained in contact with a former Afghan colleague of Hamed's, who had already left Afghanistan and who was helping other media centre staff, completed visa application forms for Hamed's family. The Priority 2 (P2) visas the soldier was applying for had been brought online at the start of August and were being offered to Afghans and their families who were at risk of Taliban reprisals because of their affiliations with the US Government.[14] But neither Hamed nor his American friends had any idea how long the P2 visa-approval process would take, especially when there was no guarantee the US Embassy would even remain open.

Before Hamed went to sleep at 3 a.m. on 15 August, the American soldier told him that if there was any trouble, he should get away from his apartment but remain in regular contact. Hamed says, 'We had no idea what would happen the next day.'

3

Shah Shahid, Kabul
I

'I was living my life in dreams only,' says Nadia Amini, referring to when she was sitting for exams at the end of her third semester at a madrassa in Kabul, in August 2021. The school, Abu Hanifa, was named after an eighth-century theologian whose grandfather was said to have been sold as a slave not far from Nadia's home village, two hours north of Kabul.[1] But Nadia, who was 19, didn't like referring to the place where she studied as a madrassa. Among her friends, that word was synonymous with another that evoked pure loathing: *taliban*, the Pashto word for 'religious student', which a group of zealous young fighters in southern Afghanistan had adopted just before taking control of the country in 1996. Nadia instead referred to Abu Hanifa as a 'university'.

It wasn't Nadia's choice to study there, and she didn't fit in with many of the 3000 other students.[2] For one thing, Abu Hanifa was in Bagrami, a poor, conservative district on the eastern outskirts of Kabul, and home mostly to Pashtuns. The Pashtuns comprised the largest of Afghanistan's ethnic groups and their tribes had ruled the region for centuries. Nadia's parents were both of Tajik descent, and although she tried to avoid judging people based on their ethnicity, at Abu Hanifa this contributed to a sense of alienation that at the time seemed to have been colouring all aspects of her life.

Nadia did make friends with a small group of students who, like her, were not so serious about Islam but who, unlike her, had chosen to study at the madrassa because of the prestige bestowed on graduates. They would surreptitiously roll their eyes when other young women scolded them for laughing too loudly or dressing in a way they deemed immodest. 'Everyone was trying to present themselves as a good Muslim,' says Nadia. Students weren't allowed to take phones to school because they could be used to take photos, and they were warned, when speaking to men *and* women, not to look them in the eye. Female students wore long, grey hijabs which they also had to tie across their faces, leaving a crescent-shaped opening through which they could see. Many wore slim, black gloves that also covered their wrists. Heels taller than an inch were strictly forbidden. Punishments were not meted out to students who infringed, but the madrassa, much like Afghan society, had a way of self-regulating, ensuring that only a minimum of resistance to conservative standards was tolerated.

'It was like living under the Taliban,' says Nadia. Indeed, as the Taliban's grip on the country strengthened, the self-appointed arbiters of such standards were emboldened. Abu Hanifa was, in many ways, a trial run for a day Nadia hoped would never come: the day the Taliban returned to Kabul.

Nadia lived with her mother and father and two younger brothers in the Kabul neighbourhood of Shah Shahid; her older brother Rahim and sister Bahira had moved to Germany in 2015. The Aminis had left their home province of Kapisa in 2016 because of unrelenting threats from the Taliban over Rahim's work with the local police. However, even in Kabul, a maze of unnamed streets packed with six million residents, Nadia's father, 66-year-old Amin, remained vigilant, renting homes for no more than a year before moving to another. With Rahim out of the country, he thought, the Taliban might try to take revenge on the family instead, and he wanted to make it as difficult as he could for them to be found.

The Aminis weren't rich, but they owned a few acres of farmland in Amin's ancestral village of Mir Bacha Kot, between Kabul and Kapisa province, on the Shomali Plain. There, Amin grew grapes, peaches, pomegranates and walnuts. The trees and vines had taken years to recover after Taliban fighters had destroyed every orchard, vineyard, crop, water well and home, and forced residents to leave, during a 1999 scorched-earth campaign aimed at quelling pockets of resistance in Tajik villages across the Shomali.[3] Amin paid the sharecroppers who worked the land a portion of each harvest. Along with the rent from a couple of homes they also owned, the sales sustained the family after Amin had retired.

Their father would give Nadia and her younger brothers pocket money each morning—no more than 100 Afghani (a little more than an Australian dollar)—which Nadia collected in a clay pot, like the ones that farmers on the Shomali preserved grapes in and sold by the highway to Kabul. Hers was painted gold and had a slit in the top through which she poked folded-up Afghani notes. The only way to retrieve the money would be to smash the pot.

Amin had bought an old, single-storey home in one of Shah Shahid's quiet residential streets. He planned to knock it down and build a new house. The street ran off a busier road that had small shops selling flour, rice and lentils from woven plastic grain sacks, and a primary school which split classes for girls and boys into morning and afternoon sessions. Early in the morning, hundreds of girls would hurry through the streets in a tide of white hijabs, stopping to buy popcorn or sweets from street vendors who would come and go as the school sessions began and ended. On the far side of the street that ran perpendicular to Nadia's, beyond two concrete barriers that prevented anything larger than a rickshaw from passing, was a high concrete wall topped with a chain-link fence covered in green 'sniper screen' and coils of razor wire, and which ran for several blocks in either direction. Men in uniform stood watch in guard towers above signs that forbade photographs. Behind the wall was a compound used by ANA military intelligence personnel. In 2015, a truck filled with explosives was detonated by its driver outside the compound in the middle of the night, flattening a decrepit hardware bazaar opposite and leaving a 5-metre-deep crater in the road.[4]

In spite of that attack, in May 2021, as the Taliban were creeping closer and closer to Kabul, cutting off major highways as they approached, Amin had moved his family to the house in Shah Shahid because of the sense of security that being close to an important piece of military infrastructure provided. By August, the idea seemed almost fanciful. In provinces across Afghanistan, government security forces were capitulating day after day. 'Every morning there was news,' says Nadia. 'I was so tired of it. "The Taliban took this province, the Taliban took that province ..."' The mood at home was becoming tense. The Aminis were beginning to feel trapped. Reports of Taliban fighters forcibly marrying young women when they moved into newly conquered territory sent chills up Nadia's spine. The entire family knew that if the Taliban ever captured Kabul, it would be impossible for them to hide forever.

Nadia and her younger brothers Hanif, who was 17, impetuous, and less mature than 14-year-old Elham, who the family often called 'grandfather' because of his wisdom, berated their parents for allowing the family to become so vulnerable. 'Why are we in Kabul?' Hanif would ask. 'You should be taking us out!' Elham remembered the time, when he was just seven or eight, that local Taliban fighters had come to their home in Kapisa looking for Rahim—he was still terrified of the long-haired insurgents.

Nadia sympathised with Amin, though. 'It was very difficult for my father,' she says. 'He did everything for us without a care for himself.' Amin had even considered moving the family to Turkey, as he'd heard that country granted citizenship to foreigners—even Afghans—who purchased land or a home there.

Rahim, on vacation from work in Germany, was getting anxious as well. He sensed that time was running out for his family back in Kabul. 'If anything happens to my family,' he thought, 'it will be my fault.' He was calling home every day, trying to coax his family into being positive, but it rarely worked. Talking to Elham, he felt helpless. 'The Taliban are coming!' Elham exclaimed one night. 'They'll kill us! Do something!'

Rahim was pushing Nadia and Hanif to apply for scholarships overseas as a way of getting out. To do so, however, they'd have had to pass a TOEFL—a Test of English as a Foreign Language. Hanif, who was in his final year of high school and had taken on the affectations of a Kabul thug, wearing sneakers, his pants legs high on his calves, and with his hair greasy with olive oil, barely spoke a word of English.

Nadia's mother, Shukria, who was 51, short in stature, her eyebrows eternally furrowed, was as stoic as ever. Her strength had always been a comfort to Nadia, who, even at the age of 19, slept most nights cuddled up beside her. One night a year earlier, Nadia had steeled herself to sleep alone, taking her bedding into another room. But at midnight, woken by a nightmare, she ran back to Shukria, clutching her sheet and pillow. 'I'll never sleep another night alone,' she told her mother.

Before August 2021, the Aminis had spread out among their home's four rooms: Amin in one, Nadia and her mother in another, and Hanif and Elham each in their own room. A week into that month, however, they were all sleeping in the one room. They'd wake at the sound of gunshots they'd ordinarily have slept through. Alarms from foreign embassies practising drills for evacuations and rocket attacks echoed eerily through the Kabul basin. One night, a terrifying roar broke the silence: kilometres away, at Hamid Karzai International Airport, American soldiers were testing a Counter Rocket and Mortar system. The weaponry fired hundreds of rounds per second towards an imaginary rocket flying over Kabul. Self-destructing in midair, the deadly slugs peeled open like petals from a flower bulb and fell to the ground with a clink.

Although he'd given up on getting himself and his family out of Afghanistan, Amin did what he could at home to protect them in the event the Taliban overran Kabul. As had become common practice among Afghans during violent changes of regime in the past, with the inevitable purging of dissidents—first by the

Soviets and their thuggish Afghan intelligence agents, then by the Taliban, and in 2001 by the US and their allies from the Northern Alliance—Amin built a false wall in one of the rooms of the house in Shah Shahid. If the government collapsed and anarchy took hold, he'd be able to hide the family's valuables, particularly its gold, which—like many Afghan families—he'd bought because it was safer than entrusting large amounts of money to a banking system known for multibillion-dollar frauds. More likely, however, was a Taliban takeover, and Amin knew it wouldn't take long for their fighters to begin systematically hunting enemies from the previous government, its armed forces and intelligence agencies, and their families. Inherently distrustful, Amin bought a load of bricks and constructed the false wall himself. He used leftover cement as render, smoothing it down with a wooden plasterer's float, then leaving it to dry.

For Nadia, it wasn't just the Taliban's approach that was a source of distress. Since she'd graduated from high school, her family had become increasingly uneasy about her leaving the house alone, Hanif especially so. He'd always been protective of his older sister, but in the last year or two he had become more controlling, more aggressive. He'd protest to his parents that it wasn't safe for Nadia to be out on her own, that she could be kidnapped or harmed because of Rahim's work with the police. When Rahim had encouraged his siblings to take the TOEFL test, Hanif had rattled off the reasons why Nadia shouldn't: 'It's too dangerous for her to be on the streets in unfamiliar neighbourhoods in Kabul. How would she survive on her own in a foreign country anyway?'

Their father, and even the younger Elham, began to embrace Hanif's cynicism. 'He was only a child, but everyone is accepting his wishes,' says Nadia. 'In Afghanistan, the family often goes with the son's wishes.' Nadia knew the constraint they commanded had little to do with her safety and everything to do with the propensity most Afghan families have—and which few young Afghan women escape as they begin to explore life outside the confines of the home—for maintaining control over the lives of women. It was as if permitting any kind of independence could only result in behaviour that would reflect poorly on the family.

For Nadia, Abu Hanifa provided the perfect ruse: her family saw it as a place of great piety, but for her, in spite of the eagle eyes her fellow students and faculty had for sin, the pressure to conform was somehow less there than it was at home. During her end-of-semester exams in early August, Nadia studied at Abu Hanifa rather than at home like her friends—and much to their consternation, in the past her grades had always been higher than theirs, despite her studying for a fraction of the time they had. She even treasured the unpredictability of the shared taxis she rode to and from the madrassa: mini-vans crammed with strangers; conductors hanging out the sliding doors, crying out destinations and collecting fares; and the short walks at either end.

One day, overwhelmed by the limits imposed by her family, Nadia told them she was going to Abu Hanifa to study. Instead, she took a taxi to the other side of the city to see her oldest friend, Mariyam. They had lived close to one another in southern Kabul until the year before, when Mariyam's family had moved across the city's eponymous river, which runs north-east to south-west and effectively cuts Kabul in two. The distance separating them, and the Aminis' intensifying scrutiny of Nadia's behaviour, had made it hard for them to see one another more than once every few months. 'It was a moment I needed to cry,' says Nadia. 'I was so sad about family problems and there was no-one at home I could talk to about them.'

Soon enough, however, the disquiet at home was usurped by the cause of the angst gripping much of Kabul. By 14 August, Nadia had completed her exams. The results would be announced in the coming week, before the fourth semester commenced. It was a Saturday, the first day of the Afghan week, and Nadia, who was eager to be anywhere but at home, had organised to meet a friend at Abu Hanifa. 'We didn't have class,' she says. 'We had just gone to enjoy the day.' By the time she left the madrassa, there was a palpable tension in the streets. It was the middle of the day, when traffic in Kabul usually flows the most freely, but in Arzan Qimat, not far from Abu Hanifa but still in Kabul's far east, it was at a standstill. Beside Nadia's taxi was a tan-coloured ANA armoured combat vehicle, one of the thousands of humvees the Americans had lavished on the Afghan army and police forces, but which they had long since abandoned. There was a soldier standing in the turret behind a machine gun; other soldiers sat on the roof beside him and on the bonnet. An Afghan flag was draped over the turret.

'They were so young, like 17,' says Nadia. 'They looked tired and dirty, dust through their clothes and hair.'

Nadia tried to get the attention of one of the soldiers. 'I'd heard how they had not been receiving their salaries and thought maybe they hadn't eaten,' she says, 'so I was trying to give them some money.' Judging by the direction from which they had come, she thought that maybe they'd escaped from the Taliban in the district of Surobi, to the east. 'Everyone,' she says, 'was looking at them with pity.'

< >

Nadia was born in the Pakistani city of Rawalpindi, the headquarters of the country's military, in 2003. Her mother and father had moved there with their oldest son, Rahim, an infant at the time, soon after the Taliban had taken control of Afghanistan in 1996. They joined the millions of Afghans who'd fled the Soviet war of the 1980s and were still living in Pakistan as refugees, doing so when Amin's past with the Soviet-sponsored communist-regime army finally caught up with him.

Amin had been sent to the former Soviet state of Bulgaria so as to study to become an explosive ordnance disposal technician (EOD). He returned to Afghanistan as one of only a handful of qualified EODs, with his services in high demand. Millions of land-mines had been buried across the country throughout the 1980s and remained a deadly threat, even for the army responsible for laying many of them. So Amin was posted to one military base after another, living with Shukria in government housing in villages close to the installations.

When the communist government of Dr Mohammad Najibullah—and his army—collapsed in 1992, Amin no longer had an employer with use for his skills. He went to ground for four years while civil war engulfed Kabul, until the Taliban emerged to defeat and disarm the factions vying for control of the country. For Amin, the Taliban's narrow-minded zealotry was antithetical to more secular endeavours, such as pursuing knowledge and curiosity, to which he'd been taught to aspire. Amin also knew that, as a former communist soldier, he would be on one of the new regime's lists for arrest, imprisonment or maybe even execution. He decided to present himself to those who would otherwise eventually hunt for him, as an asset rather than a threat, offering to work for the new Taliban Ministry of Defence.

Amin was posted to a military facility in Logar province, located immediately south of Kabul, where the Taliban were holding dozens of prisoners. They were former soldiers who had voluntarily surrendered and handed over their weapons, but who were later arrested anyway. Amin, an army veteran just like the prisoners, imagined himself as one of them. He began hearing rumours from the Taliban guards that the prisoners were awaiting execution. Deciding he couldn't stand by, Amin freed around 20 of the former soldiers and fled with them into the night. He made straight for home in Kapisa, collected Shukria, young Rahim and a few possessions, and travelled with them by taxi over rocky roads through southern Kapisa's famous pomegranate orchards, across Surobi and the provinces of Laghman and Nangarhar, to the border with Pakistan.

The Aminis rented a small apartment in Rawalpindi, in a block already filled with large Afghan refugee families. Young Rahim played with the other Afghan children—during the monsoon, they would climb the stairs to the roof and make miniature swimming pools with the rainwater they collected in plastic tubs. In 1999, Shukria gave birth to the couple's first daughter, Bahira. Amin found enough work cleaning dishes in restaurants or selling fruit from a roadside cart to pay the rent and provide food for his young family, but having owned land and a home back in Afghanistan, where he was a respected member of his community, in Pakistan he felt diminished.

A year and a half after the Taliban was overthrown by the Americans in 2001, and eight months after Nadia was born, the Aminis returned to Afghanistan. They moved back into their home in Dara-i Farooq Shah, Shukria's family's village, set in a lush, green valley in Kapisa. The Aminis' was the only home made of brick, the others being mud-brick structures that looked as though they had emerged from the earth itself; the water in the village's central irrigation canal, in which children swam during the summer months, was also stained a murky tan. The Aminis' house was surrounded by a high wall and built in the shape of an 'L'. In the courtyard that sat in the crook of the 'L', Amin planted a handful of apple and walnut trees, as well as a Caucasian lime tree that produced the heart-shaped flowers he loved.

By 2007, Hanif and Elham had been born. On the weekend, Amin would take the family for picnics at his farm in Mir Bacha Kot, which was an hour away, towards Kabul. On one of the neighbouring farms was a great old walnut tree that was three storeys high. Nadia and her two older siblings would leap over the narrow irrigation canal that separated the two farms in order to collect all the enormous nuts they could carry. One day, the neighbour's son, who was brandishing a shotgun, caught the three in the act. Nadia lied and told the farmer's son they thought the giant tree was on their father's land. Then, after apologising for the misunderstanding, she asked whether they could keep the nuts.

Shukria says that, as an infant, Nadia was 'shy and calm', but by the age of five or six, she was cheeky and full of tricks. The Aminis called her *shahitan cheroghak* (cute little devil). At home, Nadia used to crawl around like a cat, sneaking up on her brothers and sisters and tickling their feet. 'Sometimes,' Nadia says, 'I'd even scare myself.' One time, Nadia waited in the courtyard outside the kitchen, where Bahira was making tea for the family. When her sister came outside, she found Nadia standing in the middle of the courtyard, hair flopped over her face and tongue hanging from the side of her mouth, playing dead. Bahira screamed and dropped a tray full of glasses, dried fruit and nuts, plus a thermos of tea. Their mother ran out from the living room to find the clamour was just the result of another of Nadia's pranks on Bahira rather than a serious calamity. 'What if you give her a heart attack?' Shukria scolded.

Nadia's antics were never expressions of rebellion or disobedience, though. She was a bright student who challenged her teachers. At the end of grade two, she even passed a test which allowed her to skip a year and go straight into grade four. Her parents—and even their parents—had always prioritised their children's education. Her grandfather Allahdad established the first ever primary school for boys and girls in Mir Bacha Kot. Local families had never before sent their girls to school, but when Allahdad, a respected elder in the district, enrolled his own daughter—Amin's sister—others followed suit. At home in Dara-i Farooq Shah, Amin and Shukria both helped Nadia learn to read and write.

Nadia demanded to be treated as older than her age. During Ramadan, the ninth month on the Islamic calendar, during which most adult Muslims fast during daylight hours, she was incensed that she wasn't able to take part. 'It wasn't because I was religious,' she says. 'I just wanted to be a grown-up.' When her parents and older siblings woke for *sehri*, the meal taken before dawn during Ramadan, prior to a day's fast, they refused to rouse her. If she woke herself, Rahim would tell her to go back to sleep. If she slept through *sehri* and woke with the sun, she was furious. Nadia was around ten when she first fasted. 'My eyes were almost falling closed,' she says. 'It was as if I was drunk.' Late that day, when Rahim realised why his sister was so lethargic, he and Bahira held her and poured water into her mouth. 'I was so angry,' says Nadia. 'I complained to my mother that I'd been fasting all day and only had a couple of hours until *iftar*'—the breaking of the fast, which the family held on a woven plastic carpet in the courtyard.

Nadia adored Rahim. Ten years older than Nadia, he followed his father into the armed forces, joining the Afghan National

Police (ANP) after graduating from high school in 2011. He was posted to a training academy in Maidan Wardak province, where he taught incoming recruits. Wardak had become central to the Taliban's revival in central Afghanistan. The police academy sat beside the highway that runs south from Kabul to Kandahar, then west to Helmand and Nimroz, north to Herat, then east across northern Afghanistan, before turning south again towards Kabul, completing a loop of the country. Travelling on this road was like running a gauntlet, which is why the Americans referred to it as the Highway of Death. In August 2011, an American Chinook helicopter flying under the call sign Extortion 17 was shot down by a rocket-propelled grenade fired by a Taliban fighter in the Tangi Valley, only a few kilometres away, behind the mountains at the rear of Rahim's academy. Thirty Americans and eight Afghans were killed after the missile struck the tail rotor of the aircraft, sending it into an uncontrollable spin. It was the deadliest event involving foreign troops in the entire 20-year war.[5]

Rahim would brave the highway to Kabul every second weekend, driving a police-issued forest-green Ford Ranger pick-up truck two hours' north to Dara-i Farooq Shah. When they heard the familiar gurgle of the diesel engine, Nadia and her younger brothers would rush outside and climb into the tray, which had twin seats on either side, and demand to be taken for a ride through the village. Nadia loved it when Rahim let her sit in the driver's seat, even though her legs couldn't reach the pedals. However, although he enjoyed a sense of elevated status when returning to Dara-i Farooq Shah, Rahim came to understand that the pride it brought him and his family was matched by the quiet contempt of others.

Even though the Afghan Government's forces controlled Dara-i Farooq Shah and Kapisa's predominantly Tajik-majority northern districts, the Taliban were becoming increasingly active in the Pashtun-dominated southern district of Tagab. From there, they could fan their influence throughout Kapisa, not only by planting IEDs and ambushing government and foreign military convoys, but through intimidation and coercion achieved via an expanding network of agents and informants. Night letters began appearing, pinned to walls around Dara-i Farooq Shah, warning that those working for the government should leave their jobs, and that failure to do so would result in consequences, and their families would have no right to complain. The first direct threat to Rahim was written in chalk on the outside of the Amini house.

Her brother wasn't the only person in Nadia's extended family receiving threats. Gul Agha, as she knew her uncle, was a police officer in the Kama district of Nangarhar. For as long as she could remember, Nadia and her family had spent Februarys in Kama, where, nearly 2000 metres below Kapisa,[6] the winter temperatures were comparatively mild. Nadia's favourite thing about going to Kama was seeing Gul Agha's daughter—her cousin—Nargis, who was four years her senior. They would watch films together at night and cook. When the families sat and chatted around the *sandali* heater, warming their legs beneath a blanket that helped retain the heat, Nadia would sneak underneath and push her feet towards the fire. 'Save me from the little devil!' Nargis would yell in mock horror.

By the winter of 2012, Gul Agha had also received threats like the one directed at Rahim. Taliban agents were quietly infiltrating Nangarhar's mosques, spreading news of atrocities—both real and imagined—committed by foreign soldiers and their counterparts in the government security forces, and encouraging worshippers to expose such people who lived among them. One night during the Aminis' visit that year, after dinner, Nadia was asleep in the guestroom with everyone in her family except for Bahira, who was in the main house with Nargis and her family, across a central courtyard. Amin was woken by a noise and saw flames coming from the main house. He ran across the courtyard and charged through the door just as an explosion took his feet out from under him. Gul Agha and his one-year-old daughter Shabana were killed instantly. Nargis, who had been trying to carry her infant sister from the room, was still breathing, but shrapnel from the explosion had torn the flesh from her jaw and nose. Her clothes had either been completely burned away or had melted onto her body. Amin, whose feet were badly wounded, found and carried out Bahira— her body had large patches of raw flesh and blackened scraps that curled at the edges where the skin had stopped melting.

'Nargis was alive for two days,' says Nadia, who visited her in a hospital in Jalalabad. 'But she had terrible injuries. We could see her teeth and the bone of her nose.' Bahira survived but received burns to 80 per cent of her body. 'It was like a bad dream,' says Nadia.

The Aminis were sure that it was a deliberate attack, a petrol bomb thrown through the high window that faced the street, they thought, followed by a grenade. Of Gul Agha, Shukria says, 'He had been receiving threats, but he never took them seriously.' Rahim, who had been on duty in Wardak at the time, felt partly responsible for what had happened because of his work with the police. He was especially devastated by Bahira's injuries and vowed to one day find her the treatment she needed for her burns, which caused her constant pain, outside Afghanistan. His family all wanted Rahim to leave the police. But while neither Amin nor Shukria trusted the Taliban—they had seen their brutality and betrayal in the 1990s before fleeing to Pakistan—the only other option was to return to Pakistan and live as refugees. And after the indignity of their years in Rawalpindi, Amin had sworn he would never live as a refugee, anywhere, ever again.

‹ ›

The threats towards Rahim and his family in Kapisa for a long time remained just that—threats—never escalating to violence like they had in Kama. Then, on a Thursday night in late 2014, soon after Ashraf Ghani had been sworn in as Hamid Karzai's successor, Rahim collected his mother from home and drove to Kabul for a cousin's wedding, planning to stay with the family overnight. Nadia was at home with her father, sister and two younger brothers when they heard banging on the front gate. When Amin opened the gate, a group of men burst through, swinging their fists and grabbing at

Amin as he stumbled backwards. When he tripped over and fell, the men rounded on him and continued punching him and kicking him in the side as he tried forlornly to protect himself, all the while pleading with the men to tell him what they wanted. Hanif and Elham, who was only eight, ran from the house towards their father but were swatted away like flies: Elham's nose was left bleeding from a backhanded blow, and Hanif was kicked when he resisted. Nadia and Bahira, still inside the house, watched in horror through a window.

The young boys' intrusion proved enough to interrupt the attack's violent momentum. The men stepped away from Amin, who was cowering on the ground, his *peran tunban* torn and askew, gasping for the air that had been pounded from his lungs. 'We know you're an honest person,' conceded one of the men, just a shadow against the night. 'We know you're a respected member of the jirga,' he continued, referring to the local tribal council. 'For that reason, we will be merciful and make a proposal: your son can stay in his job, but he will work for us.' The men did not say who they were or whom they represented, but Amin didn't need to ask, nor was he confused about their offer. They were the Taliban, and they wanted Amin to convince Rahim to work for them as an informant. 'If you don't accept this offer, we will take her,' said the spokesman, pointing at Bahira who was standing at the window with Nadia.

When Rahim and Shukria returned to Dara-i Farooq Shah the next morning, Nadia and her siblings were told to pack their things. 'We left with only money, gold and clothes,' says Nadia, 'but we were all leaving together, as a family.' After the dawn call to prayer, Amin arranged a car and a driver and they left the village without telling anyone. He instructed the driver to go the long way to the border, first to Kabul, to avoid passing through Tagab, which would have saved hours but taken them through areas where they were sure to cross the Taliban, and then east through the treacherous, winding Mahipar Pass towards Nangarhar.

Nadia, who suffers from car sickness, sat on her father's lap in the front seat. Although the highway route was controlled by the government, the soldiers defending and travelling it came under daily attack from rocket-propelled grenades and machine guns from the mountains above. Having a child in the car who was clearly visible was a subtle indicator to both suspicious government soldiers and Taliban fighters that the passengers weren't a threat. Still, Nadia grew sick on the switchbacks dropping down from the pass where it levelled out alongside the Kabul River, which had slowed to a trickle, the past winter's snow long since melted. She threw up in a plastic bag and tossed it out the window.

At the Torkham border crossing, truck drivers lounged in the shade beneath their 18-wheelers, smoking cigarettes and boiling tea on gas burners. Lorries decorated with childish pastoral scenes painted in primary colours and chain-link skirting jostled for position, each jolt sending them into a jingling cadence. Young boys hurried between the lines of traffic selling bottled water from plastic buckets with melting chunks of ice for 10 Afghani. The Aminis got the taxi to go as far as it could, then they got out and walked. They didn't have visas, let alone passports. Amin disappeared into a room with an Afghan border guard. They came out a few minutes later and the guard escorted the family towards Pakistan. All Nadia had was the backpack she used for school, which contained some clothes and a packet of biscuits. On the Pakistani side of the border they climbed into a waiting van. The driver pulled up next to a Pakistani border guard who began speaking with Amin. After the pair had agreed upon a sum, and Amin had handed over a roll of Pakistani rupees, the guard waved them on.

The Aminis first made for the home of an Afghan family they had befriended during their time in Rawalpindi more than a decade ago, staying in a guestroom for a little over a week before renting an apartment of their own in Islamabad. 'It wasn't a good time,' says Nadia. 'Our finances were poor.' Amin did some daily labour now and then, but he grew increasingly withdrawn and glum: he'd failed to protect his family and had forsaken his own vow—never to leave home again. In-between looking for work, Amin tended to Shukria, whose blood pressure had shot up with the stress and uncertainty of the move. 'When someone is sad in your home when you're a child,' says Nadia, 'it infects them too.' Rahim, too, was suffering, from the guilt brought on by the consequences of his work—initially by the Taliban's beating of his father, but also for forcing the family to leave their home for a second time. Still, he and his parents continued to try to come up with escapes from their predicament.

'They hadn't only threatened Rahim,' says Shukria, 'but our daughters as well. So the threat wasn't going to automatically disappear.' But they all agreed they couldn't live in Pakistan forever, and there was no future for them in Islamabad. They'd never shed their refugee status, which would make finding decent work for Amin and Rahim, and good schools for Nadia and her younger brothers, virtually impossible. So a decision was made which the Aminis hoped would solve all their problems at once.

The Aminis weren't the only Afghans taking desperate measures to find safety in 2015. After the contested presidential election the previous year, confidence in the Afghan Government among the population had plummeted. At the same time, foreign donors were losing interest in what appeared, more and more, to be turning into just another chapter in an intractable war, upon which no amount of spending could make an impact. Investors were turning away as the risk–reward calculation that had drawn them to Afghanistan in droves a decade earlier began tilting out of their favour. Unemployment soared, and the value of the national currency tanked. Meanwhile, international combat troops were being drawn down, having officially handed responsibility for Afghanistan's security over to the Ghani government on the first day of 2015.

The Taliban had reignited their insurgency as foreign forces began pulling back from the front lines. Without the command, support, firepower and morale provided by the Americans, who were backing them, the Afghan army and police forces withered in the face of an adversary who could see that, after 15 years of punishing war, their fortunes were beginning to change. Victory over the foreign invaders was no longer just a quest for which the

Taliban, as Muslims, were obliged to fight, but a realistic possibility. As the Taliban advanced on population centres across the country— particularly in the north, where populations were historically more aligned with the government—entire communities moved ahead of the fighting to the provincial capitals and Kabul. Others did the same in the hope of finding work, as the internationally bankrolled war economy was dismantled, blast wall by blast wall. Hundreds of thousands left the country altogether, joining the world's largest migration flow since World War II.[7] In total, some 200 000 Afghans applied for asylum in Europe in 2015, a figure believed to be far smaller than the total number of Afghans who attempted the journey.[8]

The Aminis pooled together the equivalent of A$15 000 to pay a smuggler to take Rahim and Bahira, the two who were most in danger, to Europe. Rahim was 23, Bahira only 17. Because Amin wanted to retain enough money to re-establish the family in Afghanistan once they returned, they couldn't afford to send any of the other children as well. They also hoped that Bahira, whose health had been of constant concern since the attack in Kama four years prior, would be able to find treatment in Europe for her burns. 'My brother is tall,' says Nadia, 'and when I hugged him for the last time my arms couldn't reach all the way around him.'

From Islamabad, Rahim and Bahira went south and then traversed Pakistani Baluchistan, clinging to the southern side of the border with Afghanistan before crossing into Iran. The brother and sister had a phone between them, which they used to call their family in Islamabad whenever they could find the right combination of phone credit and network coverage. Approaching Iran's border with Turkey one night, their car was fired upon. Bullets punctured the windows and doors. One passenger was struck in the hand as he tried to protect himself. Another bullet grazed Rahim's forehead before instantly killing the Afghan asylum seeker sitting beside him. Bahira clambered from the car while Rahim helped the wounded passenger, now faint and disoriented, with all of them crossing into Turkey together—covered in blood and in shock, but alive. From there, Rahim and Bahira made their way across the Mediterranean to Greece, then north through Macedonia, Serbia, Hungary and Austria, finally arriving, nearly two months after having left Nadia and their family in Islamabad, in Germany along with nearly 450 000 other asylum applicants.[9]

As a minor, Bahira was allowed to apply for family reunification visas on behalf of the rest of her family.[10] In the meantime, with his two eldest children safely in Germany and confident of having their asylum applications accepted, after just under a year in Pakistan, Amin took Shukria, Nadia, Hanif and Elham home. After crossing the border, they stopped by the side of the road in Jalalabad for a bag of raw sugar cane, chopped into pieces that Nadia could barely fit in her mouth, but which oozed with sweet, syrupy juice, until all that was left were the dry husks which she'd toss from the window of their vehicle. 'I was happy leaving Pakistan,' she says. 'When you're in a country where you don't know the language, it's like you're deaf and mute.' But while they had made it back to Afghanistan, the Aminis decided against returning to Dara-i Farooq Shah. While the Taliban could no longer touch the two children they'd threatened directly, the Aminis knew that retribution could be administered in a number of ways, and that their debt to the Taliban would one day have to be repaid.

Like most Afghans, Bahira didn't know her exact birthdate. It wasn't until after 2001 that birthdates started to be required for some official documents in Afghanistan, and even then, it was mostly only needed for non-Afghan documents, or passports. Most people simply picked a date on the Gregorian calendar from the year they were born, or thereabouts, which henceforth became their 'date of birth'—1 January was a popular choice. According to the date Bahira had nominated, from the time she was granted asylum in Germany, she only had 56 days remaining until she turned 18, after which she would no longer be entitled to apply for family reunification as a minor. The Aminis steeled themselves before spending several days navigating queues and bureaucracy at the Directorate of Passports in Kabul. By the time the passports were issued, though, Bahira was 18 and the family reunification option had lapsed.

The Aminis bought a house on Street 2 in the Kabul neighbourhood of Karte Naw. They were among thousands of returning Afghan refugee families in Karte Naw who had owned land elsewhere in Afghanistan when they'd left between 1979 and 2001, only to find it, years or decades later, pilfered by others enjoying a turn at the top of the food chain in their absence.[11] 'Who has the guns,' says Patricia Gossman, a Human Rights Watch Afghanistan veteran of four decades, 'gets the land.'[12]

The house was close to the government-run Rahman Mina High School where Nadia was enrolled in grade nine, in the same class as Mariyam, the daughter of old family friends. Nadia was eager to make up for the year she'd spent out of school in Pakistan and was most looking forward to her maths, biology and English classes. Out of class, she would try to speak with her teachers in English and often requested extra homework. 'My classmates were so lazy and my teachers' English wasn't great,' she says, adding like a true multilinguist: 'I was at the top of my class but look how bad my English is.'

< >

Three years after returning from Pakistan, the Aminis were still being cautious, even in the ever-growing metropolis of Kabul. To mitigate against the possibility of kidnapping, Amin forbade the children from attending classes more than three days each week. The tactic would make it harder for potential plotters to establish their patterns of movement and grab them from the street. The Aminis continued to move house every year or so, but never far from Rahman Mina or the school where Hanif and Elham studied. It was in grade 12 that Nadia's friend Mariyam left Rahman Mina when her family moved to the other side of the city. 'It was the worst feeling ever,' says Nadia.

Towards the end of her final year, during a subject in which students were asked to create a hypothetical business from the ground up, Nadia, upon a suggestion from her teacher, made a business plan for a small dairy. To begin with, the imaginary business had one asset: a cow. 'It wasn't the kind of business I'd have *actually* started,' says Nadia. Outside class, she started thinking about getting into the wedding hall business. In the last 10 years, Kabul had become littered with them: garish, leviathan brick boxes clad in mirrored glass, with replicas of landmarks such as the Eiffel Tower or Dubai's Burj Al Arab hotel distinguishing one from the next. 'I don't know anything about business, but everyone chooses a profession—medicine, journalism, engineering—and I chose business. I wanted to be a businesswoman,' says Nadia. And, in reference to her idea of building a wedding hall business, she adds: 'You think I'm the kind of person who thinks *small*?'

After graduating, Nadia sat for the national university entrance exam, the Kankor,[13] and, around the same time, she enrolled in a course at an English-language institute. When taking the Kankor, Nadia was asked to nominate five faculties she would be interested in studying at university. 'I chose a Bachelor of Business Administration,' she says. 'The other four, which included Sharia Law and Dari Literature, the family chose.' It was the first instance Nadia could remember where choices she felt were hers to make were instead made by her family. Just as she was embracing the independence she'd earned from four years of hard work after Pakistan, or perhaps because of it, it was being taken away from her.

Hanif was driving the shift towards control. He was now the oldest male child living with the family, and, despite being two years younger than Nadia, he wanted to assert the authority he felt his new place in the family pecking order warranted. 'You know,' says Nadia, 'when you become older in Afghanistan, you think you have power.' But before she'd even received her Kankor results, Hanif told her: 'If I don't want you to go to college and study Business Administration, you will not be allowed.'

By the time the Kankor results became available, Nadia's family had turned completely, forbidding her from even retrieving them. Mariyam did it for Nadia when she searched for her own results.

'I didn't pass,' Mariyam told Nadia, 'but congratulations! You passed and have been admitted to Business Administration.'

'I was so happy,' says Nadia. 'But my family said, "Why are you happy? Grade 12 is enough for you."' In the end, Nadia and her family came to a compromise: Islamic Studies or nothing.

Hanif says the decision not to allow Nadia to study business was one made with her safety in mind. The university, he says, 'was too far from home and not safe, so we had to choose another faculty. Nadia was sad about this, but because of the threats to the family, we couldn't allow it'.

'This is just an excuse,' Nadia tells me. 'You have a dream and someone tells you "You have to change it", or "You're not allowed" …' She trails off.

Preserving the safety of women is a common sleight of hand used by Afghan men to keep those within their family under control. Neglecting such a duty and allowing a young woman the freedom to walk when they wish in the streets, to socialise with unrelated men, and to develop their understanding of the world outside the home and their ideas about their place therein, is deduced by many *outside* the immediate family to imply the woman is what Nadia refers to euphemistically as a 'bad girl'. Boiled down, a 'bad girl' is one who cavorts and sleeps with men out of wedlock—a prostitute in Afghan terms, a great stain on a family's honour. To avert such a possibility, rather than confront those who deliberately misinterpret the young woman's ways and use it to undermine her family, instead, her brothers, father and male members of the extended family more often elect to restrain her behaviour.

Although Nadia had little interest in Islamic Studies, she settled for the compromise she'd made with her family because 'it was better to study something rather than nothing at all'. She began diluting her dreams, recalibrating her aspirations in line with what her family would permit and holding on to even more modest ones to keep herself from losing all hope. But Nadia was stubborn. She would seize on any concession her family made and take it as far in her mind as she could. She learned that if she completed Islamic Studies, she could go on to study Islamic sharia law.

'Why did I want to study Islamic law?' she asks herself. 'Force. I taught myself to like it, and TV shows helped me to embrace it.' Nadia was referring here to *India Alert*, a true-crime program broadcast on Afghan television.

She wouldn't be able to begin learning sharia law for another six months, but already she was warming to the idea. In her room at home, she'd stand pillows along the side of her bed to represent a jury, and then she would act as a judge, practising the delivery of verdicts in the mirror. If I have to study this, she thought, I might as well try to like it.

While Nadia was contemplating her future as a judge, she continued attending as many classes as she could at the English-language institute without angering her family. By the time Nadia was ready to sit the final exam, however, they had soured on that course as well and forbade her from sitting for the test. Throughout the family's gradual turn towards oppression, Shukria had maintained a careful neutrality. But as the treatment became increasingly severe, with Nadia continually singled out and hounded by her father and brothers, Shukria entered into an unspoken alliance with her daughter. Neither of them could ever acknowledge it in front of the others, but her mother's support buoyed Nadia. 'She told me to sit the exam secretly,' says Nadia.

Despite attending less than half her classes in the weeks leading up to the exam, Nadia scored one of the highest marks of all her classmates. 'When I was presented with a certificate,' she says, her classmates, many of whom didn't recognise her from previous classes, 'were whispering among themselves: "Who is she?" I was so proud.'

When she went home that afternoon, she placed the certificate, which congratulated her for her hard work, on a table, leaning it against the wall so her family would see it. 'It was a big thing I'd done and I thought they'd be proud,' she says. Her mother was the first to see the certificate. 'She doesn't show her emotions and didn't really acknowledge it,' says Nadia. 'But I knew she was proud.' However, when Amin and Hanif spotted the certificate, Nadia says 'they behaved like animals with me. It was the first day my father struck me with his belt'.

Nadia says it was Hanif who urged their father to punish her, which he did so as not to appear weak in front of his son. 'He said I'd disrespected him by sitting for the exam,' she says, which he'd told her she wasn't to do. Nadia argued that she didn't think she'd done anything wrong, and then stated: 'If you must beat me, beat me as you can.' Hanif held her hands in front while Amin struck her several times across the back. She stood silent, wincing with each blow. There was little Shukria could do.

'This is Afghanistan,' says Nadia.

< >

In Kabul in mid-2021, aside from the continuing slew of assassinations and several attacks against the Hazara ethnic minority by Islamic State militants, there was scant evidence of the war for the control of Afghanistan, but the Taliban's nationwide military advance was closing in on the capital. For the Aminis, the closer the insurgents came, the more critical it was to escape. But they felt as though they'd now run out of options. Amin refused to endure the indignity of living as a refugee in Pakistan yet again, and the gates to Europe, which had been open to Rahim and Bahira in 2015, had long since been boarded up. As well, attempting the perilous route with his young family was a risk Amin was not prepared to take.

Amin took all the precautions he could, including cutting off all contact with the family's neighbours in Dara-i Farooq Shah, lest someone find out where they now lived, but these seemed as futile as the day of reckoning with the Taliban felt inevitable. The family had no idea what had happened to their Kapisa home or the fruit trees within. Elham, now 13, had spent half his life away from home and could barely remember the canal in which he'd swum as a child, nor the weekend visits from his oldest brother Rahim.

Nadia's world continued to shrink, too. Between her days at Abu Hanifa and her nights at home, it was as if the future under the Taliban that everyone around her feared, and from which her family had been running for the past six years, had already arrived. 'After my youth,' she says, 'I have no good memories.'

PART II

Mid-August

'The Taliban Are at the Gates'

4

Emirate City, Kabul
I

On 15 August 2021, Hamed Safi woke to the news that the governor of Nangarhar province had surrendered Jalalabad, the gateway to Kabul from the east, to the Taliban. Aside from Logar, which lay to the south of Kabul, it was the first province bordering the city to fall. Hamed knew that unless the Taliban faced resistance on the Kabul–Jalalabad Highway, it would take barely three hours for their fighters to start arriving at the capital's eastern gates.

Hamed called his father, who was on his way with his wife and daughter to the second day of an engagement party in the southern suburb of Darulaman, and asked him to turn around and drive to his sister-in-law's apartment in Macroyan 4. Next, Hamed called his driver to Emirate City and requested he take his wife and children to another aunt's house in Taimani, which, like Macroyan 4, was near the centre of Kabul. He didn't live with his extended family, as most Afghans did, but now he wanted to bring everyone close. As for his wife Zarifa, who was six months pregnant, and their two young children, he says, 'I didn't want them to be alone for a single hour.'

At 7.30 a.m., before his driver had arrived to collect his wife and children, Hamed had dressed in a business suit and left Emirate City in his Toyota Corolla. He drove around the western end of the airport and through a corridor of high concrete blast walls painted with colourful murals of heroic-looking soldiers, which ran between the Ministry of Interior Affairs and the end of the airport runway. Before reaching the palace, he stopped at his bank. More than 100 men were crowding around the entrance. Two security guards with Kalashnikovs were struggling to maintain order as another controlled the heavy security door. A smaller group of a dozen women stood to one side. Hamed jostled for position for 90 minutes. This was no time for civility, so when the door finally opened, he angled his shoulder in front of the man beside him and pushed through. Because of the rush on local banks in recent days, a withdrawal limit of US$2000 or 200 000 Afghani (approximately US$2500 at the time) had been imposed. Hamed took out the maximum in Afghani and traded them for US dollars through a moneychanger on the street outside.

From the bank, Hamed drove to a private parking station close to the palace in Shash Darak, a heavily protected neighbourhood that also housed the Ministry of Defence, the NDS offices, a prison, and the homes of some of the government's most senior officials. He checked the time: it was 10.30 a.m. As Hamed left his car, he noticed that most of the men coming and going from the palace were wearing traditional Afghan clothes. He suddenly felt self-conscious in his suit, before realising that he was among a minority of pedestrians heading towards the palace. But he was used to working on days when administrative staff were told to stay home. The streets around the palace were occasionally blocked by demonstrations or closed altogether because of attacks or when the threat level was high. 'Even on the most dangerous days in Kabul,' says Hamed, 'I had to be in the office—it was my job.'

Before heading for his office, Hamed stopped at a cafe between the palace's outer entrance, the First Gate, and a second entryway which palace staff referred to as Flag Gate, for the Afghan tricolour that flew above it. The cafe was in an elegant building of grey stone, glass, and bare timber beams, and surrounded by towering pine trees. A few staffers mingled in the broad, outdoor seating area that looked out over a manicured lime-green lawn fringed with pink, red and coral roses, but there was nothing like the normal comings and goings for the time of day.

Hamed's brother Mahmoud called and the two agreed to meet at the cafe. When Mahmoud arrived, he said to his younger brother, 'Please, leave the palace as soon as you can. The Taliban are at the gates of Kabul.' According to the intelligence the PPS were receiving, the Taliban were planning to make their way to the palace and, because Hamed wasn't with the armed forces, Mahmoud thought he should leave. 'Take your family and go. But don't go to your own house, it's too dangerous, they might come and ...' said Mahmoud, trailing off.

Wahid Omar, Hamed's boss, now showed up with some other people. Hamed and Omar were friends as well as colleagues. Omar took Hamed by the hand and pulled him away from the group.

'Do you have your passport with you?' Omar asked in a whisper.

'Yes.'

'I'd prefer it if you went directly to the airport.'

'But what will I do once I'm there? I don't have any tickets and I can't leave my family.'

'I know you have a visa for the US,' replied Omar. 'A lot of people are going to the airport, you can join them. Maybe there will be a chance of finding a seat.'

< >

Hamdullah Mohib rose at 6 a.m. on 15 August after two hours of fitful rest. He and his wife Lael, who was in Abu Dhabi, had spent some of the previous night corresponding by text about which of Mohib's heirlooms she was to pass on to each of their children. It was a pragmatic exchange, but when it ended, Lael cried. 'We were preparing for him to not make it,' she says. She reminded herself of a quote by the author Haruki Murakami that a friend had recently shared: 'Pain is inevitable. Suffering is optional.' She told herself: 'Now is not the time to suffer. There's work to do.'

Lael had left more messages for her husband after he had gone to bed in the early hours, one of which was a request that he distribute cash to their house staff. After scrolling through his other messages and bringing himself up to speed with the morning's developments, Mohib went to a desk drawer in his study and took out a tall stack of 1000 Afghani notes (each worth approximately US$12.50 at the time) that were separated by elastic bands into six wads of 100 000 Afghani. He gave one wad to each of their four staff and returned the remainder to the drawer.

Mohib was soon headed for the Haram Sarai Palace, where president Ghani had begun the day reading a book beneath an enormous Oriental plane tree in the palace courtyard. Since the COVID-19 pandemic had begun 18 months earlier, Ghani, who had recurring health problems, had made a habit of holding meetings outdoors to minimise the chance of contracting the virus. Before meeting with Mohib and agreeing on a list of representatives to attend the upcoming meeting in Doha, the purpose of which was to negotiate a settlement with the Taliban, Ghani spoke in the courtyard with Abdul Salam Rahimi, one of the most senior members of the government's existing negotiating team, and a key personal ally. Rahimi had been developing back-channel relationships with senior insurgent leaders. He informed president Ghani that the Taliban had agreed not to enter Kabul by force. More of Ghani's advisors joined the outdoor discussion, during which it was decided that an emergency cabinet meeting would be held to straighten out the confusion miring the ministries after the previous day's on-again-off-again posturing.

The government's team for the meeting in Doha—which included the Ghani allies Rahimi, the president's chief of staff Matin Bek, and Massoum Stanikzai, Ghani's senior negotiator, who was already in Doha, as well as, at Ghani's insistence, Mohib—was finalised around 11 a.m. 'This was a meeting,' says Mohib, 'which would decide the fate of the republic, including the fate of the president.' However, when it was discovered that vice-president Amrullah Saleh, who had taken on a role as Kabul's de-facto security chief, had left the capital for his home province of Panjshir, planning for the meeting was abandoned.

Now at the NSC's offices, Mohib was visited by Qahar Kochai, the head of the PPS. Kochai informed Mohib that, according to his sources, Taliban fighters had entered the south-western Kabul neighbourhood of Company. Maidan Shahr, the capital of Maidan Wardak, had fallen to the Taliban soon after sunrise that morning, and that city was only an hour by road from Company, so there was every chance that the reports were accurate. Kochai also passed the information on to Rahimi, who told Kochai what he had already told the president: that the Taliban had agreed not to enter Kabul. But he said he would speak to his Taliban military interlocutors about the breach. A senior Taliban commander then asked Rahimi to provide the specific locations of the supposed fighters, so that their commanders could be identified and the fighters ordered to stand down.

Mohib then received another visitor. After the vague response to his request for evacuation assistance from the Americans, he had reached out to his contacts from the UAE. The visitor, Saif, who worked inside the Emirati Embassy in Kabul, had come to brief Mohib and the president on an evacuation plan his government had approved. The two walked to the Haram Sarai courtyard, where Saif told the president that a chartered plane would arrive at Hamid Karzai International Airport by the following evening, 16 August. The plane would be refuelled and its crew put on stand-by to leave at short notice. 'It was a relief,' says Mohib. He'd thought to himself that if things got difficult, at least now they had an exit.

The relief was short-lived. As Saif completed his briefing, the sound of gunfire erupted outside the palace and the president's bodyguards ushered the three men inside.

‹ ›

From his office overlooking the apartment block that incorporated his Kabul residence, Ross Wilson could see embassy staff hurrying across the courtyard that connected the two buildings. They were exiting the apartment building with armfuls of belongings and piling them near the perimeter of the compound, to be burnt.

At around 9 a.m., Wilson was joined by his deputy, Scott Weinhold, and Admiral Peter Vasely for a call with Jake Sullivan, the US National Security Advisor, and Antony Blinken. According to Wilson, there were still around 1500 staff inside the embassy. He says that, given the alarming developments, 'we made the decision … that we had to evacuate everybody immediately'.

A month earlier, on 13 July, diplomats from the US Embassy had warned Blinken in a dissent channel cable that the Afghan Government and its security forces were on the brink of collapse. The caution had come a week after President Biden had played down the risk of a complete Taliban takeover as 'highly unlikely'.[1] The cable, of which Wilson was aware but did not sign himself, urged the Biden administration to expedite efforts to evacuate Afghans perceived to be at risk from the Taliban because of their work with the US Government and military over the course of the 20-year war. In fact, at the same time embassy staff were decrying the lack of urgency in evacuating at-risk Afghans, the US military was strug-gling to rally the support of Wilson to prepare for an evacuation of the embassy itself. 'We had ad-hoc meetings with the embassy,' said a military officer who was involved in the withdrawal effort, 'but they didn't want to talk about the [evacuation]', which was ulti-mately planned only in the days leading up to its commencement.[2]

Wilson denies that he and his senior embassy staff were ill-prepared. 'My senior staff, including the deputy chief of mission, assistant chief of mission, consul general, and security officer and his staff,' says Wilson, 'engaged repeatedly over the weeks before mid-August with the senior military planners, and I met with [Brigadier-General Farrell J] Sullivan in July to be briefed and discuss outstanding issues.' Operation Allies Refuge, for Afghans perceived to be at risk from the Taliban, was announced the day after the dissent channel cable was received but didn't commence until later in July. By 15 August, only 2000 of the 20 000 eligible Afghans had been flown out of Afghanistan.[3]

Inside the embassy, the process of destroying sensitive documents and other items—including passports belonging to Afghans desperately waiting to be issued visas,[4] American flags and framed photographs of president Trump—which had begun the day before, now sped up. Boxes and equipment were stacked up before being carted off to an incinerator. A pall of acrid, black smoke billowed over the embassy. Compounding the sense of urgency was the 'band, bang, bang' of hammers smashing computer hard drives, and the echo of embassy loudspeakers calling for groups to proceed to the helicopter landing zone inside the international military mission's headquarters next door. Although some had lived in the embassy compound for more than a decade and had turned their apartments into homes, as evacuees, embassy staff were permitted to take a maximum of one suitcase per person.

As a crew member of one of the Chinooks charged with carrying out the evacuation of embassy staff to Kabul's airport, Andrew Romine had flown until 3 a.m. on the morning of 15 August. 'There was less of a *how* things were to be done,' he says, 'and more of a what *needs* to be done. It was just up to us to get it done any way possible.' The crew had flown laps of the route—three minutes' flight time each way—for five hours, pre-staging embassy personnel at Camp Alvarado, on the military side of the airport where the State Department's aircraft were stationed, for a pre-scheduled charter flight departing that day. By mid-morning, with rumours filtering through the camp that 20 000 Taliban fighters were converging on Kabul, some, says Romine, 'were visibly worried and at times distraught'.

Wilson says at that time in Kabul's Green Zone, where most foreign embassies, including that of the United States, as well as UN agencies, the World Bank and international media bureaus were located, 'security arrangements had ceased to function. The soldiers left and the contract personnel who supported it were gone, so we no longer had any confidence in the international zone security perimeter'.

Even more worrying for Wilson beyond the dwindling protection of the Green Zone were the reports he was receiving from the outskirts of Kabul. Taliban forces, he was told, were not only moving towards but into Kabul province from the south-east. As Rahimi had explained to the president, Taliban leaders in Doha had told Zalmai Khalilzad, the US peace envoy, that their forces would stop at the gates of Kabul. 'They weren't stopping,' says Wilson. The reports, he continued, 'posed this spectre of the armed takeover of Kabul, an extremely chaotic and dangerous situation in which our ability to stay now looked really non-existent'.

< >

Hamed Safi had worked at the presidential palace for 12 years, and, before he left, as his brother had implored him to do, he wanted to go to his office to delete the data from his laptop. Not all palace staffers had the same concerns. Many working in service ministries like water and energy or public health were leaving their files and data intact, assuming that an incoming Taliban administration would prioritise continuity in apolitical sectors, like resources and health, rather than reprisals. But Hamed didn't count himself among them. He knew that if the Taliban managed to get inside the palace, their technicians would mine staff computers for incriminating data, building cases for the inevitable purge that many believed would come once the group had consolidated power. He didn't want to take the risk.

'I trashed *all* my data,' says Hamed. 'Files, photos, everything. I was in a hurry. I was hearing gunshots.' The gunfire was coming from the direction of Zanbaq Square, where one of the five main entrances to the Green Zone—and the closest of those to the palace gates—was located. Hamed called Mahmoud, who reassured him that the gunshots were from a bank near the square, warning shots from security guards trying to disperse the increasingly desperate crowd of people trying to withdraw their savings. Similar scenes were playing out across Kabul, triggering panic on the streets and declarations on social media that the Taliban were inside the city.

As Hamed was leaving his office, he ran into Wahid Omar, who was looking increasingly harried and who again pushed Hamed to leave. A group of a dozen or so senior PPS officers, including Mahmoud, were standing nearby. 'They were looking toward Gul Khana,' says Hamed—referring to the palace that housed the president's office—as if asking what the president would do. Hamed approached his brother, who again told him to leave, adding: 'The situation is deteriorating.' Mahmoud offered his car keys to Hamed, thinking, 'I'm going to be killed, but at least I can save my brother.' Hamed explained that he had his own car parked nearby. He was reluctant to leave his brother, but he had confidence that Mahmoud would survive, as he had countless times in the past, if things got worse. 'I told him to stay in touch and to take care of himself,' says Hamed. Mahmoud hugged his brother and cried quietly over his shoulder.

When Omar walked towards the president's office, his two secretaries followed, as did Ghani's three deputy spokespeople and two others from the Office of Strategic and Public Affairs, as well as Hamed. Omar could sense their desperation. He turned, his face tired and remorseful, and said: 'I don't have a plan. Everything has happened so fast.' He said that if anyone had plans of their own—to resign and leave the palace, to travel to another country—he would do his best to help.

Neither Hamed nor his colleagues had any such plan. In fact, because Omar was one of Ghani's closest aides, Hamed's instinct— his *plan*—like the others, was to stay close to him. At the gate to the Gul Khana Palace, Omar, frustrated by his powerlessness, told the group to wait outside. He would speak to the president and return. But after an hour, with no sign of Omar, one by one, Hamed and his colleagues said goodbye and left.

Inside the palace, meanwhile, around lunchtime, Ghani recorded a rushed video message that would be distributed to the media in the hope of reassuring the public. 'I have guided the defence ministry to take full responsibility for the security of all residents,' he said into a camera that was askew, before vowing that 'those people rioting, looting and killing, we will deal with them with full force'.[5]

Hamed walked beneath Flag Gate's stone archway, past the cafe, then through the outer perimeter of the palace via 15th Gate. As he approached Shash Darak, where he'd parked his car that morning, he received a call from the PPS office: the president would be meeting with the defence minister. He was energised by the news. It was the first time that day he'd had reason to believe the government was in control and planning a defence of Kabul.

Hamed promptly returned to the palace and joined protocol and PPS officers in the advance team leaving for the Ministry of Defence, a short drive from the palace inside the Green Zone. It wasn't unusual for the president to have unscheduled meetings for which the advance team had little time to prepare, especially for urgent security matters, and Hamed assumed his counterparts in Defence would know more than he did. However, no-one could tell him where the meeting was to take place, or what was to be discussed. 'I saw a few PPS guys standing outside of the main building,' says Safi. 'They said, "Nobody is even aware the president is coming."' The PPS in the advance party were equally confused. They called their team leaders back at the palace and were told to await further instructions. Bismillah Khan Mohammadi, the minister of defence, was nowhere to be found either. Around 2 p.m., Hamed called Omar, but there was no response.

< >

'The day unravelled from the moment the firing began,' says Hamdullah Mohib. At 11 a.m., he was joined on the porch of the NSC offices by Abdul Salam Rahimi and Matin Bek. Mohib asked his secretary to arrange some tea. A few minutes later, the secretary himself, rather than the usual waiter, returned with the tea. 'They're all gone,' he said of the kitchen staff.

Mohib had marvelled in the past at the ability of Kabul's residents to get on with life within hours of the most harrowing attacks. On 31 May 2017, the driver of a water tanker packed with more than a tonne of explosives had detonated the lethal device outside the German Embassy, a few hundred metres from the NSC. At the time, Mohib was staying with his parents, having just returned to Kabul from Washington, DC for a visit. He remembers waking up to what he thought was a severe earthquake. 'The chandelier was shaking rapidly,' he recalls, and by the time the audible thump of the blast reached his parent's house, he was running out of the room with his phone. More than 150 people were killed in the blast, the vast majority of them workers in nearby offices and motorists. The government blamed the attack on the Taliban's ruthless Haqqani Network.

'But by that afternoon,' says Mohib, 'traffic had opened on one side of the road there. Yes, there was a lot of fear, but people were moving on with their lives. There was an unshakable resolve … And I always assumed that if Kabul came under attack from the Taliban, these people are not going to give up. I even thought maybe civilians would come to the rescue and start fighting back.'

Mohib then says of 15 August: 'But that day, that one little incident—just firing in the air—had created such a huge panic that people had vacated and left the palace grounds and the ministries. And more and more reports started pouring in as we were sitting there. We received reports that some police were coming to work that day wearing civilian clothes underneath their uniforms, and that they were taking off their uniforms at the first sign of danger to blend in with civilians. At the airport, the police had abandoned their security checkpoints, which had resulted in people entering the airport.'

Kabul was descending into chaos. Armed gangs impersonating Taliban fighters were looting police headquarters around the city even before the police had cleared out. The usually heavily secured entrance to Street 15 in the upscale diplomatic enclave of Wazir Akbar Khan in central Kabul had been abandoned and whitegoods were being wheeled out the gate on trolleys. As businessmen and government officials abandoned their homes and tore through the streets towards the airport in armoured LandCruisers, neighbours walked through the open doors and helped themselves to whatever had been left behind.

The group gathered on the porch at the NSC quickly came to a realisation which, in the 20 years since the Taliban had been removed from power, none of them could have ever imagined: they agreed the best way to bring calm was for the Taliban to issue a statement. 'There were now concerns that these shots were fired by the Taliban inside the city,' says Mohib. 'It wasn't true, but it had triggered a panic.'

Rahimi set to work calling his Taliban counterparts in Doha and, according to Mohib, 'said that he would tell them that it would help if they issued a statement'.

Bek tweeted to his 33 000 followers: 'Don't Panic! Kabul is safe!'

At 12.30 p.m., Zabihullah Mujahid, a Taliban spokesman, tweeted to his 500 000 followers:

Praise be to God that with the help of God Almighty and the overwhelming support of our people, all parts of the country have come under the control of the Islamic Emirate.

However, since the capital, Kabul, is a large and densely populated city, the Mujahideen of the Islamic Emirate do not intend to enter the city by force or war, but rather talk peacefully about entering Kabul peacefully. Negotiations are underway to ensure that the transition process is completed in a safe and secure manner, without compromising the lives, property and honour of anyone, and without compromising the lives of the people of Kabul.

The Islamic Emirate instructs all its forces to stand at the gates of Kabul and not try to enter the city. Also, until the transfer process is completed, the security of Kabul city, which must be maintained, is referred to the other side.

We reiterate that the Islamic Emirate does not intend to take revenge on anyone, all those who have served in the military and civilian sectors in the Kabul administration are forgiven and safe, no one will be retaliated against. All should stay in their own country, in their own place and home, and not try to leave the country.

We want all Afghans, from all walks of life, to see themselves in a future Islamic system with a responsible government that serves and is acceptable to all. God willing.[6]

By the time the Taliban statement was issued, Mohib was at Palace Number One, the presidential residence. 'The statement is conditional,' Ghani said to Mohib. 'They have said that order in Kabul is the responsibility of the government. It's a trick statement. They've issued it but at the same time they're going to continue to do what they want.'

Ghani attempted to contact the minister of defence and the chief of army staff, but neither could be reached by phone. He was successful in contacting his minister of interior and the chief of the NDS, instructing them to get their officers onto the streets to restore order. When the two security chiefs told the president they no longer had the necessary personnel to secure the city, even if defending it from the Taliban was no longer an immediate concern, Ghani and Mohib agreed that non-essential staff, including Rula Ghani, the first lady, should be evacuated. Emirati officials arranged for 10 tickets for their 4.30 pm flight from Kabul to Dubai to be made available.

While walking back to his office, Mohib was texted by a former minister, who told Mohib he was about to receive a call from a Pakistani number. Mohib told the man that, because of the way he'd configured his phone, he couldn't receive regular calls, but that he could be contacted via the Signal app. The person who got in touch was Khalil Haqqani, whose brother Jalaluddin had founded the Haqqani Network, and who had himself risen to the senior ranks of the Taliban's military commission. Haqqani, calling from Peshawar, reaffirmed that the Taliban didn't want to enter Kabul by force. In a claim that was as menacing as it was reassuring, Haqqani told Mohib the Taliban had been in contact with all senior government officials except the president, the vice-president and Mohib himself. They had, said Haqqani, promised not to harm those who agreed to their demands, and they intended to keep that promise.

According to Mohib, Haqqani then told him that, once the government had issued a 'statement of surrender', he would inform Mohib where they could negotiate. Mohib says he pushed back, suggesting they negotiate first, before Haqqani ended the call.

Mohib called Tom West in Doha, to ask whether he thought a meeting with Haqqani on Afghan soil might eliminate the need for the Doha meeting, saving time, and perhaps bloodshed, in Kabul. West, according to Mohib, said it wasn't a good idea: 'He didn't want me to be found in a room with a bullet in the back of my head.' The Doha meeting remained the objective.[7]

Mohib went to his residence to collect his passport and toiletries for the trip to Doha, as well as a suit, which he preferred over the local attire he wore most of the time in Afghanistan. Opening the desk drawer to take his passport, Mohib noticed that the 200 000 Afghani he'd returned there after giving money to his staff earlier in the day, was gone.

< >

By 1.30 p.m., the presidential palace had almost entirely emptied out. The only people remaining were ministers, senior advisors, security officials and the PPS. Inside the US Embassy, meanwhile, efforts intensified to burn documents and destroy hard drives and weapons, including anti-rocket systems that Mohib had requested be handed over upon the Americans' departure. Every available helicopter and crew assigned to the embassy evacuation were dispatched. Two completely shut down from overuse. 'We essentially put as many aircraft and crews in the air as possible,' says Andrew Romine. 'And [we] flew the helicopters till they broke.'

At around 1.45 p.m., an abbreviated flag-lowering ceremony was held in a courtyard of the embassy, during which Ross Wilson was handed the folded American flag. After another 30 minutes had passed, Wilson and his deputy were asked to move to the helicopter landing zone. They hoicked on their body armour and Kevlar helmets, as they would do for any flight from the embassy, and joined colonel Joe Becker, the defence attaché, who was carrying the folded flag Wilson had passed him, up the cargo ramp of a waiting Chinook. They were the last civilian personnel to leave the embassy, lifting off from the soccer-field-turned-helicopter-landing-zone at around 2.30 p.m., before hurtling above the now-gridlocked Airport Road.

Earlier, at 2 p.m., the minister of defence had called Mohib hoping that he would have the situation under control. Mohib recalls that Mohammadi said he was inside the ministry but that 'there was no-one else left. Just him'. Mohammadi then said the Taliban were in Kabul, acknowledging that the fighters may have been from existing cells rather than external groups from the provinces. Regardless, and in spite of the Taliban's assurances that they would not enter Kabul by force, their fighters were now in the neighbour-hoods of Kotal and Khair Khana in the north-west and Deh Sabz district in the north-east, adding to the growing sense of anarchy. Without understanding that the Ministry of Interior Affairs, which controlled the police, and the NDS were barely functioning by then, Mohammadi said that the ANSF needed to come up with a joint plan. In fact, the ANA, of which he as defence minister was at the helm, was also in the midst of death throes.

President Ghani now told Mohib he would go to the Ministry of Defence to meet Mohammadi himself. While Ghani made his preparations, Mohib corralled Rula Ghani and eight or nine directors and senior advisors, including Wahid Omar, towards a helicopter landing zone behind the Dilkusha Palace. The recently constructed landing zone was in the eastern corner of the citadel, adjacent to Ariana Square, where the former Afghan president Dr Mohammad Najibullah had been publicly hanged and castrated by the Taliban when they took control of Kabul in 1996. The group of travellers, who would be flown to the airport for the 4.30 p.m. Emirates flight, boarded one of three waiting Mi-17 helicopters from the presidential fleet; the president's fourth helicopter was nowhere to be seen, having been forcibly grounded at the airport.

A crew member told Mohib that, because of the hot weather and extra weight, due to the helicopters being fully fuelled, he could only take six passengers. As Mohib remonstrated that the airport was only three minutes away, Qahar Kochai approached and said to Mohib: 'If you leave, I cannot secure the president.'

'Do you want me to stay?' Mohib asked.

'No, I want you to take the president with you.'

Rahmatullah Osuli, the commander of the presidential helicopter fleet and the president's personal pilot, who had just flown in from the airport, now spoke up: 'The airport is not safe ... the Americans are controlling the airspace and are not giving us permission to fly.'

Crews aboard the American Chinooks trying to reach the embassy were getting frustrated, too. 'It was very slow getting in and out of the airport to make runs,' says Andrew Romine. 'There were so many aircraft trying to get in and out of the airport at once. Air Traffic Control [ATC] was still trying to follow all safety protocols and it created a standstill ... there were [times] when that had to be thrown out the window to get anything done. ATC was overwhelmed, as was every pilot out there. It's seriously a wonder there were no collisions.'

Sometime around midday, the air traffic controllers were evacuated from their tower on the civilian side of the airport. As a stop-gap, US AH-64 Apache helicopter crews overhead stepped in to assist. Aside from the presidential fleet, most Afghan helicopter pilots were disregarding ATC commands altogether anyway. 'They were just doing what they wanted and not talking to ATC or anyone,' says Romine. 'I personally saw one Mi-17 departing HKIA [Hamid Karzai International Airport] that crossed above the departure roll of a C-17. It wasn't super close, but it made me think this is some crazy shit and we'll be lucky if no planes crash today.'

'We have enough fuel to fly to Termez,' said Osuli. Termez was several hundred kilometres north in Uzbekistan, over the towering Hindu Kush range, but only a few minutes beyond the Amu River and the border with Afghanistan. This, he said, was the safest option for the president.

Recollections of the bloody downfall of Afghan leaders past started flooding Mohib's mind. Dr Najibullah had been blocked from reaching the airport during an attempted escape in April 1996, several months before his eventual murder, by the militiamen of his former general-turned-warlord, Abdul Rashid Dostum. And another warlord, Ismael Khan, had been surrounded and captured in Herat only a few days ago. Mohib started to envisage a calamity at the airport if they attempted to make the Emirates flight.

Also on his mind was the potentially dwindling loyalty of the PPS and the pilots, on whom his survival, and that of president Ghani, was entirely dependent. He recalled conversations with Abdul Rassoul Sayaf, yet another warlord-turned-politician, who had told him his own story of escaping the Taliban in 1996. His own people, Sayaf told Mohib, had turned on him, at one point arguing over whether to kill him or to arrest him and hand him over to the Taliban in the hope that the Taliban would spare them as a reward.

Mohib didn't feel his security would turn on him, but the PPS guards were probably no longer under singular command. He looked at the waiting helicopters and pictured the PPS officers hijacking one or more of them. Mohib says, 'I understood at this point that the security forces, the PPS, are only interested in their own security. If they're rescued—if they themselves are part of it— it will happen; if they're not, they're not going to care about the safety of the president or anyone else.'

The same went for the pilots. 'Most important was the safety and security of this crew,' continues Mohib. 'That was going to be the lifeline for the president. Had they not felt protected … I looked in their eyes and saw that these people don't really care what happens to anyone but themselves.' Mohib realised that the pilots had already decided to fly out of Afghanistan.

Everything—the question of the PPS' loyalty, the pilots' safety and the country's history of violent transitions of power, not to mention the Americans' unwillingness to factor the president into their evacuation plans—was pointing towards the fact that Kochai was right. So Mohib drove with Kochai in a PPS vehicle to Ghani's residence, where he found the president preparing to leave for his meeting at the Ministry of Defence. 'Mr president,' said Mohib, in a tone that left no room for argument, 'it's time to leave.'

According to Ghani himself, he was actually preparing to fly to Khost province, where he had strong ties with the Tanai tribe, a proposal that had been abandoned by the rest of his cabinet 48 hours earlier.[8] Ghani also says Mohib was 'literally terrified' and gave him no more than two minutes to leave. 'The PPS has collapsed,' Ghani recalls being told, prompting him to think: 'If I take a stand, they will all be killed. And they are not capable of defending me.'[9] He asked if he could go upstairs to gather some belongings. 'No, there's no time,' Mohib told him. 'I thought we were in a ticking time-bomb situation,' says Mohib.

Kochai escorted the president to where his driver and car were waiting. A convoy was also there, waiting to transport Ghani to the Ministry of Defence. Hoping to evade attention while driving to the helicopter, Kochai broke protocol and ordered the drivers not to follow him. Mohib and Kochai did not speak about it at the time but, according to Mohib, they had a mutual understanding: 'If it was going to work, it was going to work small, it was going to work without people knowing what was happening. The more people that got involved, the larger the risk.'

At the landing zone, Mohib and Kochai boarded the helicopter carrying Rula Ghani and her close protection team, as well as several other officials. On another helicopter were PPS officers who, according to Mohib, carried approximately US$200 000 in cash, as per normal protocol, and Mohib's security detail and administrative staff, who had close to US$500 000 of operational cash in local currency. (Numerous accusations that the president and his entourage absconded with suitcases full of American dollars were later made, but with little evidence to back them up. I was not able to substantiate the allegations.) Staff and bodyguards fought for the remaining seats on that helicopter and the third aircraft.

Osuli conferred with the president about where he wanted to fly. Pakistan was the closest destination but, because of the longstanding acrimony between its leadership and Afghanistan's, it was out of the question. Tajikistan was the next nearest, followed by Uzbekistan. Ghani chose the latter, confirming Termez as the landing point, and Osuli gave the order for the crews to start their engines. One of Mohib's secretaries was thrown from a door as the Mi-17s strained to climb, before finally lifting off, pointing northwards, and leaving the palace and the staff that remained behind.

The three helicopters passed the enormous Afghan flag that hung from a 70-metre flagpole atop Bibi Mahru Hill—it was visible from almost anywhere in Kabul—then skirted around the unfolding chaos at the airport. The grids of Kabul's rooftops were soon replaced by the vineyards, orchards and brick-kiln chimneys of the Shomali Plain. Trailing the fleet was the fourth helicopter, which had managed to escape the airport. The passengers watched as black smoke rose from Bagram Airfield, before the pilots steered up the Salang Valley. The crew on one of the helicopters informed their passengers they would need to offload weight if they were to make it over the 3900-metre Salang Pass, so the PPS officers onboard wriggled out of their body armour and threw it from the aircraft.

Mohib scanned the hillsides below. 'We were still in survival mode,' he says. The pilots had to fly low to conserve fuel, and although they weren't aware of any Taliban with surface-to-air weapons in the Salang, the lumbering helicopters would be vulnerable to small-arms fire and rocket-propelled grenades until they cleared the pass, through which Taliban convoys from the north would be travelling towards the capital. Mohib had several shouted conversations with crew members to confirm they were on track to make it across the Uzbekistan border. 'It would have been better to die in Kabul at the palace than to be killed on an aircraft on our way out,' he says. 'That would look very bad.'

Once the ground started to fall away after they cleared the Salang Pass, Mohib, for the first time in days, had time to think. Reflecting on this later, he says: 'I came to the government from a very idealistic viewpoint, thinking, "We now have the opportunity to build the country ..." and then we ran into politics. I think we were all unprepared, president Ghani included, for the kind of politics it takes to run a country, especially one like Afghanistan, and the unfortunate games that get played, both locally and internationally. I never imagined leaving Afghanistan, leaving my post, without being able to say a proper goodbye ... I imagined that when my time in government was over, there would be an event, a goodbye, time for me to say what I've learned. There would be thank-yous for the efforts that I had put in. It would be a celebration. It wouldn't be a day where we had just evacuated, not even sure whether we were going to make it—and then, even if we did, at the other end, what kind of a reception would we have in another country. A president, literally in a time lapse, from being the president to being in exile. The minute that helicopter landed in Uzbekistan he was no longer the president, and we as his staff around him were no longer what we were.'

< >

'It happened very suddenly,' says Hamed Safi. 'We were looking toward the palace and one helicopter was taking off, and then another, and then another. We thought they were coming to the MoD, where there is also a parking area for helicopters.'

When the three presidential helicopters had grown small in the sky, Mohammadullah Amin, one of the president's bodyguards, radioed the palace's Tactical Operations Centre (TOC). 'Where is the president going?' he asked. 'We don't know,' came the reply. 'This was strange,' says Hamed. 'The TOC should know every move the president makes.'

'Something isn't right,' said Amin. 'We need to go.' As they drove back to the palace, Amin called Qahar Kochai, but his phone was switched off. Hamed called Wahid Omar: his phone was off as well. The protocol officers with Hamed had the same result with their boss, Aminullah Atifmal. 'That was when we knew they'd escaped,' says Hamed.

As they neared the palace, one of Amin's PPS colleagues radioed to tell him an altercation was taking place between some of the president's bodyguards over bags of cash. When they turned into the gate leading to the PPS offices, two of the bodyguards were standing by the side of the road arguing over a small suitcase. Two other bodyguards were approaching to try and separate the first two. 'Everything was destroyed,' says Hamed. 'I knew it was time to leave the palace.'

When Amin was called to Palace Number One, Hamed returned to the Office of Strategic and Public Affairs once more, this time to destroy travel documents, passport photos and visa application forms belonging to the colleagues whose official travel he managed—or used to manage. He then walked through 15th Gate, turning once again towards Shash Darak. He saw a friend from the palace who he knew lived in Macroyan 4, close to his aunt Shahla, and offered to drive him, relieved to have company.

Outside the palace was bedlam. At Massoud Square, the main traffic circle between the Green Zone and the airport, cars were at a standstill. Chinooks were disappearing behind the concrete barricades separating the US Embassy from the world outside, emerging minutes later with another load of evacuees. The drivers of armoured four-wheel drives carrying foreign passengers rammed vehicles out of their way. 'There was chaos on the street,' says Hamed. 'It seemed like everyone was going to the airport to save their own lives.'

The drive from Shash Darak to Macroyan 4 usually took Hamed five minutes. On 15 August, it took him nearly an hour. His mother and father, with whom Hamed had pleaded to spend the day at his aunt's house, embraced him when he arrived. Hamed called Mahmoud, who by then had changed out of his PPS uniform, and stayed on the phone to distract him from his thoughts as he made his way home on foot. When he walked in the door, his mother took his face in her palms and kissed him again and again. 'You're alive!' she exclaimed. 'Thank God.' Hamed then called Zarifa, who was at another aunt's in Taimani, to tell her he'd made it safely to Shahla's.

Everyone from Hamed's extended family, although spread across several different homes, was now safe and accounted for. But the joyous relief ebbed as night fell. 'You could see the sorrow on everyone's face,' says Hamed. His parents and his aunt willed breaking news from the television, clicking through the channels looking for updates, while he, Mahmoud and their sister Samira scrolled social media on their smartphones.

Soon after 10 p.m., the news channel Al Jazeera cut to a live feed. 'The Taliban weren't just in the palace,' says Hamed. 'They were in the president's office.'

Mohammadullah Amin, with whom Hamed had returned from the Ministry of Defence a few hours earlier, had been asked by former president Hamid Karzai and Massoum Stanikzai to remain in the palace after Ghani fled that afternoon—the Taliban had assured them he wouldn't be harmed. At 10 p.m., Amin unbolted one of the gates he had earlier ordered his remaining subordinates to lock, and he ushered a group of around 20 mainly southern Taliban fighters and their commanders inside the citadel. He led them to the first floor of Gul Khana Palace and the president's office.

The fighters stood around the glass-topped timber desk that Ghani had delighted in telling visiting journalists once belonged to Amanullah Khan, the reformist leader who guided Afghanistan to independence from Britain in 1919 and later fled into permanent exile, but which in fact most likely belonged to Mahmoud Tarzi, his foreign minister. One fighter sat with downcast eyes in the chair from which Ghani had delivered his rushed address earlier that day. His silvered Kalashnikov sat on the desk in front of him like an offering. One young fighter had a bandage wrapped around his hand. Another carried a loudhailer. There was little fanfare. They were victorious, but right now, they were mostly exhausted.

'I'll never forget it,' Hamed tells me. 'I worked in that office for 12 years. I arranged a lot of interviews for the president there. And then I saw these people. My God.'

Hamed turned to his family: 'Now everything is finished.'

5

Resolute Support Mission Headquarters, Kabul

On the morning of 15 August 2021, lieutenant-general Haibatullah Alizai, the newly appointed army chief of staff, had driven from the Ministry of Defence to Resolute Support Mission Headquarters, the international military base beside the US Embassy in Wazir Akbar Khan. A large contingent of US Army Delta Force soldiers had arrived in Kabul and their commanders wanted to meet with their Afghan counterparts to discuss plans for securing four key areas of the capital: the airport, Bagram Airfield, Kabul City and the city's outskirts. By the time the meeting had concluded, however, one of the locations the Deltas had marked for protection had fallen to the Taliban: Bagram Airfield had been overrun and thousands of prisoners from the Parwan Detention Facility—mostly Taliban fighters—were now running free.

The scope of the plan was narrowed and new orders were handed down. The Afghan National Army's most formidable fighting unit, the Kteh Khas Afghan (KKA), was to join the CIA's proxy forces, the National Strike Units, or Zero Units, in securing only Hamid Karzai International Airport. KKA personnel were duly called back to their headquarters, Scorpion Camp, from the prisons they had been ordered to protect in the early hours of that morning, and, along with the other KKA members present, they were instructed to prepare to move to the airport.

Scorpion Camp lay deep inside the Kabul Military Training Centre off the Kabul–Jalalabad Highway in the east of the capital, nestled in-between drab concrete barracks, a Soviet tank graveyard and boundless live-fire ranges. Beside the KKA headquarters was another camp, home to the Afghan Reconnaissance Unit (ARU), which comprised the most elite fighters from the KKA, other army special forces units and commandos. The ARU had been established in 2012 as a niche unit of less than 100 personnel whose primary task was locating high-value targets behind enemy lines. Publicly, the ARU didn't exist. 'We pretended we were KKA,' says the unit's commanding officer, major Behzad Behnam, 'but we were using it as a shield.'

Lieutenant-general Alizai had taken charge of the Afghan National Army Special Operations Command (ANASOC) earlier that year. Subsequently, in July, the ARU, until then under ANASOC command, was expanded in both size and scope. A further 200 soldiers were recruited with the aim of turning the unit into the Afghan equivalent of Delta Force. The ARU would be reserved for only the most critical missions and deployable countrywide. In addition, while the unit previously had been part of the Ministry of Defence's regular chain of command, it was now directly under Alizai's control, answerable only to him. 'This was a very elite unit,' he says, 'and I didn't want it to be misused by any other individuals or organisations.'

Since early August, Behnam, a KKA veteran himself, had been in contact with the commander of Delta Force. The unit was planning to bring an element into Kabul to secure the city and its surrounds during the final days of the American evacuation, and the commander had asked Behnam for his support. Behnam proposed creating an entirely new force, Eagle Unit, which would be composed of 400 soldiers primarily from the ARU and the KKA's prized 4th Company. To carry out the ambitious operation, Eagle Unit would join forces with the CIA's Kabul-based Afghan proxy force, the 01 unit, whose American advisors and commanders Behnam had already met with several times. However, when Delta Force had arrived in Kabul and met with lieutenant-general Alizai that morning, Behnam was nowhere to be seen. An American colleague whose information Behnam trusted more than anyone else's had texted him on 11 August: 'Move your fucking arse. Move your family out of Afghanistan. This is the last warning I'm giving you.' Behnam had flown with members of his family to Islamabad and hadn't yet returned to Kabul.

Among the men major Behnam recruited into the ARU in the months beforehand was a 28-year-old KKA captain and father of four, Arman Malik. The captain had been recommended to Behnam by a special forces battalion commander when he went scouting for recruits. Behnam had been immediately impressed by the way in which captain Malik grasped the bold ideas he had in mind for Eagle Unit.

< >

Arman Malik was born in the northern province of Takhar in 1993. After the Taliban first came to power in 1996, Takhar became a strategically vital region for the anti-Taliban Northern Alliance. Linking Tajikistan to the north and the Panjshir Valley to the south, it served as part of a critical supply route for the resistance being led by a charismatic Panjshiri commander, Ahmad Shah Massoud, and his Shura-e Nazar faction.

In the early years of the war between the Taliban and the Northern Alliance, the Taliban made inroads into Takhar on several occasions and control toggled between the two groups. Malik's father, Ahmad Sakhi, developed a reputation as a peacemaker, first with Massoud's fighters, who were demanding land from an ethnic minority, and later with the Taliban, whom he implored to treat the people of his community with respect and dignity, and to whom he passed on the gifts of livestock the minority community gave him as thanks for his mediation with Massoud's men.

The mobile phone tower after which Antenna Post is named.
14 September 2021

Dasht-e Langar, Chak, as seen from the ruins of Antenna Post.
14 September 2021

Sunrise over Kabul. 7 October 2020

Taliban fighters ride through the streets of Kabul on a captured police humvee hours after president Ashraf Ghani fled the Afghan capital.
15 August 2021

Taliban fighter Abudajanah, who oversaw the capture of Antenna Post, prays near the remains of a Soviet tank in Chak, Maidan Wardak.
9 October 2021

Taliban fighters admire the crater left by a tunnel bomb that precipitated the May 2021 collapse of the Afghan government in Nerkh district, Maidan Wardak province.
20 September 2021

With the Taliban at the gates of Kabul, a US Army Chinook lifts out of the US embassy, evacuating staff to Hamid Karzai International Airport.
15 August 2021

During a spate of assassinations in Kabul in 2020, a man is carried from the scene of a roadside bomb targeting vice-president Amrullah Saleh, who was uninjured in the blast.
9 September 2020

Government security forces and firefighters near an entrance to Kabul's Green Zone soon after what government officials estimated to be 1500 kilograms of explosives carried in a water truck were detonated during morning peak hour, killing a reported 150 and injuring more than 450. 31 May 2017

Nadia Amini in Kabul.
2 November 2021

Taliban fighter Hejratullah on his former prison bed in the Parwan Detention Facility
8 October 2021

The knife Najma bought after the Taliban took control of Kabul, which she said she would use to kill herself if their fighters came for her.
1 September 2021

Queueing outside Kabul's passport office at sunrise as the Taliban's military advance gathered momentum.
12 July 2021

Bullet holes and bloodstains on a wall in an abandoned police station where nine escapees from the Parwan Detention Facility were last seen in the custody of the CIA proxy force known as 01. 19 September 2021

Hundreds of Afghans wait outside a perimeter gate on the northwestern side of Hamid Karzai International Airport as a military transport plane departs during the mass-evacuation operation that saw a reported 120 000 non-combatants airlifted out of the Afghan capital in the last two weeks of August.
24 August 2021

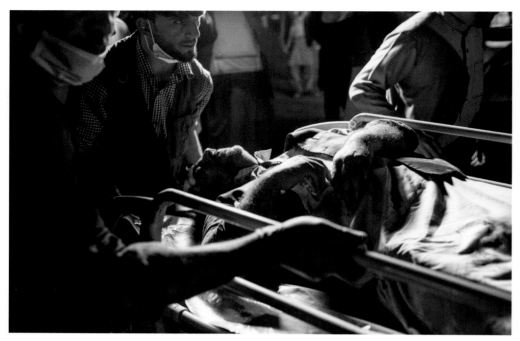

A man is helped onto a hospital gurney outside Emergency Hospital after being injured in the bombing at Abbey Gate.
26 August 2021

The canal beside Abbey Gate where an estimated 180 people were killed—mostly Afghans trying to enter Hamid Karzai International Airport, but also thirteen US servicemen and women—after an ISIS suicide bomber detonated an explosive device in the final days of the evacuation. 7 October 2021

But eventually, Sakhi's interventions saw his immunity withdrawn. The Taliban commander with whom he had broken bread asked Sakhi, whom he knew to have relations on both sides of the front line, to introduce him to his rival Massoud. Sakhi arranged the meeting through a close friend, one of Massoud's commanders, Mohammad Daoud Daoud. The Taliban commander was so impressed by Massoud that he defected to the Northern Alliance. Massoud, in turn impressed by such a high-profile revolt, asked Daoud to introduce him to the man who had facilitated it, and promptly offered Sakhi an administrative job with the Shura-e Nazar.

The first time the Taliban infiltrated Takhar, beyond its capital city Taloqan, Sakhi and his family were living in a village to the east, halfway to neighbouring Badakhshan province. Malik was shepherding sheep one afternoon when two Taliban fighters approached and asked for the name of his father. Malik was only six at the time but he already had an innate ability to understand the local conflict dynamics, and so he gave the militants the name of a cousin instead. 'This was the experience of the time,' says Malik. 'The Taliban were looking for anyone associated with Massoud.' Unbeknown to Malik, his father had been forewarned, and, lacking enough time to collect his son from the fields, he had moved with the rest of the family to a neighbour's house, where the Taliban fighters wouldn't expect to find him. Sakhi then left his family and moved to Badakhshan for several months, until the Taliban were again driven from the family's home province.

By the time the Taliban returned to Takhar, Malik's family had already moved further east to the district of Kalafghan, bordering Badakhshan, where the Northern Alliance still held sway. While the fighting didn't often affect him and his family directly, Malik recalls how in Takhar, all the schools had been closed when the Taliban were in control, while next door in Badakhshan, boys and girls studied in the same classes until grade 12.

The more time Sakhi spent in Massoud's circles, the more he began to feel that his commander's motives weren't in the national interest. He suspected Massoud was behind the deaths of several influential leaders within his own ranks, and, after an argument with a then-mid-ranking commander named Mohammad Qasim Fahim, he left Shura-e Nazar. Still, despite his father's misgivings about Massoud, Malik says Ahmad Sakhi didn't eat for one week after Massoud was assassinated on 9 September 2001.

One of Malik's first memories of the post-Taliban era was seeing American cargo planes dropping crates of food into Takhar. As the Taliban retreated, Sakhi and his family moved to Taloqan, and, in 2002 Malik was enrolled in school. 'First we were learning under a tree, then UNICEF provided a tent and later we had a building,' he recalls. 'Every day there was new reason for hope.'

That same year, Sakhi, Malik's mother Aigul and a younger brother, Mutaqi, as well as two uncles and an aunt, were travelling on a rough road to a funeral in Kalafghan when the jeep Sakhi was driving careened into a river. The only survivor was Malik's infant brother, who was found in his mother's arms.

Malik continued his schooling in Taloqan while studying the Qur'an under his sister Parwana's husband, a local mullah. In 2009, after graduating from high school, he travelled to Kabul. He planned to sit for the university entrance exam but, after surviving on the proceeds of the sale of his family's land after the death of his parents, Malik was more interested in finding a job and making an income. Mohammad Daoud Daoud, his father's friend, was now general Daoud, Afghanistan's top counter-narcotics official in the new Karzai government. Daoud found Malik a job in the external affairs department at the ANA, where part of his work involved organising overseas military education for members of the KKA. Malik was impressed by the discipline of the unit and he envied its members' salaries, which were significantly higher than those of regular soldiers.

Malik joined the regular ANA, whereupon he was assigned to the 203 'Thunder' Corps and stationed in their corps command in the eastern province of Paktiya. Malik trained every day in preparation for the KKA's gruelling requirements, and, during a short period of leave, he fronted for their physical examination in

Kabul—he was one of less than 100 out of 1400 applicants to be accepted. In 2011, after a week of health and background checks, Malik returned to Paktiya to inform his superiors of his transfer, then moved to Kabul to train and eventually graduate as a member of the KKA.

That spring, he again met Daoud, who had become something of a surrogate father to Malik after his own father's death, and who was now the chief of police for the 303 'Pamir' zone, named after a mountain range in northern Afghanistan, and in Kabul for a short visit. After the call to prayer at sunset, Daoud took Malik's hand and told him in a whisper that he was being recommended for promotion to a senior post in the Ministry of Interior Affairs. 'But I don't think I'll make it to the position,' Daoud said. 'Keep this to yourself.' Daoud left that evening for Takhar to attend a regional meeting with senior government officials and German troops who were heading security and development efforts in the north. As they left the gathering at the provincial governor's office in Taloqan, a suicide bomber struck, killing six, including Daoud and two German soldiers.

In his early years at the KKA, says Malik, he and the other Afghan soldiers acted mostly as muscle for American counter-terrorism operations. 'The CIA was collecting the intelligence, providing packages and planning the operations,' he says, while the US Navy SEALs and Army Rangers were implementing the operations and taking KKA units with them, mentoring the young fighters with the intention of slowly handing over responsibility. 'We were under direct control of the US,' says Malik. 'They decided what we did and where we went. Often, we didn't know where we were going [on operations] and I suspect that sometimes we may have been outside Afghanistan.'

The KKA, also known as the Afghan Partnering Unit, was established in the wake of widespread criticism of the raids conducted by American counter-terrorism units in the first decade of the war. In rural areas, the home incursions roiled communities that, unable to protect their families—particularly women—in the face of overwhelming force, saw them as a blight on their honour. So the KKA was set up by the offending US units as a 'partner force' with whom they could continue to conduct raids against high-value targets, ostensibly with more consideration given to cultural sensitivities. Critics of the American raiders were reassured that the creation of Afghan counter-terrorism units would, from then on, ensure accountability for the secretive operations. But in reality, the KKA, which comprised three operational and five support companies, became a proxy force built in the mould of the American units, from whom it would continue to take its orders and without whom it would never be able to function. Although it wasn't believed to be deliberate, the KKA recruits were overwhelmingly ethnic Tajiks and Hazaras from central and northern Afghanistan whom the Pashtuns in the south considered almost as foreign as their American progenitors.

Captain Malik says that the tactics taught by the American advisors to KKA recruits—especially those in reconnaissance roles—weren't only about the application of overwhelming violence, however. For one mission, Malik was sent to Paktiya province where, disguised as a humanitarian worker and armed only with a notebook and a camera, he surveyed residents in a village about a fictitious illness for which he said a vaccine would soon be distributed. 'I made notes and took photos and located the target, who was later eliminated,' says Malik. 'Foreigners taught us all these kinds of tactics.' In 2018, such practices resulted in bans on house-to-house vaccination campaigns in Taliban-controlled areas and subsequent spikes in the spread of the polio virus.

After only a handful of operations, Malik was transferred to the KKA's personnel department, which kept him off the battlefield but close to the unit's leadership and the advisors who lived onsite inside Scorpion Camp.

The KKA became a formidable fighting force: they had the best fighters, the most advanced weaponry, highly motivated advisors who accompanied them on operations, and a remarkable success rate. 'They conducted impossible operations and hit impossible targets,' says Behzad Behnam. 'Even the Americans were impressed. All the high-value targets that the KKA managed to kill [as many as 80 or 100 each month] were behind enemy lines.' But the KKA were heavily reliant on American support. So, too, the ANA's conventional forces and the police, who were dysfunctional, unmotivated and corrupt, but who had proved capable of preventing a total Taliban takeover provided they had the backing of the United States.

'The Americans provided us with every single element for an operation,' says Behnam, 'the intelligence, the planning, everything. Then they briefed the troops on how to conduct the operation. Also, while on operations, they were watching you constantly … controlling you, telling you what to do, where to go—starting with motivation, then the logistics, landing on the target, executing the [mission] and flying or driving back to HQ … Basically, the soldiers on the ground just had to execute it. Everything is so well-planned that you can't go wrong.'

But while the KKA were extraordinary at carrying out operations under the command of the Americans, with their seemingly infinite resources, they were ill-prepared for the day it disappeared. That day came on 29 February 2020 with the signing of the Doha Agreement. 'That changed everything,' says Behnam. 'It was a huge shock.' Overnight, the KKA, like all Afghan forces, were forced to take responsibility for all aspects of their work—intelligence gathering, planning, fire and air support, and aerial surveillance—not just their execution, as in the past.

The Americans living at Scorpion Camp started winding back their involvement almost immediately. Even then, as equipment was removed and support reduced, the KKA didn't believe the Americans would ever actually leave. It was political theatre, they thought. The foreigners had invested too much to depart before the soldiers they had trained were capable of taking full responsibility for the country's security. The idea of a Taliban government, of a terrorist safe haven like that which had allowed al-Qaeda to plan the 9/11 attacks, would never be allowed to become a reality.

'On a daily basis, the Americans started distancing themselves,' says Behnam. 'Until one day they came to my office and said, "We won't be here tomorrow."'

Malik says that, until April 2021, CIA advisors lived with the ARU and KKA at Scorpion Camp. After that, they would fly in and out morning and night by helicopter. Then, in July, says Malik, 'they said goodbye altogether, and we realised they were leaving Afghanistan'.

‹ ›

The Taliban had no worse enemy than the KKA and the ARU, and the soldiers who served in those units knew they would be at the top of the incoming regime's list for reprisals once the group had consolidated their power. Being caught in uniform, or worse, inside Scorpion Camp, where an affiliation with either unit would be undeniable, was likely a death sentence. Of the 300 KKA fighters present inside the camp the night before, 14 August, dozens slipped away, changing out of their uniforms and quietly deserting. Others who would ordinarily have been on the base had been sent to the southern province of Helmand for the futile attempt to prevent it from being overrun. Many had been killed. Others were stuck at the 215th Corps headquarters there or were on overdue leave after returning, while many of the wounded from the fighting in that province were undergoing treatment.

From the ARU, only five soldiers, including Malik, remained. Around 130 men had been dispatched to gather intelligence on Taliban movements around Kabul and the surrounding provinces; 60 were waiting in the 215 Corps headquarters for air transport back to Kabul; and 12 had been killed in Lashkar Gah, Helmand's capital. Several others, Malik concedes, had deserted. 'All the soldiers were tired of Ashraf Ghani's devilish lies,' he says. 'Trust was no longer there.'

Eagle Unit, which comprised the best fighters from both the ARU and the KKA's 4th Company, and the plans its commander, major Behnam, who was in Islamabad, had been making with Delta Force, were by now virtually defunct. In Behnam's absence, his deputy ordered Malik to make an inventory of the ARU equipment that was being loaded into the approximately 60–70 vehicles in which the remaining soldiers would depart for the airport. Among the tally, 174 M4 carbine rifles, 60 Beretta M9 pistols, 60 Harris tactical radios, 30 M240 and M249 machine guns, 160 sets of night vision goggles and 40–50 AT4 single use rocket launchers. They would hand the weapons over to the Americans, who were coordinating the mission to secure the airport.

As the day progressed, and news of the last of the provincial capitals surrounding Kabul—and Bagram Prison—falling to the Taliban filtered through the camp, Malik, in spite of the dread rising inside him, tried to remain composed in front of the remnants of the ARU. Although he had lost faith in the ANSF's ability to fight its way back from the brink of military defeat, Malik still hoped that the special forces in Kabul could defend the city until the United States forced president Ghani to agree to an interim government and a peaceful transfer of power. With that, he believed, assurances of mercy would be made to those, like him, who had spent the past decade trying—and ultimately failing—to bring about the demise of the Taliban.

'I believed in the survival of the republic and the support of the international community,' says Malik. 'I never thought about the collapse of the republic. I didn't even get a passport for myself or my family members.'

But it was becoming increasingly difficult to maintain the stoic facade, even to himself. 'I was devastated,' says Malik. 'Many soldiers and commanders had already left; they knew Kabul was falling. I thought of all the soldiers we lost over 20 years at war with the Taliban. I never believed that they would be handed victory like this.'

The ARU was so short on numbers that Malik called his brother Kabir, a computer science student with whom he lived in Qasaba, on the northern side of the airport, and asked him to come to Scorpion Camp to bolster the unit's numbers for the drive to the airport. Kabir had never been in the military, but, as Malik had done with several young women from government ministries, Kabir had been brought to the firing range at Kabul Military Training Centre a few times in the past. Any other day, arranging access for family or friends to the fortress-like camp would have taken Malik several phone calls and favours. But by the early afternoon of 15 August, the ANA gate guards had abandoned their posts, and the soldiers inside the perimeter were too preoccupied with survival to question Kabir as he walked through the gate and up the hill to meet his brother.

Malik would be driving his own unmarked Ford Ranger. He positioned his brother in the turret of an ARU humvee and reminded him how to operate the M240 machine gun mounted on an arm behind a slanting armour plate, cranking the charging handle so it was ready to fire. In the mid-afternoon, as the convoy prepared to leave, colonel Khalid Amiri, the commander of the KKA, who was among the few from the KKA and the ARU deployed to Helmand who had managed to get back to Kabul, stood before his men and those of the ARU. Six weeks earlier, after government forces had pushed back Taliban fighters in the northern province of Balkh, Amiri had declared: 'As long as we are alive and have blood in us, we will not allow the enemy to rule the people of Afghanistan.'[1] Now, seeing the pitiful state of his unit, and having heard about the departure of Ashraf Ghani less than an hour before, Amiri offered a choice to the remaining 100 or so men who had assembled alongside the convoy of idling vehicles: 'It's up to you. Either you are coming with us to secure the airport or you can go to your homes. You decide.'

Before stepping into their vehicles, some soldiers began changing out of their military uniforms and into civilian clothes. Malik couldn't believe what he was seeing. It looked like defeat. 'Seeing them change out of their uniforms, it was very disappointing to me,' says Malik. 'But I still didn't think everything was lost.'

The dozens of vehicles, piled with weapons but with no more than one or two occupants each, wound their way out of Scorpion Camp. The last government forces still fighting in large numbers in Kabul, between Darulaman and Rish Khor, about 20 kilometres south-west of the airport, had held off the advancing Taliban until word reached them of president Ghani's unannounced exit from the palace. Lieutenant-general Alizai says that, inside Resolute Support Mission Headquarters, he proposed to the Americans the institution of martial law, but he was quickly rebuffed.

Malik was in the middle of the convoy as it drove onto the Kabul–Jalalabad Highway, civilian traffic having been blocked by a KKA humvee so that the vehicles remained a single, unbroken unit. A 12-kilometre drive to the airport lay ahead. Members of the ARU's reconnaissance team had dressed as civilians and melded with the growing chaos around Kabul, and were now reporting back to Malik. He also instructed his four men to mine their sources and social media for whatever information they could find on the circumstances in Kabul.

As the convoy crawled west along the highway, drivers cut in-between the unwieldy armoured vehicles, despite the machine gunners trying to warn them off. As they passed through Ut Khel, home to Mullah Tarakhel, an influential member of parliament who had lobbied to prevent the KKA from basing themselves in the neighbourhood, pedestrians lined the road and glared. 'When I wound down the windows,' says Malik, 'I could hear them talking. "Look at them," they said. "They're leaving because the Taliban are here." They were happy the Taliban were coming.'

But Malik refused to betray his resignation to his men. The government would convene, he assured the men, perhaps at the airport. They would create a council, disavow Ghani, and arrange a smooth transition. His private thoughts were darker: like Hamdullah Mohib, Malik was thinking back to Dr Mohammad Najibullah's undignified demise. He was also watching in disbelief as drivers of vehicles in front of and behind him broke away from the convoy and sped off, escaping down side roads headed he-didn't-know-where. Other drivers pulled to the side of the highway and stepped out, unarmed and dressed in civilian clothes, to disappear into the tide of pedestrians.

Before reaching the city, one of the ARU's reconnaissance officers reported heavy traffic on Airport Road between the American Embassy and the main civilian entrance to the airport. The officer suggested the convoy divert through the narrow streets of Yakatoot, which it did. Steep speed bumps then forced Malik to a virtual halt at regular intervals. He cursed the jolting lumps of concrete, each one forcing him to look into the eyes of passers-by who no longer looked back with respect, but with pity or contempt.

But it wasn't until the convoy emerged onto Airport Circle that Malik grasped just how far the government had fallen. 'Airport staff were fleeing and huge numbers of people were trying to get inside,' he says. 'The situation was out of control.'

Once Malik and the others made it through the circle, the train of tactical vehicles continued along a wide boulevard separated by a median strip lined with young pine trees and red-and-white dividers, steering towards the gate to which they'd been instructed to report. After all the desertions, the convoy was barely half the length it had been on departing Scorpion Camp an hour and a half earlier. 'I felt beaten,' says Malik. 'I felt like I had lost the game.'

At around 6 p.m., the convoy turned into the entrance to the ANSF's Joint Special Operations Command (JSOC) headquarters, midway along the southern side of the airfield. Malik stood with the guards at the gate to ensure that everyone aboard the vehicles was authorised to enter. He then left the airport entrance and drove his brother to a relative's house in Taimani. 'I told him I had to go back to the airport to hand over ammunition and weapons and that I would be fine,' says Malik. 'It was almost dark. The police had left their posts, and it was quiet on the streets.' While driving back to the airport around 7 p.m., from behind the tinting on the windows of his Ranger—which he had added, along with a coat of white paint, after a crash the year before, in order that the car didn't stand out as a government vehicle—Malik watched a car drive by with a white Taliban flag flapping from the aerial.

‹ ›

At 4 p.m. that day, just as Malik was preparing to set off in his convoy, lieutenant-general Haibatullah Alizai arrived at JSOC headquarters at the airport with the commander of the Afghan Air Force and the head of military intelligence. Lieutenant-general Sami Sadat, who had cancelled his plans to travel to India to have his battle wounds treated and taken up the post of chief of security for Kabul, was surprised to see him: 'Brother, please go back to MoD.' Alizai replied: 'There is no-one to protect MoD.'

The two young generals drove to the presidential palace in an armoured convoy with a coterie of bodyguards and support staff. The few PPS officers guarding the First Gate admitted the convoy, which then wove around the palace perimeter to the Ministry of Defence—the gates were open and the guards were gone. The generals then made their way to the Resolute Support Mission Headquarters, where Admiral Peter Vasely was preparing to depart for the airport.

'I need some of the newly arrived troops to deploy with my troops and conduct a couple of patrols inside Kabul,' Sadat said to Vasely. 'We just need to take care of tonight. Tomorrow, discipline will come back to the city.'

'No,' said Vasely. 'My orders are to evacuate the city and move to Kabul airport.'

'What about the people who are left in Kabul City?'

'That's not my problem,' replied Vasely.

'It is a fucking big problem because we can't fit all the people in Kabul airport.'

'I'm taking orders from the Pentagon,' said Vasely. 'I've been told to evacuate my forces and the US Embassy to Kabul airport. If you want, you can fit in one of the helicopters.' Vasely then said:

'Sami, you don't have a president, you don't have a government. Who are you fighting for?'[2]

Alizai now turned to Sadat and said he wanted to join his men who were fighting from the ANASOC headquarters in Rish Khor. Sadat said it was a bad idea. When Alizai pushed, Sadat pulled rank as chief of security for Kabul: 'General Alizai, I don't allow you to go back to *my* corps headquarters. You will either be captured alive or you will be killed miserably and I don't want to see that.'

Alizai and Sadat returned to the JSOC headquarters, arriving around 7.30 p.m. Bismillah Khan Mohammadi, the minister of defence, was at the airport as well. He told Sadat he wanted to fly out of the country and regroup, with a view to mounting a resistance from abroad. Sadat acquiesced and saw Mohammadi off on one of two Emirati C-130 military planes that Assadullah Khalid, one of Mohammadi's ministry predecessors, and who was in Dubai for medical treatment, had arranged with UAE military officials.

At this time, says Alizai, 'we were still considering announcing martial law'. But the idea was finally abandoned when a message was transmitted to the remaining ANA commanders with functional units, a message that sounded almost identical to what Vasely had told Sadat less than an hour earlier. 'No-one is left,' the voice on the radio announced. 'What are you guys fighting for?' The soldiers from ANASOC's 1st Battalion, who had been holding the line in Rish Khor, heard the declaration of defeat and retreated to the airport. From that moment on, says Alizai, neither the KKA nor any of the other units standing by would fight.

'The defence minister, plus his deputies, plus his corps commanders, all of them lost control over the army,' says Behzad Behnam. 'They didn't know which units were available, where in Afghanistan they were, which units were in Kabul and which units were able to fight.' Behnam adds that, aside from Mohammadi, none of the corps commanders, including Sadat and Alizai, had enough experience to know how to deal with such catastrophic circumstances. 'To say there weren't forces available to defend Kabul is absolutely wrong,' he says, pointing to the special forces battalion fighting in Rish Khor, and another that had withdrawn to Kabul from Kunduz and was ready to fight. There were also police and NDS special forces. 'As an army commander,' continues Behnam, 'if you can't manage to lead, saying "The soldiers stopped fighting" or "There weren't any forces available to fight" is a very good excuse.'

The plans for Eagle Unit to join forces with the CIA's 01 unit and Delta Force in securing Kabul and Bagram Airfield, meanwhile, had been made redundant by the Taliban's final advance that day. Alizai and colonel Amiri had also fallen out of the loop with the Americans. Most KKA soldiers were languishing in corps headquarters across the country, waiting for transport to Kabul, or had already deserted. The 01 unit and the other CIA proxy units, on the other hand, were still intact and under effective command. The Americans could sense that the ANA, including the KKA, were falling apart. Alizai says, 'We were part of their morning plan, but not their afternoon plan.'

‹ ›

After captain Malik returned to the airport, colonel Amiri moved his KKA and ARU convoy from the southern side of the facility, where JSOC and the commercial terminals lay, to the northern military side. With the ANA now all but disbanded, Amiri announced that, yet again, the plans had changed. As he'd done at Scorpion Camp, he gave the remaining soldiers a choice: 'Go to your homes, or come to Panjshir with me for the resistance.'

He was referring to the Panjshir Valley, where Ahmad Shah Massoud had staged his 20-year fight, first against the Soviets and later against the first iteration of the Taliban in the late 1990s. A handful of ANA commanders, mostly natives of Panjshir, had been in talks with Massoud's son, Ahmad Massoud, who had pledged to lead another resistance against the Taliban in the event of the government's collapse. Amrullah Saleh, the vice-president, who had been notably absent for a security meeting in the presidential palace that morning, was already in Panjshir.

Malik was torn. He had met the younger Massoud two months earlier at his home in Wazir Akbar Khan and hadn't sensed that he was capable of leading an anti-Taliban resistance, as Massoud's father had. 'I was reluctant,' says Malik. 'I didn't believe in Massoud.'

Around a dozen KKA members were willing to go to Panjshir with Amiri. They took four humvees from the 30 that had made it from Scorpion Camp to the airport, loaded them with as many weapons and as much ammunition as they could carry, and drove off for the JSOC gate. Standing at the entrance to an aircraft maintenance hangar that faced the Afghan Air Force's flight line, Malik was left with the KKA's remaining vehicles and an enormous stockpile of weapons. He and the four ARU soldiers consolidated the weapons in four humvees and his Ranger. Nearby sat some armoured LandCruisers belonging to Alizai, Sadat and Mohammadi, some with their headlights on, doors wide open.

By 9 p.m., Malik began seeing silhouetted figures moving in large groups from the civilian side of the airport, across the airfield and towards the military side. He left his soldiers to guard the arsenal and the fleet of vehicles they'd been left with, and he approached Sadat, who was sitting in one of the black armoured LandCruisers. Malik introduced himself and asked for instructions regarding the armaments. 'Secure the weapons,' Sadat ordered.

Malik returned an hour later, again asking for instructions concerning the weapons. Sadat again told Malik to keep them secure. He also asked the captain whether he had any food. Malik had some cooked rice in a plastic bag in his Ranger, but when he offered to fetch it, Sadat waved him off.

Sometime around 10 p.m., lieutenant-general Alizai coordinated with the Americans, who had taken control of the airspace above Kabul, to allow an Afghan Air Force C-130 transport plane to fly to Kandahar Airfield, where 125 members of the CIA's 03 unit were still waiting to be evacuated; Alizai accompanied the two pilots himself. Sadat then contacted his successor at the 215th Corps, Jawed Salim, and suggested doing the same for him and his 200 soldiers, who were marooned in Helmand. 'Don't even try,' said

Salim. 'If you come to Bastion airport, there is no way people will control themselves.' He was referring to the Taliban fighters who were now in control of both the base and the remaining government soldiers. By the time Alizai returned from his flight after midnight, the 03's sister unit, 01, had been ordered by their CIA masters to spread out across the airfield and bring it under control.

The third time Malik approached Sadat, the lieutenant-general told Malik to just leave the weapons. He said he had chartered a plane with 70 seats—which in fact had been arranged by Assadullah Khalid—adding: 'I will take you with me. You're a committed soldier.' Malik didn't respond, knowing he couldn't leave the cache behind until the airport was properly secured.

Malik says that, sometime around midnight, when he returned to Sadat a fourth time, Sadat shouted: 'Go to Hell! What do I care about your weapons?' (Sadat says he has no recollection of the encounter.)

Despite the rage building inside him, Malik walked away in silence. 'My expectations of Sadat were higher than his capabilities,' he says. 'I expected he might have made efforts to secure the airport, but instead, he was just thinking about himself.'

Malik was 50 metres away from the vehicles he'd been protecting when he realised the four ARU soldiers who had remained with him throughout the day and night had finally left. He was alone with around 1000 weapons, 26 tactical vehicles and his white Ford Ranger. After his rage subsided, Malik felt a sense of calm wash over him. 'I still had my dignity,' he says. But he also knew his work wasn't over, and he prepared himself to maintain his vigil over the weapons until the morning.

< >

Just as Malik was discovering he was alone, colonel Amiri's KKA soldiers, who were still waiting inside the JSOC exit to leave the airport, began deserting him as well. The guards manning the gates had told Amiri that the Taliban were in control of the city and they had been ordered not to let anyone in or out. Now, having waited until midnight, the soldiers had had enough. 'I had my personal clothes with me,' says Safiullah, who was one of those soldiers, 'because I thought I might need them.' He'd found himself thinking, to Hell with Amiri, and had unzipped his uniform, revealing a crumpled *peran tunban*, then disappeared into the crowd outside the airport. 'I'd faced these situations before in several operations,' says Safiullah. 'This was the only way out.'

6

Shah Shahid, Kabul
II

A t home, the fear welling inside Amin Amini's boys was being expressed as anger. 'You knew the situation in the country,' said Hanif, exasperated and distraught. 'Why did you even bring us into this world?'

'It was so hard for my dad,' says Nadia. She thinks of an artwork by an American designer, Chad Knight: a three-dimensional rendering of a father holding the outstretched hand of his young son. The father's manikin-like body is drilled with holes, front to back, with the remnant dowel-like cross-sections collected and reassembled to form his son. 'The father is giving everything to his son,' says Nadia, speaking as if of her own family. 'He's doing many things for his children but he's not thinking about himself.'

But on the morning of 15 August, with the family having gone to sleep the night before burdened by rumours that the Taliban were near Pul-i Charkhi prison, where thousands of Taliban prisoners were anticipating imminent freedom, they resented their father for their very existence.

Elham, Nadia's 14-year-old brother, was crying. A month earlier he'd been fitted for two *peran tunban*, one black and one grey, in the southern style—'Taliban style,' says Nadia—collarless, with buttons running down from the right collarbone. Elham had always worn jeans and T-shirts, but buying the traditional garb had given him a faint sense of control over the impending Taliban takeover. Dressing like the fighters who would come, he thought, would infer a like-mindedness or kinship that didn't require a declaration of allegiance. The *peran tunban* would act like an invisibility cloak. It was a basic survival technique, like those used by the villagers in Maidan Wardak who were trying to navigate life on the front line between the ANSF and the Taliban. So Elham had worn the clothes with a bashful pride. But the sense of preparedness the purchase had provided a month ago now seemed quaint—Elham felt helpless and exposed.

The youngest Amini was effortlessly smart. He had picked up passable Urdu from watching *India Alert* on television, conversed in halting English with Nadia, and was learning German as had his oldest brother, Rahim. He was born into a time when opportunity and aspiration weren't just for a privileged few but assumed for all. He hadn't wanted to follow his father into the ANP, as Rahim had. He'd wanted to become an engineer. But now, he was without hope. 'I have no future,' he told his parents. 'That's because of you.'

Rahim was on the phone from Germany throughout the morning, trying to keep everyone calm. 'It's okay,' he said, 'nothing will happen. We will find a way.'

Amin was burning photos. He had never made time to paint the false wall he'd built into one of the rooms of the house to hide them, and now it was too late. There were faded photos from his own time working with the police, before the Taliban first took charge in the mid-1990s, and of Rahim with the international military mentors he'd worked with after the Taliban were toppled in 2001.

'Look at this situation,' Hanif said to his father. 'This is the country you love?'

At mid-morning, after news of the Taliban reaching eastern Kabul the night before had proved to be false, Amin and his wife

Shukria both left the house to run the kinds of errands they would handle on any other day. Although the Taliban were closer than they'd ever been to Kabul, the aggressive young lieutenant-generals Haibatullah Alizai and Sami Sadat had been appointed to key posts in Kabul and, as far as the Aminis knew, were still planning to defend the capital. For the time being, life went on. Shukria went to a local government office to sign the sale documents for the house which had been purchased under her name, while Amin went to buy fruit from the bazaar at the end of their street.

Then the sound of gunfire, rapid, from many weapons at once, enveloped Shah Shahid. Shukria's headscarf slipped from her head as she ran home. She banged furiously on the gate and called for one of the children to let her inside. 'Call your father,' Shukria said. 'The gunfire is coming from the military base.'

Amin said he would return as soon as he could. In the meantime, the gunfire was unrelenting. Shukria, worried about bullets coming through the windows, hurried Nadia and her brothers into the basement, where they sat apart on boxes and long rolls of carpet. 'We thought the Taliban were fighting the soldiers,' says Nadia.

The gunfire was indeed coming from the military base at the end of the Aminis' street, but although the family didn't know it at the time, the Taliban were nowhere to be seen. Before the soldiers abandoned the base, they were expending as much ammunition as they could. 'Maybe it happened all over Kabul,' says Nadia. 'While they were leaving, I think they wanted to use their bullets, so as not to leave them.'

The ANA gunfire in Shah Shahid, like the warning shots fired by security guards outside banks in central Kabul, were sounds to which Kabulis were inured. The sound of desultory gunfire was common in the capital, as it was across the rest of the country—it came in celebration at wedding parties and on victories by national sporting teams or the country's exalted mixed martial arts heroes; it emanated from duck-hunting hides built using river stones into valley walls on the edge of the city; it commemorated independence from the British after the third Anglo-Afghan war in 1919, and the start of Eid. In Kabul, the sound of gunfire represented ceremony and leisure as much as violence and death.

But this day was different. The tension that had been building in the capital since the Taliban had started their advance in May was at breaking point. While political leaders from both sides—along with the Americans—scrambled to organise a peaceful transition of power in Doha, the terrifying cacophony emanating from places like Shah Shahid's military intelligence hub late that morning signified a disavowal of the politicians who had led the populace to the precipice, and a public declaration of resignation, of defeat.

Amin arrived home and went straight to the basement, where he tried to calm his wife and children. Their breathing had shortened and their eyes were wide with terror. Rahim, the one the Aminis always looked to to make decisions in a crisis, called again from Germany: 'It's okay. Just stay where you are and don't go outside.' Nadia recalls thinking: 'I never thought the day would come that we'd be under the hands of the Taliban.'

Once the gunfire had ceased, Amin wanted to go outside to see what was happening, but his wife and children would not allow him to leave. Instead, Shukria laid out some of the fruit Amin had brought back from the bazaar. 'But we couldn't have eaten even our favourite food,' says Nadia. She remembers Elham being enraged. 'What is the point of eating?' he asked. 'We'll be dead soon anyway.'

When Shukria or the children needed to use the bathroom, they would run back to the basement afterwards 'like scared mice', says Nadia. Hanif and Elham would giggle with excitement, like children reaching safety in a game of 40 40 Home, before remembering themselves and why they were running.

It was hours after the gunfire had died down that Nadia and her family left the basement together. Exhaustion had finally overcome the fear that had seen them descending the stairs in search of shelter earlier in the day. Aside from Hanif, who went to his own room, the family gathered in the room Nadia ordinarily shared with her mother and lay down to sleep.

In the room next door, Hanif was back on the phone to Rahim—Nadia could hear him through the thin partition wall that separated her room from his. Hanif's voice was in the process of breaking, and under the weight of the turmoil that day, he sputtered and sobbed through a jumble of high and low peaks. He told Rahim he wanted to try to leave the country, just as his older brother had, paying a smuggler to get him across the border into Iran, after which he would find his way to Germany. Rahim made him promise he wouldn't. Rahim explained to Hanif, as Amin and Shukria had done earlier that day, that it was a different time when Rahim and Bahira had fled in 2015. Now, the risk was too great and the likelihood of success almost nil.

When Hanif joined the rest of the family in Shukria's room, he turned his argument to another means of escape he'd heard about in phone calls with friends. They were going to the airport, he declared. 'There's a way to leave.'

Shukria said they couldn't leave because their house in Shah Shahid hadn't yet been transferred into their name. Hanif became impatient, demanding they leave immediately, and Elham began to cry again. Nadia didn't voice her opinion—she thought the idea was nonsense—but was relieved when her parents rejected Hanif's appeals.

A schoolfriend of Nadia's called around midnight. Helai was on her way to the airport with her family. She told Nadia the Taliban were in control of the city, confirming the rumours and media reports being shared on Facebook: she had seen them herself. Ashraf Ghani was gone. And the Taliban were not only inside Kabul but within the presidential palace. Helai's father had been living in Canada and she and the rest of the family would try to reach him.

Nadia says, 'That was when I changed my mind.'

7

Parwan Detention Facility, Bagram District, Parwan Province

Sunday 15 August 2021 was yard day for Hejratullah and Fawad. Every second day, they and their cellmates in the Parwan Detention Facility, which was encircled by Bagram Airfield, were given time in a caged-in pen accessed directly from the backs of the cells, where they would eat their breakfast of bread and green tea on the concrete in the sun. On this day, the inmates sitting in the sun were even more buoyant than usual, singing anthems as they slurped their tea. Word had arrived that freedom was near.

Around 30 inmates shared each of the dozen cells in each prison block. Hejratullah and Fawad's cells were around 10 metres long and 6 metres wide. The inmates slept shoulder to shoulder on thin mattresses, with their toes pointing towards the centre of the room. They made space by bundling in scarves all their belongings—including handmade boxing gloves, and sneakers made from the remnants of prison garb—and hanging them from torn lengths of fabric tied to the cage ceiling; the web of fabric strips also allowed scarves and shawls to be draped between the mattresses for privacy. Piles of religious texts were stacked in the corners. Some prisoners collected date seeds in a jar, then shaved the sides until they were smooth, drilled narrow holes into them, threaded them onto twine, and tied them into loops of Islamic prayer beads. Toothbrushes and disposable razors sat in juice boxes that had been cut in half and bonded to the wall with thick layers of toothpaste. Tea cups dangled from hooks that were actually the handles of broken drinking cups, and which had been attached to the wall using the same blue, green and white cement.

Prisoners smuggled Nokia phones inside the detention centre by bribing guards, then sold them for as much as 60 000 Afghani (approximately US$750 at the time). In Hejratullah's cell, in the corner furthest from its heavy sliding door, two hanging blankets created a cubicle large enough for a single person to stand within. It was from this makeshift phone booth, where calls were limited to a maximum of two minutes, that news arrived from the outside world and was then passed around the prison. And by 10 a.m. on 15 August, some momentous news had been received after a succession of calls: Charikar, the district centre of Parwan province, and only 20 minutes by road from the prison, had fallen into Taliban hands. Soon after, a guard who worked as an informant for the Taliban came to the cell and informed the prisoners that Pul-i Charkhi Prison in Kabul had been taken over by the Taliban and all the prisoners had been released. 'You're going to be released soon too,' said the guard.

Fawad and his cellmates, who were in another block, weren't given the same courtesy. When a guard ordered the prisoners into their cell before their allotted time, the cell leader protested, drawing senior prison officers who threatened to send in the riot squad if the inmates didn't comply. When the prisoners heard gunshots in the distance, they halted their protest, worried that the guards might use the moment of tumult to shoot them and then claim they were killed in combat. The cell leader suggested everyone recite from the Qur'an. 'Today we might be martyred,' he told them.

Before long, the prison guards in both Hejratullah and Fawad's cellblocks had disappeared altogether. Not long after that, shouts could be heard echoing through the concrete buildings—sounds of disorder, confusion, elation. Men in prison uniforms started appearing in the corridors to open the cells' sliding doors and urge the prisoners to get out. 'No–one's here,' they said. 'No soldiers, no commanders. The mujahedin are here and they've come to release us.'

Hejratullah and his cellmates were still locked in the caged outdoor area, but they managed to climb above the access door and through a window that the inmates had always resented because of the sun that poured through in the mornings and the cold draft that blew in during winter. When they dropped down into their cell, the door was open and the guards were nowhere to be seen.

Fawad and the inmates in his block were more wary. Two months earlier, there had been an attempted breakout. The ringleaders, whose ill-fated plan relied on creating overwhelming anarchy, had urged everyone to rush for the cell doors once collaborators among the prison staff began to unlock them. But when the prison guards realised what was happening, they responded with overwhelming force, opening fire on those who led the mob and killing two. Then the riot squad was called in and they unleashed on the prisoners with their nightsticks. Scores were injured—two of Fawad's cellmates were so badly hurt that they had to be fed by hand for several weeks. 'So when they told us to leave this day,' says Saeed Rahim, one of those who shared Fawad's cell, 'we remembered the incident that happened a couple of months ago.'

However, once the sounds of footsteps and voices within the block had faded and been replaced by the more distant noise of larger numbers of men, Fawad and his cellmates left as well, walking out through the area where ordinarily they would be shackled and blindfolded before attending court or meetings with their defence lawyers. 'The treatment of mujahedin,' says Hejratullah, 'wasn't very good. They could do whatever they liked with us.'

The only doors the inmates couldn't open were the deadbolted main entrances to the cellblocks, which from the outside looked like industrial warehouses. But the escapees pried away just enough of the iron sheeting that lay where the walls met the doorframes to allow them to crawl through. Once out, they would help liberate those in the other blocks.

Senior Taliban inmates maintained mobile phone contact with commanders outside the airfield throughout the escape, who reminded them to be patient. 'We were told not to leave the prison until 2 p.m.,' says Hejratullah. There were hundreds of prominent Taliban commanders and functionaries inside the prison, and the group's military commission wanted to ensure the facility was properly secured before the inmates rushed for the front gates. But for the first prisoners to break free from the cellblocks, many of whom had been imprisoned there for more than a decade, the impulse to continue towards the perimeter of the airfield was too strong. Around midday, a large group of prisoners pulled away a strip of cyclone fencing from one side of the tin-roofed walkway that connected the cellblocks, and they ran for freedom. Many of them were obliterated by a strike from one of the Afghan Air Force's attack aircraft which had been prowling the skies above. Even then, inmates continued to squeeze through the holes in the outer shells of the cellblocks to fill the covered walkway, while the scattered figures and body parts of those hit by the airstrike remained where they'd fallen: a warning for any who wanted to push further into Bagram Airfield.

With the aircraft still circling, the prisoners at first hid under the walkway's tin roof. Around 1 p.m., they lined up in five long rows, more than 100 men in each, faced Mecca and prayed. 'The happiness on the prisoners' faces was a happiness that couldn't come from anything else,' says Hejratullah. By the designated time of 2 p.m., they began running, looking for a way out. Of course, none of the prisoners were familiar with the sprawling airfield outside their cellblocks, which was divided by endless rows of demountable concrete blast walls that obscured the horizon at every turn. The inmates who headed east came to its perimeter after a few hundred metres, but those who fled west ventured nearly 5 kilometres before they even reached the airfield's dual runway, let alone the perimeter wall beyond it.

'Bagram is a big place,' says Hejratullah. 'But I only ever saw the inside of my cell. When they took us out they put blacked-out goggles on us.'

As the escapees dispersed into smaller groups, those who commandeered abandoned military vehicles became the most obvious targets from the air. Others looted an ANA armoury and absconded with American-made weapons. Once the inmates reached the outer wall, says Saeed Rahim, 'some would go south and others would go north, looking for a gate'.

As Hejratullah and four friends from Chak district, Maidan Wardak province, stopped at an exit on the airfield's north-eastern side, contemplating which way to turn when they reached the road, a bomb fell from the sky to strike a nearby group of men, killing several of them. Hejratullah says that he saw '80, 90, 100' inmates killed by airstrikes while trying to escape.

In response to questions regarding American airstrikes in Afghanistan on 15 August, a US Central Command spokesperson denied US aircraft had conducted strikes in Bagram: 'Coalition forces,' the spokesperson said, 'conducted one airstrike in Kandahar Province on 15 Aug.' Lieutenant-general Haibatullah Alizai, on the other hand, would later tell me he ordered the Afghan Air Force to unleash all its firepower that day, and that strikes were conducted in and around the prison and Bagram Airfield.

Hejratullah and his friends, all of whom had by now changed out of their prison garb, walked out of the gate carrying M16 rifles taken from the ANA armoury and turned onto a road that encircled the eastern half of the airfield. They walked for an hour until they reached the turn-off to the New Kabul–Bagram Road.

< >

Hejratullah was born in Chak district in 1996, the year the Taliban first came to power. His father had fought with the mujahedin against the Soviets in the 1980s, and he was part of the informal network that assisted the Taliban's fighters—providing food, accommodation and transport around Chak—during the early years of the anti-American insurgency in the 2000s. Hejratullah studied until grade 10 at a school in the village of Bumbai, close to

Chak's district centre, before moving to the Kabul neighbourhood of Kot-i Sangi, where he completed grades 11 and 12 while living in a nearby hostel.

Hejratullah was the second of five brothers and also had three sisters. His older brother, despite being accepted to study literature at Kandahar University, was the first from his family to join the Taliban. 'The foreign troops behaved very badly,' says Hejratullah. 'They destroyed our mosques, they killed innocent people. That's why even university students with bachelor's degrees left university and joined the mujahedin.' It was both the influence of his older brother and the 'stories of cruelty I heard were being carried out by foreign forces in our village', says Hejratullah, that compelled him to join the Taliban before he had even completed high school in Kabul.

Hejratullah linked up with other young Taliban agents from Maidan Wardak who were living undercover in the capital, carrying out reconnaissance on assassination targets and, on six or seven occasions, he says, doing the killing himself. 'I would build a plan,' he says, 'tracking the target and working out how and when to do it.' His targets were mostly 'government people: NDS and [Afghan] Local Police. I would use a pistol, sometimes riding on the back of a motorcycle and sometimes on foot.' Hejratullah would also respond to calls from Taliban commanders from Chak needing assistance with ambushes against enemy convoys. Over and over again, he would pass through government checkpoints purporting to be a student travelling between the capital and his home province.

Then, one day in 2020, Hejratullah was arrested while having his hair cut by a barber in Kot-i Sangi. He was sentenced to three years in prison and sent to the Parwan Detention Facility.

‹ ›

Without any mobile phones with which to call their families and get assistance, Fawad, Saeed Rahim and another man began walking towards Kabul. They had been walking for half an hour when a vehicle coming from the opposite direction pulled to the side of the road. When a passenger leaned out the window to speak with the group, Rahim recognised the face of Khairullah, who was from Baghlan province to the north. Rahim was confused by the sight of his fellow former inmate driving towards the prison from which they'd all just escaped. It turned out that Khairullah had tried to drive to Kabul but had been forced to turn back just inside the gates to the city. Soldiers from the notorious 01 unit, who happened to be headquartered inside a base at the end of the highway, were stopping all cars and searching for escapees.

The 01 unit was among the few Afghan outfits that hadn't submitted to the Taliban. The reason was twofold: the 01's ruthless reputation meant that its fighters would be among the most sought after for revenge by the incoming Taliban government; and unlike other ANSF units which had developed strong working relationships with American military trainers and collaborators over the two-decade-long war, but whose ties had diminished as conventional and special US forces pulled back from Afghanistan in recent years, the 01 and its sister units were still operating alongside their CIA progenitors. Moreover, the CIA was planning to resettle the 01 unit's fighters in America, and, as a quid pro quo, it would rely on their muscle to facilitate the evacuation of the thousands of people on CIA manifests.

Hundreds of military and police bases had been ceded to the incoming Taliban since May 2021. But late on 15 August, after the presidential palace and almost every other military installation in Kabul had been abandoned, Eagle Base, where the 01 unit was stationed alongside the CIA, 3 kilometres east of the airport, remained under the intelligence agency's control. The CIA would use Eagle Base as a key staging area for their evacuation mission.

Fawad's group now split up. Saeed Rahim and the other man heeded Khairullah's advice. They would travel the long way around, heading south–east through Kapisa province before linking up with the Kabul–Jalalabad Highway and entering the capital from the east. Fawad decided to press on towards Kabul. He stopped to rest late in the afternoon with some other escapees at the Pacha Sahib mosque, a few kilometres north of Kabul. There, he borrowed a mobile phone and called his older brother, Imran, whose number he knew by heart.

‹ ›

Hejratullah and his group continued making their way towards Kabul on foot. 'At first,' he says, 'around Bagram, you could see on people's faces that they weren't happy' at the sight of hundreds of prisoners, the majority of them Taliban fighters, walking free. 'These villages were mostly Tajik,' he says. 'But as we came closer to Kabul we were being received warmly.'

One of the others in Hejratullah's group was his 20-year-old friend Muzamel. At 3 p.m., Muzamel called his older brother Amrullah to say he was free. 'Wait,' Amrullah told him. 'The situation in Kabul is unstable.' An hour and a half later, Muzamel again called his brother, saying, 'Where are you?' Amrullah, who was driving through Maidan Shahr, replied, 'I'm coming to pick you up. Stay where you are.' He then gave Muzamel the phone number of their brother-in-law, who lived in Bagram, and who would take care of them in the meantime. Muzamel wrote the number on the back of his hand with a pen, then dialled it.

His brother-in-law soon came looking for Muzamel, Hejratullah and the others, but the New Kabul–Bagram Road was crowded with throngs of escapees on foot, and cars and trucks full of Taliban fighters making their way towards Kabul from the provinces to the north. He suggested Muzamel and his companions find a place to spend the night, and he would pick them up in the morning once things had calmed down. But with Kabul beckoning barely an hour away by car, Muzamel and the others refused to sit still and continued on foot, hoping to flag down a driver who would take them the rest of the way.

Outside a village halfway between Kabul and Bagram, a group of armed Taliban fighters had set up a checkpoint on the highway and were stopping drivers on both sides of the road, looking for fleeing members of the collapsing government security forces. Hejratullah borrowed a phone from one of the fighters and called a Taliban friend from Chak who was waiting with others in the neighbourhood of Company, on the outskirts of Kabul, for orders to enter the city. He told the friend he would meet him at Company before continuing on to see his family in Chak.

An old man then pulled up at the checkpoint in a small Mazda truck he used to carry loads of handmade bricks baked in the open-air kilns closer to Kabul. He agreed to take Hejratullah and the four others with him. '"There's no problem until Kabul,"' Hejratullah remembers him saying. 'That's why he agreed to take us.'

The five fighters climbed into the Mazda's high-walled tray and sat, exhausted, with their backs against the dented walls. To the left, the tips of the hills were glowing the colour of apricots from the setting sun. To the right, layers of the Hindu Kush appeared as flat planes of blue, each ridge a paler shade than the one before it, as they receded into the smog filtering out from Kabul through the valleys in-between. As the sun sank, Hejratullah flipped the arm of a pair of handcuffs he'd found while escaping the prison over and through the pawl.

The old man drove the escapees through a village whose residents supplied coal for the innumerable brick factories to the north. Everything in the village, including the people, was coated in black coal dust. The bitumen of the highway, where it passed through the town, looked like black velvet.

‹ ›

Imran arrived at the Pacha Sahib mosque in a Toyota station wagon driven by Fawad's cousin Saifullah. The vehicle contained four other escapees the pair had picked up, three of whom Imran had recognised from Sheikabad, in Maidan Wardak's Sayedabad district, and another whom he knew from his university. With Fawad in the car, Saifullah turned onto the New Kabul–Bagram Road and headed south towards Kabul, which at that point was virtually in Taliban hands.

‹ ›

As dusk fell, the Mazda carrying Hejratullah's group pulled over so they could pray at a small highway-side mosque between a petrol station and a coal yard. Once back on the highway, the driver steered the car into the outskirts of Despacheri, in the north-eastern corner of Kabul. A row of steel bollards before a 2-metre-wide ditch, an earthen berm and a wall topped with razor wire marked the outer fortifications of Eagle Base on the eastern side of the road. Then came a series of concrete barriers and empty guard posts in the centre of the road, where government forces would ordinarily survey the people and goods entering the Afghan capital.

The Mazda's driver suddenly stomped on the brakes. One of the armed Taliban escapees in the rear stood up. 'It's 01,' he said to the others, who leapt to the bitumen and ran back the way they had come. A man called Salahuddin was the first one shot, says Hejratullah, who ran with Muzamel for a stack of paving stones beside the road. 'We had our weapons, but they had their tanks and heavy weapons,' he continues, referring to the menacing tactical vehicles used by the American forces and their favourite surrogates. The moment Muzamel raised his head above the pile of paving stones, he was struck by a bullet and killed instantly.

Hejratullah threw his M16 to the ground and climbed a fence that was just out of view of the paramilitaries trying to kill him. He fell into the scrapyard on the other side and ran past mounds of steel detritus to where five yellow American school buses were parked in a corner, awaiting dismemberment. Hejratullah crawled underneath one of the buses, where he remained undiscovered, and eventually went to sleep.

‹ ›

When Saifullah, Imran, Fawad and the four other escapees approached the checkpoint in Despacheri, fighters wearing desert-coloured uniforms with a horizontal tiger–stripe pattern appeared in the headlights and waved them to a stop. They were from the 01 unit. The fighters ordered all seven men out of the car. Imran and Saifullah, who had government identity cards and were neatly groomed, were told to drive on. The others, who wore their hair and beards long, were taken aside. 'We just need to have some words with them,' Imran recalls one of the uniformed men saying. 'We'll release them soon.'

Imran and Saifullah drove on to their homes in Company, approaching each intersection warily, unsure who, if anyone, was in control.

PART III

Late August

'The War Was Now in Kabul'

8

Fort Myer, Virginia, USA

'**N**early 16 years after the September 11th attacks, after the extraordinary sacrifice of blood and treasure, the American people are weary of war without victory. Nowhere is this more evident than with the war in Afghanistan, the longest war in American history.'[1] It was 21 August 2017, and president Donald Trump was giving a nationally televised speech at Fort Myer, a US Army base a few kilometres from the White House, abutting Arlington National Cemetery. Melania Trump, vice-president Mike Pence, secretary of state Rex Tillerson, and the chairman of the joint chiefs of staff, general Joseph Dunford, were seated to the right of the stage with senior officers from the base and other dignitaries. An army brass band sat to the left. Behind Trump, seven carefully draped flags represented the five branches of the military, the state of Virginia and the United States.

Trump had railed against US involvement in Afghanistan long before he was president. Five years earlier, he'd tweeted: 'Afghanistan is a complete waste. Time to come home!'[2] And during his 2016 presidential campaign, he'd made occasional vague references to ending 'endless wars', bemoaning the high costs of foreign military interventions for which the US received little in return, although rarely mentioning Afghanistan by name.

< >

It was a war that Trump's two predecessors, presidents George Bush, Jr and Barack Obama, had failed to end, let alone win, over four presidential terms and nearly 16 years.

After the attacks in New York and Washington, DC on 11 September 2001, the United States' initial goals of crushing al-Qaeda and overthrowing the Taliban government that hosted them were quickly, if imperfectly, realised. US warplanes began bombing Taliban targets on 7 October, by which time paramilitaries from the CIA and small teams of American special operators had already landed in Afghanistan, joining forces with anti-Taliban warlords and their militias, and directing pilots and their fearsome payloads to Taliban positions. By late November, the Taliban fighters who hadn't lain down their weapons or been captured or killed had been corralled into the few remaining cities under their control, including Kandahar, where the group was founded. Their leaders began discussing a surrender with Hamid Karzai, the tribal leader who had returned to Afghanistan from Pakistan in the wake of the 9/11 attacks to organise anti-Taliban resistance in the south.[3]

On 5 December, the day before Hamid Karzai would be announced as head of Afghanistan's interim administration at a conference convened by the UN in Bonn, Germany, a group of Taliban emissaries approached him with a letter possibly signed by Mullah Mohammad Omar, the Taliban's founder and leader.[4] They offered to transfer power and accept Karzai's incoming administration. In exchange, according to Zalmai Khalilzad, who was the US ambassador to Afghanistan at the time, but who didn't learn about the letter for more than a decade, Taliban fighters and leaders wanted to remain in Afghanistan and 'live with dignity and honour in their homes'.[5] Karzai agreed.[6]

The following day, Donald Rumsfeld, the US secretary of defense, was asked about rumours of the surrender deal. He responded cryptically: 'If you're asking, "Would an arrangement with Omar where he could live in dignity in the Kandahar area or someplace in Afghanistan be consistent with what I have said?", the answer is no, it would not be consistent with what I have said.'[7] He was referring to comments he'd made at a Pentagon press conference several weeks earlier. 'The United States is not inclined to negotiate surrenders,' he told a reporter. 'Nor are we in a position with relatively small numbers of forces on the ground to accept prisoners.'[8]

Taliban fighters handed over their weapons to tribal leaders in Kandahar the next day, but Mullah Omar had already fled.[9] Rumsfeld's denial of amnesty to Mullah Omar is widely regarded as America's first critical mistake in Afghanistan, a move that ensured the eventual return of the Taliban.[10]

As special operations forces continued to hunt for alleged terror suspects, conventional forces from the US and the international military coalition it had amassed fanned out across Afghanistan to oversee large parts of an ambitious reconstruction effort. The enormity of the task was the result of the preceding two decades of war, during which most of Afghanistan's infrastructure and institutions had been almost completely destroyed.

The trigger for the conflict was the Soviet army's invasion of Afghanistan to prop up the fledgling communist government in Kabul, an effort that began on Christmas Day 1979. Rebel mujahedin factions, equipped and funded by the US and other Cold War opponents, would fight the Soviets and their communist allies in Afghanistan for nearly a decade. An estimated 1–1.5 million Afghans died as a result, equivalent to 9 per cent of the country's population.[11] A further five million people were forced to flee to neighbouring countries before the Soviets withdrew in 1989.[12] The civil war that followed saw the mujahedin factions, once nominal allies, turn their weapons on one another in a ruthless battle to fill the power vacuum left by the absence of the Soviet-backed government. By 1996, the capital, which had been at the centre of the multipronged battle, and whose residents had endured relentless shelling, street–to–street fighting and marauding militias, was in ruins.

After the lawlessness and destitution of the civil war, the arrival of the Taliban, a group of zealous young religious students cultivated in religious seminaries in Pakistan and southern Afghanistan, and intent on restoring order and Islamic rule to Afghanistan, was widely welcomed. However, the group had no experience in governing, and it was shunned by the international community because of its uncompromising interpretation and brutal enforcement of Islamic sharia law, so it was effectively bankrupt. Corporal punishment was introduced and bans were placed on music and television, on girls attending school and women in the workplace. Men were forced to grow beards and to pray five times per day. Meanwhile, the country sank further into poverty.

So when the Taliban were finally pushed from power, Afghanistan was bereft of most of the basic foundations of a functioning state: operational institutions, infrastructure, schools and hospitals. When Karzai arrived at the presidential palace on a frigid winter's day, soon after being named interim leader, he discovered that the Arg had neither electricity nor a single working phone.[13]

The scale of the nation–building project that ensued was immense. By 2014, US spending on reconstruction in Afghanistan would usurp even that of the US$104 billion Marshall Plan enacted by America in 1947 to rebuild Europe after World War II.[14] Success, too, would be far more elusive in Afghanistan than it had been in Europe. In December 2021, following a post-mortem on Afghanistan by NATO member states in Riga, Latvia, Jens Stoltenberg, the organisation's secretary general, lamented 'the international community, including NATO, the UN, and the EU and other actors, [having] raised the level of ambition to nation-building'. He said 'that broader task proved much more difficult' than preventing another 9/11 organised from Afghanistan.[15]

The International Security Assistance Force (ISAF), which at its height comprised forces from 51 countries, was established at the 2001 Bonn conference. As well as securing the greater Kabul area, ISAF was tasked with what would grow into an even greater mission: building up the ANSF and government institutions more broadly, virtually from scratch.[16] In 2003, the command of ISAF was transferred to NATO, but by 2007 the mission's leadership was dominated by American generals, whose forces made up more than half the total international military contingent through to its final days.[17] Meanwhile, for every American military convoy whose soldiers threw sweets, pens and pencils to children as they passed through rural villages, for every British Army platoon or Australian Army taskforce that built a bridge or that dug a well and installed a water pump, there were others, usually elite special forces units, raiding houses at night and killing or capturing young Afghan men with no connection to the Taliban or al-Qaeda.

For some anti-Taliban figures who were allied with the United States, denouncing tribal or business rivals as 'Taliban' was a way of eliminating threats to commercial interests or settling personal scores. Others were induced by cash rewards to point out supposed terrorists. The operations that such accusations triggered involved small raiding teams that applied maximal force and minimal discretion when storming homes in the middle of the night. If they weren't killed in the first instance, all of the men in the targeted homes were treated as suspects, rounded up, bound, hooded and questioned. Detainees would be flown to American military or CIA bases in Afghanistan, to CIA 'black sites' in countries including Thailand, Romania and Lithuania,[18] or to Guantánamo Bay, Cuba, for interrogation and often torture. Being demeaned and defiled while languishing in prison, often without charge, was, for many, a call to arms. So too the indignity of being unable to defend women in one's own home in a country where, once married, many women are never seen by a man other than their husband or close family.

Corruption may have been less conspicuous but it contributed equally to the disenfranchisement of large sections of Afghan society, particularly in rural areas, and aroused opposition towards the government in Kabul. From the end of 2001, billions of dollars in foreign aid was funnelled through Kabul, whose ministers, even while beset by allegations of corruption, maintained ultimate control over how, where and on whom it was spent. Moreover, while major cities saw benefits from the glut of development spending, many rural communities were neglected by the government, who they began to associate with the invading foreigners more than with any improvement in the quality of their lives.

More than 70 per cent of Afghanistan's approximately 35 million people are estimated to live in rural areas.[19] For many of them, the experience of the US-led war would be marked by incidents that, whether deliberate or not, resulted in harm to themselves or their family members, including death. In areas where the fighting was so constant as to be almost endemic, even if foreign forces weren't directly responsible for civilian deaths, as outside aggressors they were nonetheless blamed for many of the estimated 70 000 civilians who were killed in Afghanistan (and Pakistan) in the first two decades of the 21st century.[20] Civilian deaths from bombs dropped and missiles launched from aircraft became almost commonplace. In the early years of the war, a succession of wedding parties were turned into killing fields by American warplanes whose crews, or the soldiers guiding them on the ground, often mistook celebratory gunfire for deliberate hostility. In one of the first incidents, in July 2002, seven 900-kilogram bombs were dropped on a marriage celebration in Dehrawud in the province of Uruzgan, the home district of Mullah Omar, killing dozens of people.[21] On several occasions, as the war escalated in intensity, the issue of civilian casualties—as they were euphemistically referred to—almost unravelled relations between president Karzai and his American counterparts entirely.

Others simply tired of having foreign soldiers—non-Muslims—in their country. Although ISAF was ostensibly in Afghanistan by invitation of the Karzai government, many began to see it as another foreign occupation.

The US military shifted its attention to Iraq, which it invaded in March 2003. The Iraqi Army was quickly defeated, while president

Saddam Hussein was captured and sentenced to death. The ruling Ba'ath Party was disbanded and, much like the defeated Taliban in 2001, excluded from the process of building a new government in Baghdad. An insurgency that grew out of loyalists from the deposed party grew to include Iranian-backed Shia militias and foreign jihadists, leading to the formation of an Iraqi branch of al-Qaeda that diverted American military resources away from Afghanistan. Around the same time, former Taliban fighters were re-arming and recruiting young men who'd suffered at the hands of foreign forces or their ANSF counterparts, or who felt neglected by the government. Most said they joined up to help rid the country of infidels out of a sense of religious obligation.

Barack Obama campaigned on ending the wars in Iraq and Afghanistan before his election in November 2008. In a speech he gave in the lead-up to his nomination as the Democratic presidential candidate in January that year, he said: 'We will bring our troops home. We will finish the job ... against al-Qaeda in Afghanistan ... We will restore our moral standing in the world.'[22] Obama later praised his predecessor, president Bush, Jr, for his 2007 troop surge in Iraq, because quelling the violence there allowed Obama, as president, to revert attention back to Afghanistan. 'This is a war we have to win,' he declared.[23]

In 2009, with the Taliban gaining ground, and under pressure from his war cabinet, Obama decided to follow the same playbook that had had success, at least until then, in Iraq. Counter-insurgency was the US military's latest and greatest cure-all, based on the 'winning hearts and minds' approach that had been deployed in Vietnam. If it worked in Iraq, it was thought the strategy, which involved flooding a war zone with troops, clearing it of enemies, filling the liberated territory with quality infrastructure, imposing good governance and security, and spurring job growth and general prosperity, could work in Afghanistan, too. Obama reassigned the architects of the counter-insurgency campaign in Iraq—general Stanley McChrystal in 2009 and general David Petraeus in 2010—and their strategies, to Afghanistan. On their advice, Obama boosted troop levels from 50 000 when he took office to 100 000 by mid-2010.[24] But 'the surge', as it was known, came with a caveat: the troops would have to start withdrawing in mid-2011.

David Kilcullen, a former lieutenant-colonel in the Australian Army who went on to co-write the US Army's 2006 counter-insurgency field manual, was based in Kabul as an advisor to general McChrystal when Obama announced the surge during a speech at the West Point military academy in December 2009. Kilcullen recalls hearing the speech while he was dining with a small group of Taliban interlocutors in a guesthouse popular with foreign visitors. He remembers how Obama 'simultaneously, in the same speech, announces the date when it's going to end'. The Taliban seated before him were dumbfounded, asking Kilcullen: 'Are you seriously trying to lose this war?' Kilcullen says, 'We basically told the Taliban exactly how long they needed to wait until we'd be gone.'[25]

With the surge in troops came a surge in violence. Directives aimed at mitigating civilian deaths were handed down to battlefield commanders in 2008, but in 2010, Petraeus, under pressure to show results from the surge he'd lobbied for, lifted the restrictions on air strikes and other aggressive tactics. The approach produced tangible results on the battlefield, but it caused civilian deaths to rise,[26] undermining the broader strategy of winning over the population. Even Karzai distanced himself from his American benefactors, railing against what he called 'arbitrary and unnecessary operations [that] cause death to innocent Afghans',[27] and echoing the growing public sentiment that the US-led coalition was acting like an occupier. 'History,' Karzai warned, 'is a witness to how Afghanistan deals with occupiers.'[28]

Kilcullen recalls how, civilian casualties aside, at ISAF head-quarters in Kabul, general Petraeus and other senior officers celebrated their apparent success in forcing down Taliban activ-ity levels. Their strategy was working—or so they thought. The Taliban *had* taken heavy casualties, and their battlefield activity *had* dropped, but, Kilcullen says, it wasn't for the reasons his superiors believed, or wanted to believe. The Taliban, says Kilcullen, were simply 'holding back most of their forces in Pakistan, having a breather, building them up ... waiting for us to leave'.

The green flag of the ISAF was lowered inside its headquarters on 29 December 2014, formally ending NATO's international combat mission, Operation Enduring Freedom.[29] In its place came Resolute Support, a pared-down 'train, advise, assist' mission that saw most of the remaining 14 000 international troops pulled back from the front lines and into roles supporting the ANSF, which took over responsibility for Afghanistan's security.

The fallout was swift. Just as Kilcullen's dinner guests had warned in 2009, as soon as the better trained and better equipped international forces handed over to the ill-disciplined, unmotivated and poorly paid ANSF, the Taliban went on the offensive. As it had been built up, the ANSF, much like its architects in the US military, had grown accustomed to an ever-ready supply of the main tactical advantage over the Taliban: air power. It was a life-saving crutch on which ground forces could always lean when things went awry on the battlefield. Whether surrounded in a remote outpost or coming under heavy fire during an ambush on a road convoy, under most circumstances, American warplanes and attack helicopters could be called upon to obliterate Taliban lines and ensure that the ANSF and coalition units under attack weren't overrun. Injured soldiers would be spirited away in medivac helicopters and transferred to operating theatres for life-saving surgery. But when the ISAF's combat mission ended, so did the almost unlimited supply of air support. While the Afghan Air Force was growing steadily, its capabilities and arsenal were feeble in comparison to that of the Americans. The ANSF's inbuilt overreliance on American air power and on-the-ground support quickly became apparent.

In September 2015, the insurgents overran the provincial capital of Kunduz, the first major city to fall into Taliban hands since they'd surrendered the same city in 2001.[30] That same year, after the so-called Islamic State of Iraq and Syria (ISIS) took control of massive swathes of territory either side of the Iraq–Syria border, former members of the Pakistani Taliban pledged allegiance to its self-proclaimed caliph and established a foothold in eastern Afghanistan. President Obama was now faced with a stark choice: recant his promise to end the war in Afghanistan, or risk the country once again becoming a haven for terrorists with international ambitions. Obama decided to leave 10 000 troops in Afghanistan, both conventional forces which would continue to 'train, advise and assist' Afghan forces, and also special operations forces which would ramp up the more covert 'Freedom's Sentinel' counter-terrorism mission. The war, meanwhile, would continue into yet another presidency.

‹ ›

The word 'Afghanistan' was barely mentioned by any candidate in the 2016 US presidential election campaign. With American combat deaths down to less than 20 a year,[31] the war had fallen out of the American consciousness. In fact, the conflict, now being fought almost entirely by Afghans, was as deadly as ever, and the country's hard-won gains in literacy, health and human rights became more and more precarious.

When Trump spoke at Fort Myer a year later, he described his frustration with previous administrations' preoccupation with nation-building. 'My original instinct,' he said, 'was to pull out.' He then added: 'But all my life, I've heard that decisions are much different when … you're president of the United States. So I studied Afghanistan in great detail and from every conceivable angle.' Under the subsequent South Asia Strategy drawn up by James Mattis, the secretary of defense, an Afghanistan veteran himself, there would be no hasty withdrawal like that which Trump had perhaps envisaged before running for president. It 'would create a vacuum', he said, 'that terrorists, including ISIS and al Qaeda, would instantly fill, just as happened before September 11th'. Instead, much like his predecessor, Trump escalated the US commitment in the hope of turning the tide in its favour. He would, he said, deploy 'all instruments of

American power—diplomatic, economic, and military—toward a successful outcome' in Afghanistan.

Trump deployed a further 3000 troops, loosened the rules of engagement previously introduced to lessen harm to civilians, and expanded the authority of 'wartime commanders and frontline soldiers acting in real time', circumventing what he referred to as restrictive 'micromanagement from Washington'.[32] In defence of the move, he pointed to the recent successes in Iraq against ISIS, whose fighters had been pummelled by elite troops and a devastating air campaign in Mosul. In addition, the economic arm of the strategy was aimed at Afghanistan's eastern neighbour, whose government's double dealing with both America and the Taliban had rankled previous administrations as much as the war itself. 'We have been paying Pakistan billions and billions of dollars at the same time they are housing the very terrorists that we are fighting,' Trump seethed. 'But that will have to change, and that will change immediately.'

Trump also claimed that he would forgo the kinds of time-tables that Obama had required his generals to agree to in order to make military prerogatives more palatable to the voting public. 'Conditions on the ground, not arbitrary timetables,' he said, 'will guide our strategy from now on. America's enemies must never know our plans or believe they can wait us out. I will not say when we are going to attack, but attack we will.'[33]

The diplomatic part of the South Asia Strategy Trump alluded to initially appeared to have been given little thought. 'Someday,' he said at Fort Myer, 'after an effective military effort, perhaps it will be possible to have a political settlement that includes elements of the Taliban in Afghanistan, but nobody knows if or when that will ever happen.'[34] A year later, in 2018, Trump appointed a special envoy, Zalmai Khalilzad, to negotiate directly with Taliban representatives in Doha. In February 2020, after more than 18 months of fitful negotiations, the two sides signed the Agreement for Bringing Peace to Afghanistan—the Doha Agreement. But after the initial fanfare around the signing, it became clear that, for the Americans, the agreement was a mandate for withdrawing American forces from Afghanistan before the 2020 US presidential election, regardless of the consequences, rather than a bona-fide solution to a 20-year war that would continue once they were gone. For the Taliban, it signalled victory.

9

Deh Sabz District, Kabul

Early on the morning of 16 August, Hejratullah woke beneath the yellow school bus. He crawled out, forgetting the handcuffs he'd taken from the Parwan Detention Facility and removed from his pocket while trying to get comfortable during the night.

The owner of the scrapyard, a short Hazara man of 50 years named Shah Wali, had spent the previous day and night in his office. With all the yelling, screeching tyres and gunfire on the road outside, he had been too afraid to leave. He hadn't seen Hejratullah climb into his yard the evening before and was confused when he saw the young man walking past his office window from the back of the lot. He watched as the figure scaled the tall gate, and by the time Wali finally ventured outside, Hejratullah had already disappeared up the highway towards Bagram.

Still outside the gate, however, was a body, which lay beside a stack of concrete paving tiles—Muzamel. On his hand was written a phone number, which Wali called. 'I don't know you,' he said when the call was answered. 'But in front of me is a dead body with your phone number. Please come to take the body.'

When Imran woke in his family home in Company on the morning of 16 August, the Taliban were in control of Kabul. He still hadn't heard from his brother Fawad after leaving him at the 01 checkpoint in Despacheri the night before, so he decided to drive back there to look for him. He left home with his mother and father, thinking that if the soldiers who took Fawad and the others were still at the checkpoint, the presence of elders might elicit more sympathy.

The streets in the capital were still quiet, but the air of anxiety that had consumed Kabul the day before had lifted. Taliban fighters had moved into the city overnight to fill the security vacuum left when the government's forces had disintegrated. At major intersections and outside government institutions, foreign embassies and banks, fighters, bedraggled and sleepless, lounged in the back of the desert-coloured ANA vehicles and the forest-green police humvees they'd plundered during their march on Kabul. Residents, meanwhile, were tentatively stepping outside the homes in which they'd hidden the day before. Most had never knowingly set eyes on a Talib before and gawked at the long-haired fighters with a combination of wonder and fear. Many had feared a repeat of the ultra-destructive civil war of the 1990s in the battle for control of Kabul, and now, before they'd had chance to contemplate a future under Taliban rule, as one journalist wrote of a group of police the day before, they 'had the giddiness of condemned men granted a reprieve'.[1]

When Imran and his parents arrived in Despacheri, around midday, they found that the stretch of road beside Eagle Base where he and the escapees had been stopped the night before, and where he had last seen his brother, was empty. They spoke to a man who managed a petrol station a couple of hundred metres along the road. The man told Imran he had closed his doors when he'd realised the area had, all of a sudden, become a front line—one of the last involving Taliban and pro-government forces for the entire war—and that the soldiers at the checkpoint had left earlier that morning. Imran and his parents drove home, but they returned the following morning, hoping the soldiers might have re-established the checkpoint. Before turning onto the New Kabul–Bagram Road, something in his peripheral vision caught Imran's attention. He turned the car around and veered onto a road he hadn't noticed the day before. Off to the side, 200 metres away, was a pack of soldiers wearing the same uniforms—with a sandy-coloured tiger-stripe pattern—as those with whom he'd left Fawad and the others two days earlier. He approached the soldiers on foot with his mother and father. The men were guarding the main entrance to Eagle Base, from which the CIA and the 01 unit had planned and conducted secretive missions for years. They acknowledged having detained suspected prison escapees entering Kabul on the evening of 15 August, but denied knowing where they were now. 'Yes, we took them in for questioning,' one member of the 01 unit told Imran, 'then we released them.'

Imran returned to Despacheri for several days thereafter—most days, more than once. Sometimes he went alone, other times he went with his parents and uncles. Regarding the 01 unit soldiers, Imran says 'they'd swear every day they'd released them and hadn't spoken to or seen them since'. His mother, he said, implored the men at the gate: 'If you want to shoot me, shoot me, but first tell me where my son is.'

Local residents told Imran and his father, Saeed Maqoud, that on 15 August they'd seen 01 fighters at another location, 3 kilometres towards Kabul's airport on Russian Road, at an intersection known as Despacheri Square. Mirwais, a grocer in the small bazaar at the square, told Imran and his father that all the shops in the bazaar had been closed the day Fawad and the others had been detained, except for the bakery. With the escapees coming from the north and Eagle Base so close, he said, the likelihood of violence that day was great, and the shopkeepers left for their homes in the afternoon. The baker, however, had remained through the night, as is common for Kabul's ubiquitous glass-fronted mini bread factories. The baker had told Mirwais he had been outside when soldiers in tiger-stripe fatigues arrived at the square with nine or 10 detainees and began yelling at him to go inside. 'They told them [the detainees] to sit here in front of the bakery,' he told Mirwais. 'But I don't know where they took them after that.'

Mirwais apologised to Imran and his father for being unable to tell them any more. But he said 'if you give us a phone number and we find anything, we'll call you'. Imran and his father did so; Maqoud also gave his number to another local shopkeeper named Bakhtiar. At 3 p.m. on 19 August, Maqoud received a call from Bakhtiar.

Half an hour before that call, a young boy who had been collecting plastic bottles to sell to recyclers came running out of a small, abandoned police station he'd been scouring. He ran across an intersection and towards a moneychanger, Noorullah, who was sitting behind a glass box holding shallow bundles of US dollars, Pakistani rupees, Afghanis and mobile phone credit scratch cards. Noorullah says the boy was screaming, 'I saw dead bodies! I saw dead bodies!'

Noorullah walked across the intersection, rounded a wall of dirt-filled Hesco barriers, and went through the open door of the decrepit police station's main building. When he saw a body in the first room, he immediately turned around and left, returning with guards from a shipping container merchant next door. Inside the building's four rooms, including a small bathroom, strewn among discarded police uniforms, were nine bodies. The place smelled like death. Most of the faces of the dead had been destroyed by the exit wounds of the bullets that had been fired into the backs of their heads. Blood had spattered the walls around where the slugs had left divots in the masonry, and it had pooled and dried around empty shell casings from AK-47 assault rifles. Bakhtiar says, 'I saw the bodies myself. Nine bodies.'

Maqoud drove to Despacheri with an elder brother and they identified 22-year-old Fawad, despite facial wounds that had left him barely recognisable, as well as another young man—also a Talib—whom they knew from their village in the Sheikhabad area of Maidan Wardak province. They lifted the cold, stiff bodies into the back of a station wagon and drove them to the morgue inside Afghanistan's largest military hospital, not far from the shuttered

US Embassy in Wazir Akbar Khan. The seven other bodies were collected by the Afghan Red Crescent Society and taken to the same facility.

When Imran met his father and uncle at the military hospital, he also recognised the four others whom he and his cousin Saifullah had collected before they'd found Fawad. Ribbons were torn from a white sheet and tied around each of the dead men's heads, closing their jaws. Their big toes were bound, too, fastening their feet together. The bodies were then wrapped in the remainder of the white sheets and driven through Company, past Maidan Shahr, down Highway One and past the turn-off to Chak, and on to Sheikhabad for burial.

10

Emirate City, Kabul
II

Despite a change of power that was almost entirely bloodless, and the seemingly conciliatory tenor of the victorious Taliban the day before, Hamed Safi was under no illusions. 'From the moment I saw the Taliban in the palace,' he says, 'my only focus was how to survive, how to get out of Kabul.' He'd seen it all before. Once they capture the cities and consolidate their power, he thought, then they will show their true face.

Hamed worked through the night of 15 August, following up on the efforts he'd made the night before the city's fall, and reaching out to contacts at the US Embassy, whose staff had by now all relocated to the airport. The following morning, Hamed and his brother Mahmoud decided to leave their aunt Shahla's house in Macroyan 4. 'We won't solve any of our problems staying at home,' said Mahmoud. 'Let's go out and see what's going on in the street.'

The two brothers took all the precautions they could. Their uncle was Pashtun and suggested they dress as if they were, too. He handed them each a black *peran tunban* from his wardrobe, because, he said, 'the Taliban like black'. Mahmoud, whose stocky gym-honed frame and close-cropped haircut reflected his time in the thrall of the American special operators with whom he'd worked over the years, wrapped a traditional cotton shawl around his shoulders with contempt.

They took Hamed's car and drove towards Airport Road, where Hamed had become stuck after leaving the palace the day before. It was even more chaotic now. So they turned around and made their way towards Taimani, 10–15 minutes away by car, where Hamed's wife Zarifa and his children, Heela and Yasin, were staying with their other aunt, Manila—Mahmoud's family was at home in southern Kabul, too far and too risky, they thought. They drove slowly past the US Embassy, along Wazir Akbar Khan Road, past the diplomatic enclave hidden behind rings of high walls. They continued through Shahr-e Naw, with its dried fruit and clothing shops, a mall with a Turkish supermarket and a steakhouse that had become popular with palace staff, an Italian gelato franchise, and fresh juice and kebab restaurants, some of which were beginning to open after the tumult of the day before. Along the way, Hamed and Mahmoud tried to blend into the cityscape, as if they had nothing to hide from its new masters.

'You could see the Taliban in their checkpoints,' says Hamed, who'd felt adrenaline coursing through him at the time. 'We were lucky no-one stopped us. They were stopping people and asking who they were and where they were going. They had fearsome faces and awful appearances. There were only two or three of them at each checkpoint, but we were full of fear.'

He couldn't remember Zarifa and his children ever being so happy to see him as when he finally arrived at his aunt Manila's house. But Zarifa also scolded him for taking the risk to get there. 'It's fine,' he told her. 'I needed to see you and our children.'

Hamed and Zarifa had first met in 2010. When Hamed's parents decided earlier that year that it was time for him to be married, he had been embarrassed to tell them that not only did he not have a girlfriend, he didn't even have any candidates in mind. Far from discouraged, however, Hamed's mother Sahar, his aunt Shahla and sister Samira began conspiring. Samira was working as a teacher at a private school in Kabul and suggested arranging a meeting with another teacher there, a friend of hers named Zarifa. When Sahar and Shahla met her, says Hamed, 'They chose her right then and there.' Then it was Hamed's turn. To help him, Samira concocted a plan. Hamed would come to the school where she and Zarifa worked and knock on the office door where Zarifa spent time between classes, under the pretence of looking for his sister. 'I opened the door and saw a beautiful lady sitting there, behind a desk,' says Hamed.

Hamed and Samira left the school and walked to where he'd parked nearby. When they arrived at the car, their mother and aunt were both waiting eagerly in the back seat.

'How was she?' his mother asked.

'By appearance,' he replied, 'I approve. The rest is up to you.'

Hamed and Zarifa were engaged three weeks later and married the following year.

Whether Zarifa herself had been a party to the whole conspiracy or not, Hamed doesn't know. 'Women are very clever when it comes to these matters,' he says.

In Taimani, Hamed told Zarifa he had made contact with one of his counterparts from the US Embassy and that he was awaiting further instructions. For what exactly, he didn't know. He had little confidence he would be able to leave the country with his family. His contacts had told him they could only guarantee his approval to fly—he had a visa after all. But even that promise was based on the assumption that he would be able to get inside the airport. If that didn't happen, there were no guarantees whatsoever, not even for Hamed.

Despite Zarifa's protests, Hamed told her that, whatever happened, he would never leave her and their children in Kabul. For now, the agonisingly uncertain arrangements he was trying to make with the Americans were all he had. And all they could do was wait. With that, Hamed returned to Macroyan 4, while Mahmoud returned to his own family.

The next day, 17 August, Hamed received a WhatsApp message from someone at the US Embassy. He was told to prepare to leave for the airport that evening. The message also confirmed what he had been hearing from friends and via social media: that the Taliban were in control of the regular commercial entrance on the southern side of the airport. There was no mention of whether anyone else would be allowed to enter with him.

Hamed called Zarifa and instructed her to catch a taxi to their apartment in Block 11 of Emirate City—he would meet her there. Although he knew it was risky—the apartment complex was known to house thousands of government officials—it was close to two lesser-known entrances on the northern military side of the airport, from which, by now, most of the American evacuation flights were being staged.

When Hamed said goodbye to his aunt Shahla, she hugged him as if she would never see him again and cried in grief: 'Now you're leaving us, too.' After his mother and siblings had sought asylum in the United States in the late 1990s, Shahla, who had four daughters of her own but no sons, had stepped in as a surrogate for him and Mahmoud. 'She was so kind,' Hamed says of his aunt. 'She was like a mother to us. She treated us like her sons.'

Together with Sahar, Samira, and his father, Mujib, Hamed drove straight to his apartment. He didn't bother trying to withdraw more cash on the way—all the banks had been inundated by account holders trying to retrieve their savings, and leaving the country was a far greater priority than collecting the US$10 000 remaining in his account. At Emirate City, Hamed and Zarifa selected only the most important items from the belongings he had earlier piled by the front door, as his contact at the US Embassy had said that he would only be allowed to bring one bag to the airport. They gathered essential items of clothing and the several thousand US dollars in cash they kept in the apartment, which was in addition to the US dollars Hamed had exchanged for Afghani on 15 August. As well as his family's passports, Hamed also took a certificate awarded by the US State Department for the work he'd done alongside their staff before he'd started at the presidential palace in 2012, which he thought might be useful for getting inside the airport. All of this Hamed and Zarifa stuffed into two backpacks, and then they waited. 'Who dared to sleep?' says Hamed.

It wasn't until around midday the following day that Hamed received another message from his US Embassy counterpart, who was now working inside the airport. Hamed was told to make his way to an entrance the State Department was using as a staging area for evacuees. East Gate abutted a quiet residential area and a handful of small irrigated fields near the south-eastern corner of the airport, adjacent to the start of the tarmac and 2 kilometres east of the main airport entrance. The Americans inside the airport had only begun using it that morning. 'There's no crowd yet,' Hamed's contact told him, 'but hurry, because that will change once people find out about it.'

‹ ›

Beyond the chaos unfolding inside the airport and the delicate diplomatic efforts being made to convince the Taliban to assist in managing what was happening outside its walls, the scramble to facilitate entry for those like Hamed, whom international officials were trying to evacuate, was proving to be the most challenging aspect of the American-led evacuation mission. Once the Taliban had entered Kabul on the night of 15 August, they'd partially blocked the main commercial entrance at the end of Airport Road. They also deployed fighters to secure ancillary gates, those previously used by the military and airport staff, as well as the countless weak points in the perimeter wall—including a sewerage tunnel that desperate Afghan families were both pushing through and scaling to get to the runway and, they hoped, an aircraft departing Afghanistan.

There were countless instances of Taliban fighters arbitrarily forbidding entry to legitimate evacuees whom foreign officials inside the airport were trying to evacuate, including foreign citizens, dual nationals, visa holders and former military interpreters with valid Special Immigrant Visas. Panicked Taliban soldiers with no training in crowd control swung rifle butts and electric cables and fired streams of warning shots into the air in hopeless efforts to control the surging masses. Surgeons working at a Norwegian-run military hospital inside the airport treated numerous instances of what they termed 'low-velocity bullet wounds', caused by what they believed were falling rounds. On several occasions, overwhelmed fighters levelled their weapons and fired directly into the crowds.

The confusion, disorder and desperation surrounding the airport never subsided. Every day, scores were injured in stampedes; children were asphyxiated in the arms of their parents when crowds surged with a force beyond any individual's control; pregnant women collapsed from dehydration and exhaustion. Yet it could have been far worse. US peace envoy Zalmai Khalilzad, Admiral Peter Vasely and major general Christopher Donahue, commander of the 82nd Airborne Division, who was in charge of security for the evacuation, set up a line of communication with the Taliban commander in charge of security at the airport. An incongruous relationship was forged between US and other international military forces inside the airport and the Taliban fighters outside, parties that had been fighting one another for two decades. 'The scenes of those first few days at the airport weren't good, necessarily, for us,' says then US chargé d'affaires Ross Wilson, 'but they weren't good for the Talibs either. They were willing to work with us to effect and support, or at least to facilitate, the evacuation up to the 31st [of August]'—the US deadline for the withdrawal.

The arrangement wasn't only confounding for the proximity into which it brought fighters from opposing sides. The Taliban were assisting tens of thousands of Afghans who, out of fear or uncertainty, were trying to flee the country of which they had just taken control. 'It wasn't a relationship without a lot of potholes,' says Wilson. 'It was always difficult, I think probably for both sides. It was a pragmatic [relationship], I think, that helped a lot more than it hindered.'

‹ ›

After being prompted by his US Embassy contact, Hamed called Mahmoud, who offered to help drive Hamed's family to the airport; a taxi would be used as well. Altogether, including the taxi driver, there were twelve people in the two vehicles that drove from Hamed's apartment down Emirate City's long central boulevard towards the airport: Safi, Zarifa, Heela, Yasin, Sahar, Mujib, Samira and her daughter Janat, Zarifa's sister Dina, and Mahmoud and his wife Shogufa and son Massoud. However, before they even reached the road running along the northern side of the airport, several kilometres from the East Gate on the opposite side of the airfield, they saw a mass of people outside another entrance—North Gate—numbering in the thousands. The taxi driver said he knew another way. 'It will take some time,' he told Hamed, 'but trust me.'

The driver returned the way they had come, and Mahmoud followed. They took a road up the mountain behind Emirate City and over a pass, dropping down the other side into Deh Sabz and moving on to the southern reaches of the Shomali Plain. The driver then skirted around the base of the mountain until Kabul came back into view. The two cars joined Russian Road and passed the abandoned police station on Despacheri Square, where the bodies of Fawad and the eight others executed by the 01 unit lay rotting in the heat. They turned onto Jalalabad Road and turned again when they reached Green Village, since 2001 the most heavily targeted compound for foreign contractors in Kabul.

Hamed's embassy contact was tracking his progress via the WhatsApp location-sharing function, watching the blue spot on a smartphone as the Safis travelled over a patch of resurfaced road where a crater caused by a truck bomb in January 2019 had been filled in, past industrial warehouses and another heavily fortified compound for foreign UN staff who had evacuated, until a crowd of about 100 people appeared beside a spot on the road which, lined with high concrete blast walls, abutted the airport perimeter.

The uncertainty became excruciating for Hamed. 'I still wasn't sure that I'd be able to take my family,' he recalls. Hamed had heard that the spouses of US passport holders were being admitted into the airport, and as his mother and sister had received American passports after being granted asylum in the United States in the 1990s, he was hopeful this would ensure his father's admission. But neither his wife nor his children had visas in the Afghan passports he'd acquired at the beginning of the year. If he was not able to take his family with him, he had determined that he wouldn't be going either.

The two-car convoy pulled over to the side of the road. Zarifa, who since the collapse of the government had been focused on the most immediate imperatives—moving from house to house, packing and repacking, looking after their children while Hamed planned their escape—put her face in her hands and sobbed. There were so many eventualities that could transpire in the minutes to follow, in none of which, even though Hamed had promised to stay with her, could she picture their family remaining together. 'I will never leave you and our children alone,' Hamed told Zarifa. 'I will take my mother and sister, and hopefully my father, inside, and I will come back. Don't worry.' But for Zarifa, even more important than keeping their family together was that Hamed got out of Afghanistan. She wanted him to swear on her life and those of their children that he wouldn't come back for them. 'Don't be concerned about us', she said. 'We will stay here. The Taliban won't come looking for us as they will for you. Save your life and we will find a way.'

'But I had already decided I would never do this,' says Hamed. If Zarifa and their children weren't allowed into the airport, then once his parents and sister were safely inside, he would return to his family.

Hamed and Mahmoud helped their mother, who walked with a cane, out of the car. Then, with father, sister and niece in tow, the two brothers took their mother by the arms and pushed their way to the front of the small crowd, to where a few Taliban fighters were trying to maintain a buffer in front of the perimeter wall. Sahar waved her American passport and the fighters let the group through to where American Marines in desert camouflage were standing by a pedestrian gate between the concrete barriers. The Marines stepped aside, allowing them to pass through for preliminary identification checks.

A Marine asked for their documents and Hamed handed over the two US passports belonging to his mother and his niece. He also introduced his father as his mother's spouse.

'And what about you?' asked the Marine.

'I only have a visa,' said Hamed. 'But my family don't have documents. I am just helping my mother to come inside.'

'Where is your family?' the Marine asked.

'Outside the gate,' Hamed replied.

'Why didn't you bring your family with you?' asked the soldier. He then gestured for Sahar, Mujib, Samira and Janat to move inside the gate before turning back to Hamed and saying, 'Go and bring your family.'

Hamed couldn't believe it. He had never allowed himself to think this would happen. Now, with such an opportunity beckoning, the thought of this new hope being dashed sent a wave of apprehension through him.

'What if the Taliban or your other colleagues don't let me pass again?' he asked the young Marine.

'Don't worry,' he said. 'I will keep an eye on you. Just point to me and I will tell them to let you back inside.'

Hamed returned to Mahmoud's car, where Zarifa, Dina, Heela and Yasin were sitting in the back seat with Shogufa. Zarifa was furious and shouted: 'You always do what you want.' Hamed said, 'No, I'm here to take you guys inside with me. Let's go.' He then explained to Mahmoud the offer the Marine had made and suggested Mahmoud and his family try to come as well, but Mahmoud declined: 'You guys should go. We will try to come another day.'

'I don't think Mahmoud could make such a decision in such a critical moment,' Hamed tells me later. 'Maybe he hadn't prepared himself and needed more time.'

Hamed's family farewelled Mahmoud's wife and, with Mahmoud and his son Massoud helping with their backpacks, they made their way back to the crowd outside the gate. Hamed held his children close, and also Zarifa, who locked arms with Dina, as they pushed and shoved their way to the front of the pack. Then Mahmoud put his hand on Hamed's shoulder. 'Brother,' he said, 'take my son with you. He shouldn't be here in Kabul.'

There was no time to think. A Talib ran towards Hamed and his brother, swinging a length of hose, trying to force them back into the growing crowd. But an American standing atop a Hesco barrier yelled at the Talib and, with no common language, gestured to let Hamed and the others through. And so, at around 4 p.m. on 18 August, Hamed took the hands of Heela and his wife, who was carrying Yasin, and, with Dina and his nephew Massoud, walked through the gate.

The Marine who had instructed Hamed to bring his family introduced them to an American civilian who was checking names off a list and logging further details of the departees as they were funnelled through the early stages of the evacuation process. The Marine stood by the whole time, and before returning to his post by the gate he wished them good luck and a safe trip. They then moved further inside to a yard where families were waiting to have their bags searched. When Sahar and Mujib saw their son and his family with Dina and young Massoud, they were in disbelief. 'My mum was crying, my dad was crying, my sister, my wife, everyone was crying,' says Hamed. 'It was happiness, shock, I don't know. We thought, "Our lives have been saved, and now we will start a new one."' Hamed then hugged his wife and said, 'Okay, now we're safe.'

After their bags were searched, the family and the others inside the staging area were escorted onto three buses which made a long loop around the start of the runway, to the passenger terminal on the northern military side of the airport. In comparison with the relative calm of the staging area inside East Gate, the terminals and apron were convulsing with activity. As many as 10000 foreign and dual citizens, visa holders, individuals from backgrounds or professions deemed to be at risk, as well as Afghans with connections abroad or to foreigners within Afghanistan, opportunists, and even members of the Taliban—and the families of all of them, and more—were by now being flown out every day.

Hamed and his family, along with the others who had entered via East Gate, were grouped together with other evacuees in an area on the apron. They waited there for four or five hours before being directed into the terminal building sometime before midnight. Then, for the next three hours, they were led through a multitude of identification and security checks, including iris scans and fingerprinting, to ensure that any Taliban fighters, prison escapees, or al-Qaeda or ISIS suspects who had infiltrated the masses weren't being assisted out of the country. They were each issued a white plastic bracelet with a barcode linked to a biometric database, which was scanned in an upstairs waiting area. In years gone by, the waiting area, filled with rows of plastic chairs, had been a kind of purgatory for foreign soldiers awaiting flights deeper into Afghanistan, and the war, or to the quandary of post-deployment life back home.

By 3 a.m., with their security and identity checks complete, Hamed and his family had exited the rear of the terminal building and sat down among other soon-to-be exiles on a bitumen road that ran between the military terminal building and the apron where military aircraft were parked, and there they waited. Everyone was tired, hungry and thirsty. Marines distributed bottled water and the large plastic packets of military rations—Meals Ready to Eat, or MREs—on which foreign soldiers had survived in remote outposts throughout the war. Unlike much of the American military ephemera that had embedded itself in the fabric of Afghan culture after 2001—tactical wear, M16 and M4 rifles, energy drinks—MREs, crates of which often found their way into local bazaars, were a source of bewilderment to Afghans and rarely left the shelves.

Hamed was worried about the food available for Zarifa, who was seven months' pregnant, and Yasin, who was just under three. The only items that looked remotely edible were the small packets of potato chips and gummy bears. 'I didn't even know what I was looking at,' says Hamed. 'Imagine that: you cook some beef, put it in a plastic packet, then refrigerate it and heat it up months later—this is indescribable.' But one item was familiar from his time working with American advisors, and he'd developed a taste for them, too: Clif Bars. So they each made do, trading with one another for their favoured items. But Yasin remained upset. 'Why did you bring us here?' he asked his father. 'When can we go home?'

'It was very hard to explain this situation,' says Hamed, who recalled his own experience as a child refugee in Pakistan.

Hamed barely slept. They had no blankets or mattresses, so he broke down the crate-sized cardboard boxes the MREs were delivered in and laid out lengths for his wife and children to rest on. Despite the constant roar of jet engines parked on the nearby ramp, and the sound of warning shots coming from the nearby North Gate, exhaustion eventually overcame Zarifa and the children. After they'd drifted into sleep, Hamed felt a subtle sense of relief, even as he worried about the bullets from the never-ending warning shots falling from the sky.

Colour appeared in the sky before 5 a.m., just as a C-17 taxied to the centre of the apron and 100 or more Marines carrying heavy loads ambled out of the rear cargo door in single file. The night had been mild, but the Safis and the other evacuees at first welcomed the first rays of the sun and the end of the darkness that had amplified the hysteria of the night. Then, says Hamed, hour by hour, 'the sun got hotter … There was no shade'. By the time his family was called to move towards an idling C-17, they had been waiting on the bitumen for 10 hours.

Hamed's family were among the first to board the plane through the rear cargo door, but the family was separated by airmen directing them to the bench seats on either side of the fuselage—once these had filled, passengers sat on the floor. Over the noise of the engines, Hamed and Zarifa could only communicate across the cabin using their eyes. Unlike the relief and elation they'd all felt when they'd made it inside the airport gate, now Hamed and the others felt empty and grief-stricken. Then, they had been together, hugging and crying as a family with a second chance.

Now, they were within themselves, heartbroken, alone, afraid of unknown futures.

Zarifa's eyes were heavy with sadness. 'She was looking at me,' says Hamed. 'I knew she was thinking, but about what I didn't know.'

Zarifa's sister Dina was sitting further forward, her head bowed. Hamed couldn't tell whether she was praying or wiping away tears.

'We left everything in Kabul,' says Hamed. 'Everything: our dreams, our plans. But we saved our lives.'

11

Shah Shahid, Kabul
III

The decision to go to the airport came on the morning of 16 August. Tens of thousands of Afghans were doing the same, and the combination of the magnetism of mass-mobilisation and Nadia's brother Hanif's insistence was difficult for her father Amin to overcome. Shukria would stay. 'Who will protect our home?' she asked, plus she needed to complete the legal transfer of the Shah Shahid property into her name. There was no discussion about what Shukria would do if the rest of the family made it out of the country.

Amin collected the passports they'd had since Bahira, Nadia's sister, had urged them to apply for after she'd reached Germany in 2015. Nadia packed a bag with a change of clothes for herself and her younger brother Elham, and added 100 euros and a small amount of local currency she had in her purse. The Aminis then left their house and walked to the end of the street. Twenty metres along the main road from the corner where the Aminis planned to wait for a taxi was a green police Ford Ranger. The men lounging in the tray were not police, however, and the flag flapping from the tall radio antenna wasn't the Afghan Republic's. They were

Talibs, and the flag was white with the black script of the *Kalima*, the Islamic declaration of faith.

Nadia began running in the other direction, with Elham following—it was the first time she'd seen Taliban fighters since a group had forced their way inside the family's home in Dara-i Farooq Shah in 2014. 'I ran like a mouse from a cat,' says Nadia. 'I thought that if they saw a woman on the street they'd kill me,' she adds, giggling at her own melodrama.

'Don't run,' Hanif yelled. 'Don't show them that you're afraid,' added Amin sternly. Nadia and Elham then rejoined their father and brother.

While they all waited for a taxi, Amin warned the children not to look at the pick-up truck full of fighters. But Hanif couldn't control his macabre fascination. These were the villains he'd only ever heard of through the stories of his father and brother, the news on TV, and the gruesome videos that saturated social media. They were like mythical creatures, long-haired and brooding, finally emerging after years of struggle in the mountains. One of the fighters was familiar, too: a neighbour who was also the mullah at their local mosque. Hanif recognised him from his visits for prayer each Friday. He became self-conscious about the lines shaved into the side of his head and tried to cover them with the longer hair on top. The mullah, their neighbour and a Talib, had been living among them all along.

A taxi pulled over and the Aminis got in. Contrary to her usual habit, Nadia kept her window wound shut, another layer of protection from the all-threatening world outside. The passengers all laughed nervously when the driver asked whether he could turn the radio on to play music, but their father said, 'Of course, of course.'

'Everyone was suspicious of one another during these days. Everyone was thinking, "You're a Talib, you're a Talib,"' says Nadia, pointing to imaginary fighters.

The Aminis emerged from the taxi on Airport Road, several blocks from the main entrance to the airport, where Nadia purchased a small bottle of water from a roadside vendor. The crowds of people trying to enter had grown in number over the past day and spread to several other entrances. The Taliban fighters in charge were clearly outnumbered, untrained and overwhelmed. The warning shots they fired, initially to some effect, became so frequent that the crowds started ignoring them, encroaching on the Taliban lines. Then the fighters levelled their rifles and fired directly into the masses moving towards them, scattering thousands and leaving the dead and wounded at their feet. One man clutching his bleeding head hurried past the Aminis. But the family locked arms and wrestled their way to the front of the crowd, Nadia barely noticing as she dropped her bottle of water.

Beneath the sign spanning the airport entrance that welcomed travellers to Hamid Karzai International Airport, Taliban fighters had manoeuvred humvees and improvised tactical vehicles with machine guns mounted in their trays to serve as barricades. At the main entrance, meanwhile, the Taliban were only allowing women and children to enter, so Amin pushed Nadia and Elham forward. The brother and sister disappeared behind the first row of Taliban fighters guarding the entrance.

On the tree-lined avenue leading from the entrance to the commercial terminal, the police and Border Force officers who usually manned the airport's first security screening area were nowhere to be seen. The tail fin of a Soviet MiG 21 fighter jet, once the bold centrepiece of an airport roundabout, peeked over a wall behind a billboard depicting the anti-Soviet, anti-Taliban resistance leader Ahmad Shah Massoud. The commercial terminals had been abandoned—airport staff had fled their posts the day before and hadn't returned. Nadia and Elham could see people roaming throughout the airline offices, the check-in and baggage halls, and the customs area. Luggage conveyor belts had been ripped from their rails. Electrical cords lay limp where they'd been torn free of computers and phones and baggage tag printers. Piles of discarded suitcases and their spilled contents littered a rose garden. And all the doors and gates leading onto the airfield itself were open and unattended. The commercial airline crews had also fled, and flights had ceased the evening before, but a constant stream of men oozed into and out of any available opening in the crewless airliners and smaller aircraft belonging to the UN and humanitarian organisations; those who couldn't get inside climbed onto the wings and roofs of the fuselages and sat down.

Nadia and Elham, neither of whom had ever flown before, made their way through the terminal building and found themselves on the commercial ramp, where several planes belonging to local carriers loomed over them. Nadia had left her phone at home with her mother—Amin and Hanif had been in an overbearing mood and had forbidden her from taking it. But now that they were separated, Nadia had no idea where her brother and father were, nor whether they would manage to get inside the airport at all. She took Elham's hand and joined the thousands of others moving with determination, but without a clear aim, in great waves across the airfield.

‹ ›

Corporal Caleb Cummins from Charlie Company, 1st Battalion, 8th Marines was in the Middle East on 13 August when he was told, 'Pack your stuff. You're going.'

Charlie Company had spent most of the past four months at sea, departing the United States for the United Kingdom in April, then sailing to Greece, through the Suez Canal to Saudi Arabia, around Yemen, Oman and the UAE, and finally up through the Persian Gulf to Kuwait. As provincial capitals across Afghanistan began falling at an irreversible rate on 12 August, and as efforts to fly embassy staff and equipment out of the country were redoubled, Cummins and the other Marines from Charlie Company became fixated on the news coming from Afghanistan, and speculated about whether they might be tapped to fly there. Cummins had in fact quizzed a friend in an intelligence unit about the likelihood of Charlie Company being sent to Kabul. 'He told us the chances were low,' says Cummins, 'so we didn't think it was going to actually happen.' But it did.

'The first couple of days were kind of a clusterfuck,' says Cummins, who touched down in a US Air Force C-17 at 9 a.m. on 15 August, five and a half hours before president Ashraf Ghani fled the country. Charlie Company, which comprised around 150 Marines, joined Alpha Company, which had been first on the ground. 'We weren't sure what to expect. We thought we were going to pull security for the airport while everyone else did the NEO,' says Cummins, referring to the Non-combatant Evacuation Operation that, according to Ross Wilson, was officially called that morning.

Cummins dumped his pack in an office building on the military side of the airport and was immediately posted to the terminal on the civilian side.

< >

Specialist Nate Nelson was a US Army National Guardsman assigned to the 101st Artillery Battalion, 86th Infantry Brigade Combat Team, based in Massachusetts. He landed in Kabul on 4 July. When Nelson stepped onto the tarmac, he marvelled at the landscape. 'I'd spent four years in military college in Vermont and I thought *those* were mountains,' he recalls.[1]

Unlike Cummins' unit, Nelson's had been notified of their deployment seven months earlier, in December 2020. The artillerymen had spent two months being 'cross-trained' on a C-RAM (a Counter-Rocket, Artillery, Mortar system): a 20-millimetre Gatling gun coupled to a radar system that detects, tracks and fires at incoming munitions. Each weapon stands more than 4 metres tall and requires a prime mover for transportation. Bagram Airfield, from which the Americans had departed mere days before Nelson and his guard unit arrived, had been home to several of the weapons before they were relocated to Kabul for the protection of the US Embassy and the airport, as the American footprint in Afghanistan was consolidated around the capital. The sound of the gun, which is capable of firing up to 4500 rounds per minute, was that which—during a test-fire mission at the airport—had terrified Nadia and her family a few nights earlier.

Nelson hadn't expected the Afghanistan he'd learned about through the media and movies over the course of the war, nor that which he'd heard of through the stories of his National Guard sergeants who had already deployed: about IEDs, and a platoon's experiences in the Korangal Valley, in the country's north-east, as shown in the documentary film *Restrepo*. That was because he knew the American involvement in Afghanistan had declined significantly in recent years, and that there hadn't been a single American casualty since February 2020. Nelson's unit was assigned to diplomatic security, protecting the embassy and the airport using a dozen C-RAMs stationed between the two sites. The 'diplomatic security' designation meant that Nelson and his National Guard colleagues would be staying beyond the 31 August withdrawal date set for foreign 'combat' forces.

'Life really wasn't bad,' says Nelson. 'There were restaurants, all these stores. We had this cafe with a fake garden and fake grass and you could buy a smoothie. I felt like I was on vacation. You could get a massage, you could get a great haircut, the food was actually very good, and we figured we could coast like this until the end of the deployment [February 2022]. Even though the Taliban was taking ground each day, you still felt like the war was a world away.'

In fact, aside from superficial changes, Kabul was closer to the city described by Nelson's father, who had visited the capital for his work as a cartographer with the British military in the 1960s. Nelson sent his father photos of the bare mountains on the northern side of the airport. 'Oh,' his father responded. 'That all used to be forest. Then the Russians napalmed everything.' He told Nelson how Westerners would travel to Kabul to ski. 'It really was like a regular country,' he said.

Every couple of days, Nelson would check a BBC interactive map contrasting the territory controlled by the Taliban with that controlled by the government. And by the start of the second week of August, the blotches of colour denoting government control were shrinking by the day. But Nelson says there was 'this thinking that Washington had, and that our leadership had … that the Afghan forces would at least be able to hold until after the fighting season and regroup or something'.

Nelson recalls how, during pre-deployment training in Oklahoma, 'everyone was making jokes: "It will probably end up like Saigon or something."' But even after the capital of Helmand province, Lashkar Gah, fell on 12 August, Nelson checked himself. 'There's no way this will be like Saigon,' he thought. 'That was in '75, in Vietnam. We have all this technology now and we've been in this country 20 years. Things will be different.'

Nelson says that on 15 August, when corporal Cummins and Charlie Company arrived, and as thousands of Afghans converged on the airport, 'we really didn't have a lot of troops on the ground— only 600 NATO troops and the Turks', with the Americans hoping the latter would stay on after 31 August to run the airport.

That same night, Nelson was ordered to rally at the unit's command post. 'We didn't really know what was happening,' he says, but 'suddenly, everyone was wearing full kit. The mood on the base was definitely heightened.' His first sergeant stood to address the company: 'The Taliban is now in the city. We still have a job to do.'

Nelson and his gun partner drove from their command post around the eastern end of the runway and prepared for the overnight shift at gun number 8—it was in a cordoned-off yard 200 metres from where Hamed Safi and his family would enter three days later. 'There was gunfire going on throughout the city now,' says Nelson. 'It was just crazy because, just over the course of one day, or one night, suddenly, the war was now in Kabul and it was right there in front of us.'

‹ ›

Around 6 p.m. on 15 August, corporal Cummins came off the guard shift at the commercial terminal and returned to the office block on the military side to rest. Sometime in the hours before dawn, he was woken by shouting from the hallway: 'Get the fuck up! They've breached the terminal ... 400 people and reports of small arms.' Cummins and his platoon threw on their body armour, boots and combat helmets and hustled to a rally point outside. The Marines were told to chamber a round: 'Be ready to go.'

They sprinted to the flight line in front of the terminal, where they received orders to move out to the runway. As they advanced in the darkness, Cummins could see what looked like two platoons of Marines trying to hold back hundreds of civilians from the edge of the tarmac. Cummins' platoon spent the next three hours helping to push the people back towards the civilian terminal. 'That's when we started getting shot at,' he says, by 'a gunman to the east of the terminal.'

Cummins and two other Marines went to the domestic terminal building, entered the departure lounge, and made their way upstairs to the air traffic control tower. From there, Cummins could see the Marines from his platoon to the west, adjacent to the international terminal. The sun was minutes away from rising above the mountains on Kabul's eastern fringe, towards Surobi, when, immediately beneath the tower, a group of men in Afghan garb emerged, armed with assault rifles and larger RPK and M240 light machine guns. One of the men unfurled a belt of bullets and began feeding it into an M240. Cummins then received a call from one of his riflemen, who was watching the same machine gunner from his position on the ground. Cummins knew the military's rules of engagement (RoE) authorised the use of force in response to an attack or the imminent threat thereof—'hostile act, hostile intent'— but, he says, 'there were about 20 of them and I wasn't sure where in the RoE they fell'. The gunmen hadn't yet seen him in the tower, nor the riflemen further down the flight line, and therefore didn't pose an immediate threat, but Cummins had no idea who the men were, nor what they were planning with such an arsenal.

It was only when a Marine presented himself that the gunmen hurried back from where they'd come. 'We were pretty close to smoke-checkin' all of them,' says Cummins.

With all access points to the tarmac wide open, the Marines unspooled coils of razor wire along the lengths of the two terminal buildings and stood watch from the runway side. The crowd had by now mellowed and, after two hours, Cummins' platoon was relieved and returned to their office barracks to rest. But an hour later, the Marines from Charlie Company were again woken abruptly and ordered back onto the airfield. The crowd they had spent the pre-dawn hours pushing off the runway had reappeared after a military entrance on the south-eastern edge of the airport, known as Abbey Gate, had been breached by people trying to get around the Taliban blockade of the main entrance. Thousands poured across the runway from the south and south-east, past where Cummins' platoon had first joined the line that morning, charging all the way to the military flight line and beyond. A US Air Force crew stood by and watched as one group separated from the larger mass and clambered aboard their C-17. Other people almost forced their way into the military terminal, where approved evacuees were being processed.

The Marines were vastly outnumbered. Cummins noticed that his battalion commander and sergeant major were both out of their command post and among their men, trying to contain the crowd. It was only when they were joined by soldiers from the army's 10th Mountain and 82nd Airborne divisions, who had landed that morning, that the crowd slowly began to retreat. By the time the line of soldiers and Marines had pushed the crowd halfway across the tarmac, it had swelled even further, and a cloud of dust had risen from the ground to envelop the sprawling mob. The Americans hurried to clear the runway as a C-17 taxied towards them from its western end. But crowds further along broke the line and flooded the tarmac, swarming around the aircraft's low-slung belly and running abreast like Secret Service agents protecting a motorcade. Cummins saw men climbing onto the forward landing gear and hugging the main strut. In the plane's starboard armpit, beneath the wings, around 20 boys and men were sitting or standing on the retractable mainwheel door, which while open extended parallel to the ground but would fold beneath the aircraft after take-off. One man casually leaned against the fuselage, filming the crowd giving chase on the runway with his mobile phone. The American lines had disintegrated. Cummins turned to his friend Tommy and said, 'Can you believe this is happening? This is insane.'

After taxiing to the end of the runway, the C–17 turned and accelerated, lifting off before reaching Cummins and the core of the horde of people. The plane was still over the airport when the first men fell. Four landed separately over a stretch of several hundred metres near the end of the tarmac—one had been decapitated. An onlooker cursed Ashraf Ghani as others covered the twisted bodies with scarves.

< >

Even in the remote far-eastern corner of the airfield, where gun number 8 was located, the situation had been deteriorating rapidly throughout 16 August. As Nelson had approached the gate to the secure gun yard earlier that day, when he was coming on shift, he heard a burst of gunfire that sounded closer than the perpetual patter he'd heard in the distance over the past 24 hours. 'I looked to my right and the dirt was popping up and that's when I realised, "Oh, I'm, like, in contact right now."'

Nelson took cover, and a breath. 'I was kind of freaking out. I was like, "We've gone from getting smoothies to getting shot at!"' He racked a round into the chamber of his M4 carbine, popped his head up and scanned the rooftops beyond the perimeter walls to the south-east. 'I was still convinced it was just a kid who found a rifle, it wasn't like I was in a gunfight, but that's when I was like, "Shit, things are getting real now."'

Around midday, Nelson watched a mob of thousands charge towards the airstrip from Abbey Gate, just to the west of his position. The crowd's focus was kilometres from gun number 8, and Nelson had a strange sense of detachment while watching it all through high-powered binoculars from an elevated position on the C-RAM's trailer.

'At one point, we saw one of the C-17s taking off and it was like a cartoon,' he says. 'We were looking at it through the binoculars and there were just thousands of people on the runway. It was insane to me. It was at that moment that I thought, "Things are very different now," and it became clear to us that we were losing control of the situation. Overnight, the mindset went from "We're going to be here for the long term" to "Hey, we're in a war zone".'

< >

Nadia and Elham had moved out of the terminal and onto the airfield at around 3 p.m. Much to Nadia's relief, there were no Talibs, just people like her, 'running this way, running that way'. And so she and her brother joined the throng walking north, beneath the wing of an Ariana Airlines plane on which people were sitting, over the taxiway and along a fenced area of satellite dishes and air traffic control apparatus. They crossed the runway, where thousands were still milling around, some running onto the tarmac as military planes descended, preventing them from both landing and taking off—this was only three hours after several men had fallen to their deaths from the climbing C-17. Baffled American servicemen yelled into the chaos in English: 'If you don't let them land, they can't fly you out.'

Nadia and Elham continued on past the airstrip, towards where elephantine military transport planes, sandy-coloured dome roofs and rows of blast walls marked the military side of the airport, where the evacuation was being staged. 'Everywhere you looked there were people,' says Nadia. 'I didn't let go of Elham's hand for even a second. He was only a child and my father had told me not to lose him.'

Turkish soldiers in armoured Cobra tactical vehicles and Marines in towering MRAPs (Mine-Resistant Ambush Protected vehicles) moved towards the crowd in a line like a giant dragnet, some firing warning shots in the air and blasting sirens, which, to Nadia, were like songs in comparison to even the kindest words spoken by a Talib. But the crowd poured through the gaps between the machines and headed for the military terminal and the adjacent hangars. The Turks and Marines were vastly outnumbered and, on an airport-sized playing field, incapable of holding the line.

'The soldiers were telling people to "Let the planes land or we'll give the airport to the Taliban",' says Nadia. 'People were abusing the soldiers. It was embarrassing. When you're saying, "Help us," and the next minute you're saying bad words to them. It's so rude.'

'Air operations were virtually impossible,' says Ross Wilson, who was by now working from the military side of the airport. 'Afghans were streaming over toward the north HKIA terminal. We didn't know who these people were; we didn't know what their intentions were; we didn't know to what extent some of them might be armed or have specific hostile intentions toward us.'

Nadia and Elham made it as far as the buildings and hangars beyond the flight line, where they approached a Turkish soldier. He raised his rifle, yelled in Turkish and waved them back. Nadia persisted, and on realising the soldier spoke basic English, asked him for help. He brought Nadia and her brother through a gate, pointed to a wall, beside which two families were standing, and said, 'Stay there and wait for that plane,' indicating one of the military transport aircraft.

The siblings waited for two hours, by which time the colour began draining from the sky. The Taliban had entered the civilian side of the airport and were trying to regain control. Many of those in the crowd on the airfield, some of whom had been there 24 hours, had by now given up on boarding a flight and wanted to leave. Hundreds had gathered in the concourse outside the terminal, near a fountain, and the 'I ♥ Kabul' sign. But the fighters weren't allowing anyone to leave, and their heavy-handedness saw many returning to the relative safety of the terminal and airfield from where they'd come.

On the military side, soldiers from the 10th Mountain and 82nd Airborne divisions had taken over efforts to secure the runway, while the Marines were dispatched to the half-dozen entry gates around the airfield. The crowd was now sandwiched between the US soldiers on the northern side of the airport and the Taliban on the southern side. 'There was firing from both sides,' says Nadia.

'First,' says Elham, 'the Taliban were trying to scare people with warning shots, but as more people came they began shooting people directly.' On the military side, says Nadia, the foreign soldiers were only firing into the air: 'The soldiers were so patient. People were laughing at them and abusing them, but they didn't shoot.'

Even with the new influx of reinforcements, the soldiers charged with protecting the military side of the airport were overwhelmed and, like the Marines and Turks earlier in the day, they were forced to retreat once again to the terminal. Nadia and Elham and the two families were now engulfed by the mob. 'I was shivering with fear, and fainted,' says Elham. 'There was so much gunfire,' adds Nadia. 'Elham was crying and we started running. Everyone else was trying to enter but we were trying to leave.'

They wove through the masses as if wading through an incoming tide, crossing the runway and reaching the Ariana Airlines plane parked outside the commercial terminal. They sat with other families under the aircraft's belly, where they thought they would be protected from the rounds from warning shots falling from the sky. Elham was faint from exhaustion and dehydration, and Nadia cursed herself for having dropped her bottle of water at the gate hours earlier. Now and then, faint dints could be heard as slugs penetrated the top of the plane. Nadia borrowed a phone from a young woman sitting nearby and called her father. He and Hanif had made it inside the airport and soon came and joined Nadia and Elham.

The families sheltering beneath the plane joked with one another. 'Maybe the mechanic has gone to find oil,' said one man.

'Does anyone know how to fly a plane?' asked another. One man, lying on the ground trying to sleep, wished he could close his eyes and wake up in Canada.

A Taliban fighter trying to move people on grabbed a woman sitting in a group beside the Aminis. When she objected, the Talib charged his weapon. 'I'm not scared of you,' the woman said defiantly. 'Shoot me if you want, but don't touch me.' An Afghan soldier wearing the tiger-stripe uniform of the 01 unit appeared and stood between the two, placating the fighter and asking the woman in a soft tone to move aside as the Talib had demanded. 'If he shoots you,' the soldier said, 'I will have to shoot him, and there are too many of them for me to defend against—they will kill me.'

'At that moment, I cried,' says Nadia.

The soldier then pulled two small bottles of water from the side pockets of his combat pants, offering one each to the families who had watched the exchange. 'Please let the children drink first,' he said, 'and then the women.' When Elham asked if he had more, the soldier handed him a bottle that was half-full. He looked at Nadia's brother and said, 'I wish Allah could see your face and save us from these wild animals.'

As Elham rested, the Aminis convened and decided to leave the airport. There seemed little chance of boarding a plane, and the risk of continuing to try was too great. 'It was a decision [made] for Elham,' says Nadia. The family ran for the domestic departure lounge in a crouch, as if that would protect them from the invisible falling rounds. They climbed over the rows of upturned plastic chairs, through the check-in area and out onto the concourse, past the armoured LandCruisers that government officials, Kabul elites and UN staff had abandoned in their rush for the last flights from Kabul the day before. They went around the 'I ♥ Kabul' sign and along the rose-lined avenue to the main entrance, where they saw thousands of people filling Airport Circle.

Nadia, her feet aching, was angry to be leaving while so many people were still trying to get in. Overhead glowed a sign in neon blue: 'Welcome to Kabul'.

‹ ›

The Aminis arrived home at midnight on the night of the 16 August. Nadia lay awake in bed beside her mother for hours. She struggled to justify leaving the airport after having made it inside. 'I didn't sleep until early in the morning,' says Nadia. Two months later, she would tell me: 'Since those days, I haven't had a single good night's sleep.'

At 9 a.m. the following morning, Nadia received a phone call from a friend from Shah Shahid. Dina had been at the French Embassy in Kabul's Green Zone for two days, waiting to be evacuated with French citizens, visa holders and Afghans deemed to be at risk. She offered to help Nadia enter the embassy as well.

Dina's brother was married to the daughter of a Taliban commander from Logar province who, after entering Kabul, had been stationed at Zanbaq Square, the closest point to the French Embassy outside the restricted Green Zone. He could help Nadia get through the Taliban checkpoint at the square, said Dina, then into the French Embassy and out of the country. Later that day, the Taliban commander would escort a convoy of several dozen vehicles filled with French and Afghan citizens to the airport in exchange for him and his family being included in the French evacuation.[2]

'Yesterday I was at the airport,' thought Nadia. 'It's not possible to leave.' But then she spoke with her eldest brother, Rahim, in Germany, who suggested she go, but that she take her brothers as well. Soon after, with her father's permission, Nadia left home, though only with Elham, and drove to Zanbaq Square. By night-time, Dina had gone quiet. Just before midnight, the convoy left the embassy, led by members of a French tactical police unit, and passed by Nadia, Elham and the crowd waiting in Zanbaq Square. Nadia didn't know it, but there would be no more convoys departing the French Embassy for the airport.

She and Elham spent the night of 17 August in the square with a group of around 200 women and children. The next morning, her father called: 'It's over, come home.'

Elham left, but, says Nadia, 'I felt I had made such a huge effort spending the night on the ground and I didn't want it to be for nothing. So I stopped answering their calls and stayed in Zanbaq Square.' Nadia stayed for another two nights, sleeping on the ground with the friends she made among the women, who allied with one another in verbal stoushes with the fighters who guarded the square and prevented them from moving closer to the French Embassy.

It was during those two days that Nadia and I first met. I had ridden my motorcycle to Zanbaq Square to photograph the crowd waiting outside the embassy. When the Taliban guarding the entrance to the Green Zone pulled me off the street and demanded I delete the photos, Nadia was in the front row of the crowd of women waiting opposite the entrance, surreptitiously filming the encounter with her smartphone. When I was eventually escorted by two Talibs to my motorcycle a few blocks away, Nadia followed, stopping to buy an energy drink from a street vendor when she suspected she'd been spotted. After the Talibs turned back towards the square, I heard a small voice as I strapped on my helmet. Nadia told me she had filmed my scrape with the Taliban and asked if I'd like her to share it.

After spending another night camped outside the square, Nadia returned home by taxi, on 20 August. 'There was no hope left,' she says.

< >

In the time Nadia had been away from home, news had arrived from Dara-i Farooq Shah, the village in Kapisa province where the Aminis had once lived. Shukria's brother—Nadia's uncle—who still lived in the village, had called to tell his sister that his young son Masih had been taken from the street while walking to buy bread one morning, and that he hadn't been seen nor heard from since. The Taliban in the village were also asking about the Aminis.

Gone were the days when the Taliban had to be subtle about their inquiries. It was the same sort of scrutiny that had led Amin to take his family to Pakistan twice before, to send Rahim and Bahira to Europe, to hide from their past amid the sprawl in Kabul, and to risk their lives in the hope of finding a way out of the country from the airport. The reality that the Aminis had always known but had limited means with which to respond to—that the Taliban in Kapisa would never forget that both Amin and Rahim had worked for the foreign invaders, not until justice was served—began to weigh more heavily on the family than ever. For years, because the Taliban had been confined mostly to rural areas, the Aminis had been able to survive by running and hiding. And despite being momentarily swept up by the hysteria that drew thousands to the airport, Amin was adamant he would never again live as a refugee. With nowhere left to hide in Afghanistan, however, and the likelihood of evacuation via the airport—if Amin changed his mind—diminishing as the withdrawal deadline neared, there were few remaining options that would ensure the Aminis' safety.

On 22 August, Hanif left home for the bus station in Company, on Kabul's south-western outskirts, boarding a dilapidated coach for Nimroz province in Afghanistan's desolate south-west. Less than three weeks earlier, Nimroz had been the first of the country's 34 provinces to fall to the Taliban. Now, as it had always been, the provincial capital Zaranj was the casting-off point for Afghans without valid visas who sought work in neighbouring Iran or refuge further west in Turkey or Europe.

Hanif gloated as he left home. 'I'm saving my life,' he told his family. 'What about you? Why should I wait here for my death?'

'There was no way they could stop him,' Nadia says of her parents. 'And there was no reason for my mum and dad to stop him.' If they weren't willing to travel with him, they thought, why should they prevent him from trying alone?

After spending a night driving the bomb-cratered highway south from Kabul, through Maidan Wardak to Kandahar and then west across Helmand to Nimroz, Hanif and 25 others were shoved into a closed steel box on the back of a pick-up truck by a smuggler and driven a further three hours south into the desert. Hanif had one bottle of water but no food. However, he still felt he had made the right decision. In addition to the Taliban's enmity towards his family, Hanif had been hearing stories from his friends about the Taliban's first time in power from 1996 to 2001. 'The Taliban used to collect young men for the war in Panjshir,' he says of the valley from which the anti-Taliban resistance was led during the 1990s. 'I thought it was better to leave than be taken by the Taliban.'

When the driver stopped and opened the door to the steel box, Hanif saw a ladder leaning against a wall that he assumed marked the Iranian border. 'We jumped the wall and walked and ran for two hours,' Hanif says. 'When the smugglers arrived in cars, we gave the password and were driven another 14 hours to Kerman where we were stopped by police.' The Iranian police drove Hanif and the others to a small, informal border crossing and handed them over to the Taliban. They spent the night in a mosque in a nearby village and were then driven by taxi back to Nimroz. Hanif was back home in Shah Shahid within five days.

‹ ›

The shift in the family's demeanour towards Nadia became noticeable after she returned from her time spent camped outside the French Embassy. While the repression her father and Hanif had begun to impose after Nadia had graduated from high school had escalated to physical violence in the months before the Taliban took control of Kabul, she had viewed being beaten as an isolated incident—a typical male response to the loss of control felt as the young woman in their midst began to explore the world beyond the confines of her family. Now, she felt an unfamiliar animosity being directed her way at home, particularly from her father. Nadia got the sense that she was a burden on the family, 'an extra', she says. She wondered whether they might have been angry that she'd spent several days away from home, alone, but reasoned that, had that been the case, they'd have punished her for it explicitly. For the first few days, the shift manifested only as an indefinable darkening of the atmosphere between Nadia and her father, the cause of which she couldn't guess.

Months later, Nadia would tell me, 'The decision had already been made in his mind.'

She was showering one day, soon after returning home, when the water suddenly stopped flowing. Elham, who reasoned Nadia had been in the shower long enough, had turned off the water pump. It was unlike her younger brother. 'Why did you do that?' she asked. The two argued back and forth and Nadia eventually went to her mother to complain about Elham's behaviour. That evening, Amin, Hanif and Elham were sitting in the courtyard when Elham told them about the argument he'd had with Nadia, exaggerating the insults his sister had used. As Hanif's anger grew, he started inciting Amin to act.

Amin walked inside and found Nadia in the living room. When Nadia denied having used the language of which Elham had accused her, her father slapped her across the face. 'I didn't do anything wrong,' Nadia said as he left the room. A minute later, Amin returned holding the plastic hose that connected their gas bottle and stovetop.

Then Shukria entered the room and Nadia pleaded with her: 'Mum, you saw, it wasn't my fault.' Shukria repeated Nadia's denial: 'It wasn't her fault.'

Hanif now came in and moved towards Nadia, grabbing hold of her wrists when she raised her hands to fend him off, while Elham closed the windows facing the neighbour's house. 'I was crying,' says Nadia, who was more devastated over the indignity and injustice of what was happening than in fear of the physical pain she was about to be dealt. 'Mum was trying to defend me but no-one was listening.'

As Amin started flailing Nadia with the length of hose, she cried out. 'Respect your father when he's speaking to you,' demanded Hanif. 'He hit me everywhere,' says Nadia. 'Back, hands, but not my face or my head.' One of the blows left a shallow wound where the end of the hose had struck her forearm.

Hanif eventually released his sister's wrists. She ran to her room and closed the door. Shukria followed. 'She knew I was scared of being alone,' says Nadia. 'She said, "Come and sleep with me." When I told her I wanted to be alone, my father came in and said, "Are you coming or will I have to beat you again?"'

After that night, Nadia went from feeling unwelcome in the house to being terrified of putting a foot wrong—the behaviour of her father and brothers had turned into a brutal projection of their own fear. 'Like, if I was told to come to this room, I should come,' she says. 'If I was told to go to sleep at this time, or sit there, or speak with that person, I should do it [without question]. If I went to the bathroom and spent more than five minutes ...' She trailed off, then added: 'They were trying to find fault, to blame me and to find reasons for beating me.'

Late in the afternoon the day after Nadia had been beaten, the family sat together in Amin's room, drinking tea. Nadia went to the kitchen to prepare a plate of fruit, but she could still hear her family talking down the hallway. 'They were having a discussion about what the family should do,' she says. With the plate of fruit in hand, Nadia crept along the hallway and listened more closely.

'I want to leave,' said Hanif. 'I will go to Iran again. Home is like a jail. We can't go out to see friends. How many days do you expect us to live like this? There is no way we can stay here. Eventually, they will catch us, they will kill us. And we will blame you.'

'No,' said Amin, 'there is another way.'

Amin had received advice from an elder from Kapisa about his family's dilemma. Amin was the only one from the family who was present for the conversation, and while Nadia believes her father sought out the advice, the others believe the elder approached Amin, unsolicited. 'We don't know what their motives were,' says Shukria.

However the conversation came about, Amin explained that he had told the elder that leaving the country as a family was not an option. He didn't want to live as a refugee again, and even if he were willing to, he said, 'the Taliban will identify us crossing the border'. Continuing to try to hide from the Taliban, he said, was untenable in the long term. He also told the elder about his nephew Masih, who was still missing, presumed to have been taken by the Taliban, and reminded the man of what had happened to his eldest daughter Bahira years ago at Gul Agha's house in Kama.

Amin then said what the elder had advised him: 'Give your daughter to the Taliban.'

Nadia couldn't believe what she'd heard. Rounding the doorway into Amin's room, she said: 'Why don't you tell him to give his own daughter to the Taliban?'

'If you were a father and you were in my position, what would you do?' asked Amin angrily. Nadia responded that his idea was nonsense. 'Okay, then you find a way,' said Amin. 'You find a way and we'll follow it.'

< >

Nadia started to think about leaving home. 'They were feeling ashamed of the decision they'd come to,' says Nadia, 'and were looking for reasons to justify it—to prove to themselves they were right.'

On 26 August, Elham and Nadia were at home speaking with their mother about me. At the time, I was playing a very small role in a large operation assisting at-risk Afghans to leave the country. An assortment of foreign journalists, aid workers and others with deep connections to Afghanistan, working mostly out of Paris, were compiling flight manifests and making arrangements to get those listed inside Hamid Karzai International Airport. One commercial airliner had already been chartered using money donated by an American philanthropic organisation, and it was hoped there would soon be more. Nadia's best friend Mariyam, with whom Nadia had connected me so that we could remain in contact indirectly if, because of the difficulties with her family, she wasn't able to do so herself, had asked for assistance leaving the country. I had offered to include her name on a longlist for a prospective charter flight being arranged by the consortium in Paris. Nadia doesn't remember the topic of conversation with her mother and brother, but given the circumstances, I suspect it may have been about requesting my help to leave the country—inflated as her understanding of my powers might have been.

When Hanif overheard the three speaking, he demanded that Elham tell him what they had been talking about. Although Hanif was already aware that Nadia and I had been in contact, and had not previously taken issue with this, the circumstances in the house had changed—Hanif, even more than Amin, was looking for any reason to justify further estranging Nadia from the family. When Elham told Hanif that I had been the topic of discussion, he stormed into his father's room, locking the door behind him.

A few minutes passed before the men called Nadia into the room. 'Everyone was silent,' she says. '[Hanif] said, "Sit in front of me," like he was my boss. Then he asked for my money. I had 100 euros—it was in the cover of my phone. He took my phone, broke it, and took the money.'

'Why are you doing this?' she asked her father, referring to his decision to hand her over to the Taliban for marriage.

Hanif responded: 'This is the decision, and you should accept it.'

'I won't,' said Nadia. 'If you want my money, I will give it to you. If you want my phone, I will give it to you. But I will not accept this decision.'

She turned to her father, who had taken a back seat to his 17-year-old son, and asked, 'How can you just sit there while he says all these things?'

Nadia left the room and walked towards the front door. Hanif chased her and punched her with a closed fist to the back of her head. When she held up her hands to defend herself, Hanif grabbed her wrists in one hand and slapped her across the face repeatedly with the other. As Amin looked on, again Nadia implored him: 'Why are you just watching?'

Nadia describes the aftermath of the beating: 'I was just waiting for night-time. I would sit by the window, watching the sky and talking with God, about everything that happened that day, asking him why he's not responding to me.' But before night came, Nadia went to the bathroom and took a packet of razor blades from a shelf, before shutting herself into Hanif's room. She took a book of colourful sticky notes from her bag and began writing on them, one after another, and attaching them to the back cover of a book. 'I love you but I can't do the thing you want,' she wrote. 'I'm not responsible for what is happening.'

The idea of ending her own life, rather than allowing someone else to take it from her, had come from a story she'd heard of a friend of her mother's. After a group of men broke into her apartment, the woman, believing their intention was to rape her, threw herself from a window. 'She killed herself to protect herself,' says Nadia.

Speaking of the suicide attempt, Nadia says, 'When I cut it at first there wasn't much blood. So I pushed it [the razor] and it was like opening a tap. It felt warm through my fingers.' When Shukria entered the room and saw Nadia and her bloodied forearm and hand, she called for help. She regretted the impulse immediately, because Hanif rushed in and slapped Nadia. And when Shukria suggested taking Nadia to the hospital, he scoffed: 'Let her do what she wants to do.' So Shukria simply wrapped a scarf around Nadia's wrist.

'It was white,' says Nadia of the scarf. 'It became red.'

Nadia called me from Shukria's phone at 4 p.m. Unable to speak freely or for long, she tried to tell me what had happened, but cryptically, and I didn't understand. She then called Mariyam, who phoned me to explain that Nadia was having problems with her father and brothers. She didn't tell me about their decision to hand Nadia over to a Talib for marriage, nor that Nadia had sliced open her wrist with a razor blade. But even though I wasn't aware of the severity of Nadia's predicament, it still seemed serious—her plight stood out. The extraordinary circumstances of the time, which saw the ordinarily onerous criteria and process required for obtaining asylum in foreign countries suddenly done away with, meant that foreigners like me were receiving dozens of requests for help on a daily basis. However, they were mostly from strangers who appeared not to have specific reasons for fearing the Taliban, beyond the universal state of repression the group was expected to institute, but understandably hoped to take advantage of the moment and find a place on an evacuation flight out of Afghanistan. Nadia, on the other hand, despite her situation, had not once asked for my help.

On the day Nadia and I first met near Zanbaq Square, she didn't tell me she'd just spent two nights there and would stay longer; she didn't tell me about the Taliban's desire for revenge against her family, that they had twice fled to Pakistan to escape; nor did she speak of the way in which her father and brothers had been treating her over the past 12 months. At only 19, Nadia was plucky and selfless. She played down her plight, and even as she faced being sacrificed by her family to placate the Taliban, she empathised with her father's predicament and reasoned that her brothers were only acting out of fear.

It wasn't until a few days later, when circumstances at home became desperate, that Nadia finally asked for help.

‹ ›

Nadia's left hand was weak from her self-inflicted wound, but Hanif pushed her to work, demanding that she wash his clothes. And when Nadia's wound reopened, he castigated Shukria for standing in for her. 'Why aren't you telling her to learn the housework?' he asked, inferring that she needed to practise for when she was married.

Some days later, towards the end of August, Shukria received two guests at home: an old woman with white hair, and her daughter, who was around 24 years old. The elderly woman was wearing a colourful dress, all layers and folds, typical for women in rural Afghanistan. Amin and Hanif stayed in Amin's room while the women entered, allowing them to gather privately in the guestroom with Shukria, who was a reluctant host but carried out her duties as custom demanded.

Amin asked Nadia to prepare tea. Although it was a first for the Aminis, the practice of introducing a prospective bride to the women from the family of an eligible groom was innate and conducted with an air of ceremony. When she entered the room with the tea, Nadia clocked the two women—both Pashtun—and her mother's anguish, and knew immediately what was going on. In fact, Nadia had anticipated this meeting and had come up with a plan to sabotage it.

As she lowered the tea tray to the ground between the two guests and her mother, the fingers on her left hand gave way under its weight and the far edge dropped the final few centimetres, causing one of the cups to tumble onto its side. That hadn't been part of her plan, but Nadia registered the old woman's disapproval with satisfaction.

Nadia knelt, righted the cup, then lifted the thermos and began pouring green tea. Then she picked up the cup and saucer and stretched forward, causing the sleeves of her dress to retract up her arms, revealing the bandage. 'Here you go,' Nadia said with faux politesse. Neither of the guests visibly reacted, but they didn't have to.

'In Afghanistan, when a person attempts suicide … they think that she's not a good girl,' says Nadia. So, she continues, 'they reject[ed] me'.[3]

'It was my plan,' Nadia tells me, 'and it was successful. I kissed her [the old woman's] hand out of respect that I didn't have, then left the room.'

A week later, on 6 September, over breakfast, Hanif once again broached the decision to hand Nadia over to the Taliban as a bride. 'You must accept it,' he told her. Again, Nadia refused. And again, Hanif flew into a rage, this time punching her as if she were an opponent in a bout of mixed martial arts—a sport Hanif followed fanatically—striking her in the neck.

Amin stepped in. 'Okay, stop,' he said. 'For now, it's done.'

But Hanif didn't stop. Nadia went into her mother's room to get away, but Hanif followed and struck her again, sending Nadia to the floor. 'Stand up!' he demanded.

Shukria came in to protect Nadia, but Hanif pushed his mother aside and started kicking Nadia as she cowered on the floor, her knees curled up against her chest. He stomped her, striking her in the groin with his heel. Nadia screamed in pain, breaking Hanif's violent momentum. Amin and Elham rushed inside the room as Shukria forced her son away from Nadia. Then she told Amin and Elham to leave as well.

'What have you done?' Shukria yelled from inside her room. 'She's bleeding.'

'This is nothing,' said Hanif. 'She should thank God I didn't take a knife to her.'

A friend of Shukria advised that she take Nadia to hospital. So they caught a taxi to a nearby clinic. Nadia called me, explaining that she was on her way to hospital with her mother and that she feared returning home. I called a friend, Penelope, a qualified social worker who had worked for years to get Afghan girls into school, and who had single-handedly established several safe houses in the capital for women and families in imminent danger in the wake of the Taliban takeover. Penelope agreed to step in and do whatever was necessary, and suggested I pass her number on to Nadia.

Meanwhile, at the hospital, when the doctor asked Shukria what had happened, she replied that Nadia had fallen. 'My eyes were full of tears,' says Nadia. The doctor then drew a curtain around herself and Nadia, who was perched on the edge of an examination table. Nadia soon told her what had really happened and begged her to see some of her other patients, then come back to her for a full examination. She was trying to buy time because, she says, 'I was worried they'd kill me when I went home.' The doctor thought of an alternative, referring Nadia to another hospital for a procedure she couldn't perform herself. But Shukria rebuffed the suggestion and she and her daughter set off for home on foot.

Nadia was struggling to walk. But her slow pace created a little distance between her and her mother, who Nadia believes was turning a blind eye to her daughter's frantic efforts to plan an escape while not actively participating in it—just giving her more time to do so. It was at this point that Nadia called Penelope to explain her situation as quickly as she could. Penelope said,

'If you want, I'll send a car for you.' But she also advised Nadia, if she felt she could, to spend a couple of days thinking about it, 'because once you leave home, you cannot go back'. The risk of what is commonly referred to in the West as 'honour killing'—the murder of a female for bringing the family name into disrepute—was too great.

'There was no other way for me,' says Nadia. 'That day, when I was in the clinic, I wasn't thinking about what my family will think, what I will do when I leave with no money, with nothing. All I was thinking about was saving my life.'

Late that night, after she had spoken with Nadia several times, Penelope texted me: 'Formulating a plan, not immediate. Tell you more later.'

Back at home, after a brief reprieve following her visit to the clinic, the family's repressive behaviour towards Nadia continued. She was constantly surveilled and never allowed outside alone. Mariyam managed to bring her a new phone to use, but the spectre of the family's decision relentlessly stalked Nadia's mind. Nadia grew afraid of silence, of what she sensed was being discussed but couldn't hear. She tried to eavesdrop on her family's conversations, because if she knew their plans, she could make her own, keeping ahead of them while maintaining the hope—the fiction—that her father might change his mind. Sometimes she caught fragments of exchanges between her father and Hanif, but, she says, 'When I'd enter the room they'd change the topic.' There was talk of another groom—another Talib. There was also the question of Nadia's scars, and discussions about how to evade the groom's family's rebuke when they were discovered.

She didn't know it at the time, but Nadia would later discover that her instincts had been right. In fact, Amin had already arranged his daughter's engagement to another Taliban fighter, which was soon to be formalised. 'He had made a deal with them,' says Nadia. '"I will give my daughter to you, and you will protect us."'

One night, Nadia was in the kitchen cooking dinner. She had a pot of water boiling on the stove for rice and a pan of oil that was spattering as it came to the boil. Hanif and Elham entered the kitchen and took hold of Nadia from behind. As she yelled in protest, Elham closed the windows and the kitchen door, an act that had become part of the men's ghoulish routine. Hanif, while holding Nadia's scarred left arm outstretched beside the stovetop, then ordered Elham to spoon hot water from the pot over the partially healed wound. When Nadia screamed in pain, Amin entered. Nadia looked at her father, as disbelieving of his inaction as she was of Hanif's brutality. Amin's silence was all the approval Hanif needed to continue and he turned back to his work, this time flicking the bubbling oil directly from the pan onto his sister's arm. 'As if it happened during cooking,' says Nadia, to disguise his premeditated savagery. 'They were my family, but when I looked at them, I saw them as animals.'

Elham was shattered by the way his brother had drawn him into his conspiracies to save the family at the expense of their sister. 'I never thought it was the last option, to give Nadia away,' he says. 'I always trusted that God would provide another way.'

'It was red, but not like a balloon,' says Nadia of the marks left by the burns. 'The pain was like when your tongue touches pepper.'

The following day, Nadia contacted Penelope, telling her it was time: 'I want to stay with you. There are some problems at home.' That night, she told her mother. 'I trusted her,' says Nadia. 'She was supporting me—not directly, but she always did what she could.' Shukria told Nadia, 'If you can, you should save yourself.' But when Nadia moved towards her, Shukria, indomitable as ever, refused her daughter's embrace.

'The next morning, I woke up very early and cooked for my dad, for everyone,' says Nadia. 'I hadn't spoken with him since he started beating me, not directly, but the night before, after the call with Penelope, I spoke with him. I wanted to make some moments for me, and some good memories of them.' She thought back to 2015, when Taliban fighters came to their home in Kapisa, beat her father, and threatened to take Bahira: 'In that situation, we were together. When my sister's life was in danger we all left the country. Why [are they] not doing the same with me now?'

When Amin and her brothers left the house later that morning, 23 September, Nadia called Penelope, who told her to pack some clothes, medicine and anything else she needed. Nadia wanted something of her mother's to take with her. Shukria had an antique gold ring where the impression of a woman's face had been pressed into a round plate on the top of a crown—her friends always complimented her on it. Nadia had a gold ring as well, one with a flower-shaped head, which she had bought with the pocket money she had accumulated in her clay pot. The two women exchanged rings. Shukria's was too big for Nadia's fingers, so she put it in a pocket. Shukria also gave Nadia a miniature copy of the *Surah Yasin*, a portion of the Qur'an that warns of the fate of non-believers. It was small enough that Nadia could close her palm around its pink-and-white cover.

She packed everything, including some jewellery and extra money, in a backpack and walked with her mother to a nearby hospital. Penelope was waiting outside in a private taxi with another young woman she was helping. Shukria hugged Nadia before her daughter climbed into the car.

'She looked tiny and overwhelmed by the bigness of the decision,' says Penelope, 'but at the same time completely together. She emanated courage and determination.'

'I was close to crying,' says Nadia, 'but there was a man, the driver, and I didn't want to cry in front of him.'

12

Abbey Gate, Hamid Karzai International Airport

Seventeen-year-old Mujda Bahar had been sitting in the dirt opposite the airport entrance for three hours, resting in the shade after a morning of failed entry attempts. She was with her younger sister, two younger brothers, her mother Zara, a teacher, and her father Abdul Nizam, who, until 15 August 2021, had been a trainer in counter-intelligence with the NDS.

At 8 a.m. on the morning of 19 August, Nizam had taken the family by taxi to the airport's main commercial entrance at the end of Airport Road. The crowd was thousands-strong, and it seemed like the Taliban guarding the gate were firing a hundred bullets into the air for every person waiting—hoping—to get inside. 'It was a family decision to go to the airport,' says Zara, 'before they come and kill us in our home.' But they hadn't expected this. Bahar and her younger siblings were terrified.

Nizam decided they should leave Airport Circle to try another entrance. They walked east, following the tall airport perimeter wall along a road where the only vehicles were US$200 000-plus armoured four-wheel drives that had been abandoned by Kabul elites scrambling to get to the airport the day the Taliban came to the city, and which were now being used by families to sleep and hide from the sun, and by Taliban fighters to stand atop for a better view over the crowd. They passed, on the opposite side of the road, the main entrance to the Baron Hotel, the 160-room compound popular with foreign security contractors who, in the summer months, could be found lounging by the pool with pistols strapped to their hips, and which was now a staging area for British nationals and others trying to leave the country. When the road ended at Abbey Gate, they continued alongside a sewerage canal, eventually stopping at the perimeter wall for Cohan Village, another camp for foreign contractors.

The air was stifling and motionless, even though it was still the morning. When the sun rose high enough to strike the putrid water in the canal, a sour stench poured over the people sitting and standing along the 4-metre-wide dirt service road sandwiched between Cohan Village and the lip of the canal. Beyond the canal was another narrow pathway, along the length of which American servicemen and women, and soldiers from other foreign countries, maintained security, administered first aid, and took on the role of consular officials, deciding who would and who would not be allowed inside the airport. Beyond the foreign military forces was a wall topped with razor wire that marked the airport perimeter.

After the main access point to Abbey Gate had become virtually impassable in the early days of the evacuation, news of the canal route, accessed mostly via the narrow backstreets and laneways to the south-east, had spread quickly. But at 11 a.m. on 19 August, the crowd was thin enough that Bahar and her family were able to sit with their backs to the wall of Cohan Village while Nizam planned their next move.

Bahar was looking at her phone when she sensed someone crouching beside her. The young woman introduced herself as Najma Sediqi, and asked whether she and her 21-year-old brother Wasiq and her 27-year-old cousin Shahid could join Bahar's family by the wall. Bahar was captivated by Najma, who was two years older than she was, with dark features made more pronounced by skin as smooth as porcelain. Bahar didn't recognise her, but

Najma said she worked as a television presenter. She was bold and confident. When her brother made room for a woman to sit by the wall, and the woman's husband abused him for what he assumed was an attempt to get close to his wife, Najma stood up and lambasted the man for jumping to conclusions. 'We sat side by side on our backpacks,' says Bahar. 'For 12 hours, Najma told me about her school, her achievements, and later on how she got a job in TV and about the trouble she received from the public, especially men.'

Najma had thought she had a strong case for being accepted by a foreign country because of her work. 'Once I'm inside the airport I can manage everything,' she'd said at first. But when she saw the folder of documents that Bahar and her family had compiled to support their own evacuation efforts and asylum claims, Najma was taken aback. She hadn't understood how narrow was the criteria for being allowed inside the airport, and now she was worried that the YouTube videos she planned to present—some of which had been viewed hundreds of thousands of times—weren't going to satisfy the soldiers who would decide the fate of her and her family.

The two families bought *bolani* (deep-fried flatbread filled with shredded leek and potato) and bottles of water from young boys who wandered through the crowds until there was no space left to walk, much less ply their trade. The sun, meanwhile, moved over the airport, turning the service road along the canal into a furnace.

To have any chance of entering the airport, Bahar and Najma and their families would have to wade through the knee-deep sewage, which the soldiers on the opposite bank were using as a buffer to contain the crowds, and present their cases. While the criteria changed from hour to hour, the foreign forces were looking almost exclusively for foreign passport or visa holders. Few, if any, Afghans who didn't hold the priceless documents were taken inside the airport on the basis of unverified threats, regardless of how serious—or genuine—they were. Yet still they came with certificates from training courses undertaken with foreign organisations and militaries in the early 2000s, photographs with foreign dignitaries and military officers, employment contracts with embassies and international contracting organisations, letters of support from foreign officials, copies of family members' foreign passports and driver's licences, visa–application acknowledgment letters, Taliban threat letters and photos of slain family members. Some even came with electricity bills or vehicle registration documents.

The longer the two families waited for space to open up in the canal, the more people surged into the service road until, by mid-afternoon, there was no room to sit. Like a volcano that creates its own weather patterns, the crowd started producing forces of its own and the two families jostled and swayed just to keep their feet. When Bahar's younger siblings became so exhausted they could no longer stand, the adults encircled them in a protective ring while the children sat for a few minutes at a time to rest.

The hope that the dark would bring some respite from the rush at Abbey Gate faded as midnight came and went. There seemed little hope of even entering the canal, let alone the airport. The two families started talking about retreating from the heaving morass. Najma's group wanted to try another gate, while Bahar's family simply wanted to go home. Najma and Bahar exchanged WhatsApp numbers, as did Nizam and Shahid. 'Najma and the others left at 2 a.m.,' says Nizam, 'but because I had the whole family with me it was impossible. It became so crowded we couldn't leave.' The risk of losing one of his young children in the crowd, or worse, as they tried to get out, was too great. They stayed through the night, until 8 a.m., when Nizam felt it was safe to move back towards the main airport entrance. After carrying nine-year-old Muzamel in his arms for 45 minutes before finding a taxi, Nizam swore to himself that he wouldn't bring his children back to the airport.

When Bahar arrived home, she contacted Najma to see whether they had succeeded elsewhere. 'We failed,' Najma said. 'I feel sick and my feet are sore. I will never go to the airport again.'

‹ ›

The youngest of six children, Najma Sediqi was born in Kerman, Iran, in 2002. 'Iran was full of happiness and sadness,' recalls her eldest sister Fereshta. 'Home life was full of happiness because we were all together. There was a school for Afghans who could afford it but because only our father was working we couldn't go.'

The Sediqis travelled back to Kabul in 2011, collecting a small amount of cash from the UN refugee agency at the border. They came to be with Najma's grandmother, whose health was failing, making the return to their homeland—where the children could attend school for the first time—bittersweet. Najma passed an exam to be admitted into grade three at a school in Macroyan, and later she was the youngest in her class when she graduated from Ariana High School, located in the centre of the city close to Cinema Pamir, one of the Afghan capital's oldest movie theatres.

After completing her university entrance exam, the Concor, Najma was offered a place at Kabul University's prestigious science faculty, but she declined, choosing instead to study journalism. 'She was very charismatic, but could be soft and compromising,' says Abdul Wasih, Najma's father. 'She studied hard and read books and magazines. She studied the Qur'an but would always challenge the ideas of the mullahs, especially about equality.'

One time, Najma accosted Mullah Kefayatullah, the senior scholar at the family's local mosque in Shah Shahid. 'A Muslim man,' she said, 'can make a *nikah* [the Islamic ceremony for legal marriage] with a Christian, but a Muslim woman cannot. Why is this?' Mullah Kefayatullah said he would come back to her with an answer, but never did.

In 2018, as part of her second-year practical curriculum at university, Najma worked at a local television station, Khurshid TV. At the end of that year, while she continued her study, she took a part-time job at Zan TV, the only station in Afghanistan run exclusively by women. Fereshta encouraged Najma, telling her she could become a legend of the media industry like TOLONews' Anisa Shaheed (in April 2021, Shaheed would be named Afghan Journalist of the Year). When Najma left after six months to start at the health-themed Jahan E Sehat TV, Wasih, who had trained as a doctor, would stay up late helping his daughter with research for her segments. 'She made me crazy with all her questions,' he says.

A workmate at Jahan E Sehat, 22-year-old Zuhal, became one of Najma's closest friends. 'We were always together outside work,' says Zuhal. 'We were only separated by the night. We were like sisters and eventually our families became friends as well.' On Friday, they would shop for clothes and jewellery at their favourite malls—the Gulbahar Centre, Mubarak Centre and Kot-e Sangi Mall—and share chicken pizza at Yummy restaurant in Shahr-e Naw. Zuhal called Najma 'Najo' for short.

Since she'd started presenting on TV, Najma had received a constant stream of messages from admirers, sometimes several in a single day, many from as far away as America. One Afghan from the diaspora in the United States offered to buy Najma a car and gold jewellery, once sending $100 via a friend to help her with her university fees.

Najma herself admired a neighbour in their Russian Embassy neighbourhood. 'They never spoke,' says Zuhal. 'Only with their eyes.' But Rohina, a friend Najma made at her next job, at the Kabul-based YouTube channel *Afghan Insider*, which produced programs on Afghan food and culture and developed a wide audience among the Afghan diaspora, says, 'Najma wasn't interested in getting married in the short term. First, she wanted to achieve her own independence.'

Wasih concurs: 'During her last semester, she made around 36 000 Afghani [approximately US$450 at the time], which she used to pay her university fees. She would also use her salary to buy food for people displaced from their homes by the war.' What Wasih doesn't mention is that Najma was also supporting her own family.

Wasih had stopped practising medicine long ago, opening a franchise for an Iranian paint manufacturer in Kabul after returning to the Afghan capital in the early 2000s, before his family followed in 2011. But after investing tens of thousands of dollars and having several buyers default on payments, he went bankrupt. He sold his three homes, the family's gold, and his treasured Swiss watch, a Rado. Wasih took the remaining paint from the business and opened a small store in Shah Shahid where he also rented a home for the family. 'It was enough to survive,' he says, 'but, after two years, all the paints expired. I cried. I had nothing to run my life. Anything of value I had, I sold. I did daily labour, sold homemade medical ointments, and worked as a guard for 15 000 Afghani per month' (less than US$200). Wasih's eldest son, Wasil, who was living in the United States, would also send US$250 to the family most months.

When the COVID-19 pandemic struck in early 2020, Kabul's already floundering economy stagnated, and survival for Wasih and the Sediqis became even more of a challenge. Wasil could no longer afford the monthly payments from the US and Abdul Wasih's other revenue streams dried up. His wife's contract at the Ministry of Foreign Affairs, where she worked in administration, was discontinued. They moved the family to a smaller home behind the war-ravaged remains of the former Soviet Embassy in southern Kabul and began trying to sell Wasih's paintings of fantastical landscapes. He'd taught himself to paint in the past, for pleasure, and had sold his canvases in the bazaar for between 1000 and 1500 Afghani (US$12.50–US$18), but after trying to reignite his former passion, he found 'many similar paintings made by machines in China'. The family became almost entirely reliant on Najma's monthly salary of 12 500 Afghani (US$120 at the time) at *Afghan Insider* and the business Wasiq had established, completing application forms for those seeking the new electronic national identity cards, or *Tazkera*, for 100 Afghani (US$1.25) each.

'That's why Najma was determined to work, despite all the problems she'd face,' says Rohina. Najma's drive was always, at least in part, pragmatic—she wanted to support her family. Zuhal says, 'Her distant relatives are narrow-minded and suggested Najma should stop her work.' They couched apprehension about how her work would affect their family's reputation as concern for her safety. 'It would cause her problems someday,' they'd say. But her immediate family, says Zuhal, 'encouraged Najma to continue her work, saying, "We support you."'

Soon after Najma started working with *Afghan Insider*, Wasih found a note addressed to him, written on lined paper and stamped with the Taliban's insignia, outside their house in the Russian Embassy neighbourhood. The letter warned of the consequences of allowing his daughter to continue her work in the media. 'I thought maybe it was relatives,' says Wasih, 'or people from the neighbourhood.' He ignored the letter and hid it from Najma.

Of his six children, Najma was the one Wasih felt closest to. 'Our father cherished her especially,' says Fereshta, to whom Najma also looked up. 'She became a bit lonely when I was married and would often visit our home'—especially when she became an aunt after Fereshta gave birth to a girl. Meanwhile, of her siblings, it was Wasiq, the next eldest, to whom Najma was closest. They fought and argued constantly, Fereshta says. 'Wasiq would use Najma's body spray and she'd yell at him. Another time, on the birthday of a friend of Najma's, Wasiq gifted the friend a necklace and bracelet that belonged to Najma.' He drove her crazy, Fereshta admits, but they 'were good partners as well. They were always loyal and committed to one another'.

< >

On 15 August, the day the Taliban took control of Kabul, Najma rode by taxi into Kabul City. Outside Pul-e Khishti Mosque, beside a wide bridge that spanned a bend in the Kabul River, Najma purchased a folding knife with a matte silver blade and a steel handle with a black camouflage pattern. Both Najma and Wasiq wanted to leave the day the Taliban came to Kabul, but Wasiq didn't fear them the way Najma did. He was worried that he'd be prevented from continuing his studies, but, Wasih says, it was Najma who 'believed she was under direct threat. And, personally, I was very worried for her'.

When Najma showed her father the knife she'd bought, she told him, 'Before they take me, I will kill myself.' Wasih responded, 'Before you kill yourself, kill them, then you will be a martyr.'

Najma and her friends had been as surprised as everyone else at the speed with which the Taliban took control of the country. 'Al Jazeera said the Taliban would come in 90 days,' says Rohina. 'I was planning to leave in the second month.' Though neither she nor Najma had passports, they had planned to apply. 'We never thought the Taliban would come so quickly,' she says.

Najma stopped going to work at *Afghan Insider*. Then, on the morning of 19 August, before she made her first attempt at entering the airport, she sat on her bed and recorded a video which would be published later that day. 'Dear viewers,' she began, 'you might be thinking that Najma is always wearing attractive outfits, a smile, and is full of joy. But since the Taliban has come to power everything has changed. We don't have the courage to leave home, go to work, the office, or to school or university. So we are all just staying in our homes … Though the Taliban claim a lot of things, like "We don't have problems with girls studying or working outside the home," the stories and experiences from the past have taught us that we can't believe them, and we can no longer go to work, school or university with the same assurance that we had previously … Therefore, we decided to record a final video clip at home to say goodbye. We ask for your prayers.'[1]

Najma and her friends started taking precautions. When she left home, Najma would wear an undercap beneath her headscarf in order to conceal her hairline. 'We heard about what was happening in the provinces,' says Rohina. 'About girls being taken from home to be married. Even in the best case, we thought, "We'll lose all our freedoms."'

Najma completed some forms that proliferated on social media purporting to be asylum applications for Canada and Germany, but she received no response. She sent email addresses for what she said were organisations offering opportunities to evacuate to Australia and Canada to Mujda Bahar. 'Please tell your father to send his documents to these email addresses,' she told her.

But all their efforts came to nothing, and on 25 August, Najma wrote to Rohina: 'There is no more hope.'

'We didn't have a specific plan,' says Rohina, 'But we knew that if they came to our homes, we'd prefer to kill ourselves by our own hands.'

< >

Abdul Nizam was lecturing in counter-intelligence at the Department of Regional Studies at the National Intelligence Academy in the neighbourhood of Afshar when the Taliban took control of Kabul. 'Teaching about the Taliban's activities in Afghanistan,' says Nizam, 'inside the NDS, where the Taliban and Daesh had a lot of sources, I was sure they would never forget and that the Taliban would surely kill us.'

Ever since the Taliban had signed the Doha Agreement with the US in February 2020 and shifted their focus from large-scale attacks to a more discreet campaign of targeted assassinations, Nizam had felt hunted. When one of his young sons was stopped by a man he didn't recognise and asked which families on their street owned motorcycles, Nizam, who was one of only two bike owners, assumed it was part of a Taliban surveillance operation. Just as he taught his students in their earliest classes at the NDS academy, Nizam invoked basic counter-intelligence tactics, changing his routines, wearing local clothes rather than the Western outfits he favoured, and moving his family out of his father-in-law's house in the neighbourhood of Taimani.

Nizam's wife Zara had endured the civil war from 1992 to 1996 as a teenager in the Taimani house. And in October 2001, she'd lived in its basement during the American bombing raids that precipitated the Taliban's collapse. The two had met soon after, in early 2002, when they both enrolled at an English-language institute. By then in her mid-twenties, Zara had yet to shake the restrictions and fears of the five years she'd spent living under the Taliban, and she wore a burqa to and from the institute, where she had enrolled under a pseudonym: Zohra. 'I wasn't beautiful,' says Zara, 'but he was impressed by my character. We were both fond of calligraphy and he enjoyed my poetry.' Nizam convinced an administrative worker to track down the address of 'Zohra', and then he travelled to Taimani and introduced himself to her parents. After Nizam expressed his intention to marry Zohra, the confused parents denied knowing any such person. Once the misunderstanding was resolved and Zara was informed, she quit the English course and never returned. A year and a half of visits from Nizam's family followed. Zara says that 'although he wasn't rich, my father saw Nizam was educated and that he would go on to get a good job, and they finally agreed to the marriage'. Nizam and Zara had two boys and two girls—the oldest, Mujda Bahar, was named after spring, on the first day of which she was born in 2004.

As the bodies of NDS officers, as well as journalists, activists and moderate religious figures, piled up across Afghanistan throughout 2020 and the first six months of 2021, Nizam regretted ever accepting his first job with the Afghan spy agency. It was an organisation, he realised, that one could not simply leave when they wanted. 'Unless I could get political support or a reference from a senior official,' he says, 'I had no chance of leaving.' After the initial move from Zara's childhood home, in the four months before August 2021, the family moved a total of four times in an effort to keep ahead of Taliban assassins.

On the morning of 15 August, Nizam joined a frantic effort to destroy documents inside his office at the NDS training facility. He left for home at midday and, after battling through the chaos on the roads, arrived there two hours later. When he told Zara he hadn't managed to collect his own personal files and documents, they decided to return on Nizam's motorcycle. By the time they arrived, however, the uniformed guards at the entrance were gone, and, afraid Taliban fighters might have already occupied the training centre, they turned around and rode home. Under the assumption the Taliban now had access to his personal documents, Nizam started taking even greater precautions. He spent alternate nights with extended family and at a hotel in Kabul's sprawling Mandayee Market that was run by a family friend.

Two colleagues who fronted up to the NDS training facility on 16 August to collect personal belongings were surprised to be permitted inside with a Taliban escort. Before they left, however, they were given an ominous warning. 'Now we're under the watch of the international community,' said the Talib who had been ordered to escort the former NDS officers, 'but as soon as we get international approval, then we'll bring you all to justice.'

Zara says, 'We heard the Taliban were doing search operations, and one night we emptied a kitchen cupboard in which Nizam could hide if they arrived at the door. I sent emails to the embassies of Canada, Britain and the US. Time after time I'd check my phone, expecting a response. When none came, that's when we decided to go to the airport altogether.' She adds: 'We were sold to the Talibs. The flock of sheep was tied up and the fox was called to come and eat.'

‹ ›

It was Najma's cousin Shahid who prompted the second attempt by her family and Bahar's at entering the airport. He had tried to convince Najma and her brother Wasiq to join him in the repeat effort, but they declined, saying their father had forbidden them from going to the airport again. So, at midday on 26 August, he called Abdul Nizam, with whom he had remained in contact since they'd met outside Cohan Village during their first attempt a week earlier. 'Teacher,' he said to Nizam, 'let's go.'

'I was reluctant,' says Nizam. 'I was analysing all available information and assessed that, without the correct documentation, it was impossible. Yet, somehow, he managed to convince me.'

Nizam informed Zara. But recalling how they'd become trapped in the crowd last time, he concluded it was too dangerous to take the family again. 'I decided to go myself,' he says. 'I would go abroad and then work to get my family out.' When Bahar begged him to let her come, he told his eldest daughter her mother would need her help looking after her young brothers. While he showered, Zara laid out a clean *peran tunban*. As he left the house, she told her husband, 'Be strong and committed to your decision and I'm sure you will succeed.'

‹ ›

Corporal Joseph Russell was supposed to be taking leave from deployment in the Middle East in August. He and his platoon-mates from Ghost Company, 2nd Battalion, 1st Marines were in Jordan and had been planning tours to Petra and Bethany Beyond the Jordan, where John the Baptist is said to have christened Jesus. But on 14 August, Russell was told in relation to Afghanistan: 'Y'all are going.'

In April 2021, after President Biden had announced the 31 August deadline for the final military withdrawal from Afghanistan, plans for a possible Non-combatant Evacuation Operation went into effect, and in June, the Marines from Ghost Company were given training in case they were called in to take part. At Saudi Arabia's Prince Sultan Air Base, where temperatures during the day reached 48 degrees Celsius, Russell and fellow Marines role-played Afghan asylum seekers while others were trained in crowd-control techniques in a simulated holding area. 'We would mess with them,' says Russell, 'kind of stress them out a little bit. But it wasn't anything super intense.' The leadership 'were expecting us to be TSA', he continues, referring to the Transportation Security Administration officers who handle security in American airports.

Since their training, Russell and the Marines had been keeping a close eye on developments in Afghanistan. 'We knew the Taliban were rapidly taking over the country,' he says. By the time a deployment to Kabul looked like a realistic possibility, 'we figured we'd show up and [the Taliban] would be trying to get [into the airport], because at that point, we had no idea we were going to work out a peace agreement'. Russell adds: 'I was really excited. We thought we were going to show up and get into gunfights and stuff like that.' But, when he stops to think about it, he admits that, if the Taliban had wanted to take the airport, there was no way they could have prevented it.

Ghost Company left Jordan for Kuwait on 16 August. 'At first,' says Russell, 'we were full of excitement, and then we saw the videos of people storming the airfield. That's when we were like, "Yeah, this is going to be wild."'

Russell was born in California in 1999 and adopted by a family from Austin, Texas. He joined the Marines in 2016, at 17, after completing a recruitment postcard with a photo of a drill team that had come in the mail. 'There was a lot of talk about Iraq and Afghanistan and how we were defending freedom or whatever,' says Russell. 'I just joined because I wanted to go to combat.'

Russell had wanted to go straight into the infantry, where he figured he would have the best chance of a combat deployment. But with all of the infantry places already filled in his intake, Russell instead trained as a radio operator, a role in which, he thought, he might eventually get attached to an infantry unit. From 2018 through to the beginning of 2020, Russell was assigned to an artillery unit. 'I was not a happy camper,' he says. 'That unit wasn't my place and I didn't really get along with anyone there. It was the people and the culture they had—they weren't focused on the right thing, which was being combat-effective.'

In early 2020, he transferred to Headquarters Battery, where, he says, 'My job was to set up radios for important people.' Again, Russell was disillusioned by the Marines' reverence for the superficial. 'They were focused on how clean everyone's uniform was or how high your haircut was, and, honestly, that shit does not matter.' Three months later, Russell was sent to Fire Support Battery, which he describes as 'the battery for forward observers and JTACs [Joint Terminal Attack Controllers]', who control attack aircraft from the battlefield, and he was attached to 2nd Battalion, 1st Marines. 'I loved it,' says Russell. 'That was exactly where I needed to be: the infantry.'

On his assignment in Afghanistan, Russell says, 'Before we left Jordan we'd been told the Turks had taken machine-gun fire and that there was an attempted attack at a gate ... I honestly thought we were going to be in the middle of the city and it was going to be like Fallujah ... That's what they were telling us: "The country's collapsing and the Taliban are closing in on the airport."'

After arriving in Kuwait, Ghost Company discovered that the C-17 crew that had been slated to transport them to Kabul had been delayed by 24 hours due to ferrying evacuees from Hamid Karzai International Airport to Qatar. While the company waited, thousands of soldiers from the 82nd Airborne and 10th Mountain divisions arrived in Kabul, and by 18 August, a measure of control had been restored inside the airport. 'We thought we'd missed it,' says Russell.

Still, Russell's company commander rallied the Marines before they boarded their flight out of Kuwait. 'You're going to see things that are really going to bother you,' he said. 'You're going to see things you never thought you'd see and do things you never thought you'd do. But you've got a job to do and no-one's going to do it for you.'

It was dark when they finally lifted off. The Marines were up-kitted for the mission, wearing side armour and dual night-vision tubes and carrying the standard 180 rounds of ammunition. There were seats along the side of the C-17's hold, but most of the Marines, including corporal Russell, sat on the floor. Most of the men's faces were illuminated by smartphone screens. Some played video games while others watched news reports from Kabul. 'Holy shit! This is crazy,' said a Marine who was watching a video of the Afghans clinging to the side of the C-17 two days prior. Many of the Marines half-expected their plane to be turned around mid-flight because they were no longer needed.

Russell lay down, using a combat helmet as a pillow, and listened to music through headphones. 'The Lost Dog Street Band, Slipknot and Stevie Ray Vaughn,' he says. 'I wanted to listen to all my favourite music.'

The soldiers of Ghost Company, which consisted of the 1st, 3rd, 4th and headquarters platoons, touched down at Kabul's airport after midnight and were escorted to their sleeping quarters inside a gymnasium on the military side of the airfield. Russell sat on a treadmill—his bed—and got to work preparing radio equipment, while the other Marines slept. As a radio operator, Russell would ordinarily work side by side with the fire support team's JTAC. However, because of the nature of the mission to Kabul, there was little need for a fire support team, and so, after their first day—19 August—Russell and his JTAC, corporal Josh Christensen, fell in with the other Marines from 1st platoon working at Abbey Gate. The usual adherence to a chain of command was all but done away with. 'Anybody could have been in charge,' says Russell. 'There were times when a lance corporal would say something and I'd do it.'

At Abbey Gate, Russell either worked the main gate or the line, as the Marines referred to the narrow pathway running between the canal and the airport perimeter, from where they secured the entrance and helped those with the required documents from the canal, or drove an airport tug they'd commandeered—they'd named it Casper for its colour and the company's namesake—and ferried people and pallets of water to and fro.

When Ghost Company was first dispatched to the south-eastern corner of the airport on the night of 19 August, the crowd outside was pushing directly against the first of three heavy sliding doors that, combined, made up Abbey Gate. 1st platoon was ordered to push the crowd back several hundred metres in order to give them and the other international forces room to process those being admitted. Russell, who was pitching in with whichever of the three other platoons required it, joined the Marines from 1st platoon. They linked arms and, for more than six hours, from sunset until the early hours of the following morning, they used brute force to push the crowd—which stretched from one side of the street to the other and extended around 200 metres from the gate—300 metres back, beyond the main entrance to the Baron Hotel, to where the Taliban had a line of their own. The Taliban fighters then manoeuvred shipping containers forward to separate the two lines and began passing potential evacuees through the gaps in-between.

'At one point, I looked around a storage container just to see what was going on,' recalls Russell, 'and there was a Taliban guy standing there. He just looked at me and we did that thing where you make eye contact and give a head nod. I never thought in a million years I'd do that to a Taliban [fighter].'

The temperature during the day averaged in the mid-30s, and containing the unrelenting crowd was physically exhausting. Before 25 August, when Ghost Company started trying to rotate platoons on and off, the Marines slept when and where they could. After midnight one night, Russell even fell asleep standing up, while guarding Casper near the Marines' makeshift barracks in the gymnasium. But, as Russell had found at boot camp in 2017, it was the mental challenges that were the most demanding. After loading Casper with around 50 cases of bottled water one day, he and Christensen drove out through Abbey Gate to where the Marines' line met the Taliban's. After they'd deposited the water and were on their way back to Abbey Gate, the crowd swarmed the tug, trying to reach the few cases the two Marines had held onto after the delivery drop. Russell looked back and saw, standing still, in the middle of the road, with the crowd swirling around him, a father wearing a powder blue *peran tunban*, and carrying what appeared to be a dead boy, probably his son, in his arms. Russell wondered whether the boy might still be alive if he'd delivered the water 10 minutes earlier. He wanted to take the boy and the man to the hospital. But the boy was likely dead, so what good was a hospital now, he asked himself. Besides, maybe others would die if he stopped delivering water.

At the canal, the Marines comprised the largest contingent of the foreign forces, but there were also conventional forces from

Great Britain and Germany, as well as special forces from Belgium, Canada, France, Finland, the Netherlands, Australia, Spain, Italy and Portugal. 'One minute we'd be holding people back, telling them to stop pushing,' says Russell, 'and the next we're looking at their documents.' They would pull out 10 or so people who met the criteria for evacuation and escort them along the airport side of the canal, inside Abbey Gate and onto a waiting minibus, which would take them to the terminal. 'But it was very frustrating,' he continues. 'One minute we'd be told to look for American passports, visas and SIV [Special Immigrant Visa] applications, and the next minute it would be "Only passports" or "Only visas". One person would come to you and you'd be like, "No, you have the wrong documents," but 10 minutes earlier they had the right documents.' Russell says of the State Department, 'Every hour they would change the criteria, and sometimes they weren't taking anybody because it was so backed up.'

The hardest part of all for Russell was when he was told to return people to the canal who had been pulled out of it. On 19 August, a kind of holding area was established inside Abbey Gate for 'rejects', as the Marines and other international troops referred to those they had allowed inside but who had been declined by State Department officials or their equivalents from other countries further down the line. 'There was an old man, maybe 70, his daughter, whose leg was in a cast, and two little kids,' says Russell. He guessed they had been pulled inside after a crowd crush so the woman's broken leg could be treated, but were then found not to have any documents. 'I had to escort them all the way down to Abbey Gate, 100-plus-yards.' They walked slowly, the old man with his hand in the small of his daughter's back as she hobbled on her injured leg. 'They were very respectful,' says Russell. 'People who really wanted to leave and made fake documents or just tried the best with what they had—they understood. Like, "We tried."'

On 25 August, corporal Russell was on the canal when he was told by another Marine, 'Hey, you need to kick this kid out.' The boy was around 12, and he was with a younger boy of maybe eight.

Russell assumed they were brothers. They had no documents and were otherwise alone. Russell didn't know whether the boys' family had already made it inside the airport or whether they had come alone and somehow squeezed past the first line of foreign forces. The 12-year-old 'was crying and pulling at my sleeves and saying, "Sir, please, my family! My family!"' says Russell, who sensed the boy was trying to tell him their parents were inside the airport. 'I had to shove him out and send him back into the crowd,' he says. 'Fuck. That was really hard. I felt like I was essentially sending people to their deaths.'

< >

Late on the afternoon of 25 August, all three platoons from Ghost Company were stretched for 300 metres along the walkway beside the canal from Abbey Gate when word came over the radio of an imminent IED threat. Abbey Gate had been inundated with people who had left other gates that had been closed because of the threat, and the crowd had ballooned. The Marines were told to be on the lookout for a man in a tan–pink *peran tunban*, clean-shaven, carrying a black bag with a pink arrow: 'If you see him and can shoot him, shoot him.'

Soon after nightfall, Russell's first sergeant approached and said regarding the IED threat, 'Well, it's imminent. It's going to happen.' Minutes passed and the Marines and other foreign forces were told to get down on the ground. 'It's going to go off,' said the first sergeant. When nothing happened, Russell's commanding officer ordered close to 100 Marines from the three platoons to begin peeling back, one by one, from the farthest point along the canal, forfeiting the walkway on the airport side to the crowd and reassembling behind Abbey Gate.

Although the bomber's presumed target of foreign troops had disappeared, the attack was still expected that night. Russell and his JTAC friend Christensen were put in charge of a four-wheel-drive Gator, one of three vehicles that would be used to carry victims to the airport hospital in the event of an attack. Russell and Christensen slept a few hours in the Gator, waiting for the attack—Russell tucked a Dutch flag behind his head as a pillow.

The next morning, a single platoon of Marines was stationed along the canal. With the reduced numbers outside the wire to control the crowd, and with the other airport gates still closed because of the ongoing threat alert, Abbey Gate became more crowded and the people there even more desperate. 'A lot of parents were either throwing their kids to us or handing them over to get them through, and safe, so they didn't get trampled,' says Russell. He and the others manning the casualty evacuation vehicles set up a 'miniature orphanage' just inside the perimeter at Abbey Gate. Throughout the day, Russell and Christensen ferried the attached navy corpsmen who were carrying the babies and young children to where the Norwegian hospital staff and others were running a much larger orphanage of sorts. 'We would drive a kid or a couple of kids and come back and there would be more,' says Russell.

One of those with whom Russell had become friendly since deploying earlier in the year was a navy corpsman attached to Ghost Company named Matt Soviac. Soviac was the oldest child of parents who were well known in their hometown of Milan, Ohio, for the several other children they'd adopted, and for whom Soviac cared before becoming a father himself. 'Every time I saw him that day,' says Russell, 'he had a baby.'

Soon after 4 p.m., the Marines were again notified of an imminent IED threat. An hour later they were given a countdown to when the blast was expected: 'It's going to happen in 20 minutes … it's going to happen in 10 minutes … it's going to happen in five minutes.' But the countdown lapsed, and with no explosion, combined with the previous night's false alarm, Russell and the others from Ghost Company grew sceptical.

Just before 6 p.m., Russell and Christensen were returning to Abbey Gate with their corpsman passenger after another trip to the hospital with a child. 'You know you just saved that baby's life?' said the corpsman. Russell shrugged it off—'Sure, whatever'—and the

three continued on, around the start of the runway, back towards
Abbey Gate.

‹ ›

Abdul Nizam took a shared taxi to Pashtunistan Square in central
Kabul, passing the Serena Hotel, where hundreds crowded outside the entrance in the hope of boarding one of the bus convoys
to the airport that were being organised by Qatari diplomats. From
Pashtunistan Square, he rode another shared taxi to Macroyan 4 and
then walked to the Ahmad Yar petrol station on Jalalabad Road,
opposite the office of a local TV station, where Shahid had suggested they meet. From there, the two walked north along the road,
through the ramshackle neighbourhood of Yakatoot, towards the
airport. They were aiming for the same entrance they had tried a
week prior: Abbey Gate. This time, however, they were hoping to
avoid the crowds and the vicious Taliban fighters trying to control
them that had become a fixture of the area between that gate and
the airport's main entrance.

Yakatoot was a labyrinth of winding streets, laneways and paths,
most of which were inaccessible to vehicles, and Shahid hoped it
would deter others from trying the same route. They walked for
half an hour, stopping occasionally to ask locals to confirm they
were heading in the right direction. Nizam had never been to
Yakatoot before and was surprised to see a football field–sized area
of farmland filled with rows of iridescent-green vegetable leaves
amid the urban sprawl. They passed the home from which a group
of Taliban fighters had launched a mortar assault on the airport in
September 2017, on the day of a visit by the US secretary of defense
and NATO's secretary general in the wake of Trump's South Asia
Strategy announcement. Another house they passed was mistakenly
struck by an American Hellfire missile, fired in response to the
Taliban attack—it was occupied at the time only by a local family.

Further on, irrigation water from the farmland had flooded
the street. Nizam and Shahid continued on a raised footpath until

they reached a five-way intersection, asking again for directions and then following a narrow footpath until it reached the rear entrance to the Baron Hotel. Around 100 people were crowded outside the sliding steel security door, on which a sign, made from a row of A4 sheets and attached with masking tape, read in English: 'BRITISH PASSPORT HOLDERS'. They had been walking for 45 minutes when they passed another row of small farm plots where families sat against the side wall of Cohan Village, in the block of shade that it cast, and then the pathway opened up where it intersected with the sewerage canal.

Nizam barely recognised the service road where he and his family had met Shahid, Najma and Wasiq the week before. The Taliban had twice cleared crowds from the area that morning,[2] and the strip running alongside the canal was now virtually empty in comparison. He and Shahid wasted no time. 'There was an opportunity to get inside,' says Nizam. They walked halfway down the canal to where American Marines were lined up along the far side, in front of a guard tower that sat behind the airport perimeter wall; there were British soldiers and Italian and Australian special operators as well.

Shahid barely hesitated before lowering himself into the putrid cesspool from the low concrete wall that ran along the lip of the canal. Nizam stood on the wall, reasoning that it was only a few metres to where the Americans were standing and he could speak to them across the gap. Shahid waded through the shin-deep stream and, holding out a plastic folder full of documents, caught the attention of a Marine. Sensing the Marine's indifference, Nizam pulled his NDS ID card from his pocket and called out from the other side of the canal in English. The Marine raised his hands and said, 'Please, be patient.'

It was around 2 p.m. when Nizam called Zara. 'He told me he had reached the airport and that, this time, the crowd was smaller and he hoped to get inside,' says Zara. 'I told him, "Best of luck. Try to be committed and you will get inside."' When Nizam explained that he had heard rumours of an attack planned for one of the airport gates, Zara dismissed them. 'This is just a rumour,' she said. 'It's a rumour to discourage the people from coming to the airport.'

While Nizam spoke to Zara, Shahid called his cousin Wasiq, who was in his room at home with Najma, playing on a PlayStation with their mutual friend Milat. 'Come to the airport,' he told Wasiq. 'The crowd isn't so big.' But Wasiq's father was home and wouldn't let him leave. Abdul Wasih knew that Najma and Wasiq hadn't entirely given up hope of making it inside the airport and aboard one of the scores of planes flying out each day. But he had also heard the growing rumours of a security threat at the airport, and he had stayed home throughout the day to ensure they did, too.

'I kept them at home until 4 p.m.,' says Wasih, at which time he was called by an old friend who asked him, as a former doctor, to make a house visit. As soon as he had left, Wasiq and Milat knocked on the door of Najma's room—she was now sitting on her bed reading the Qur'an—and told her to get ready, because they were going to meet Shahid and Nizam at the airport. Najma was reluctant to go against her father's wishes, but she didn't want to be left behind. Wasiq packed a small bag with some clothes and some food left over from Fereshta's birthday dinner the night before, and the three walked from the house and along a laneway to where it deposited them on Darulaman Road.

A local taxi driver, Jamshid, who had become a friend of Wasih's family, was waiting in his usual spot near the entrance to the lane. As they set off, Jamshid began quizzing Wasiq. 'What are you doing at the airport?' he asked.

'Because I know English, I'm going to help with translation.'

'So why do you have your bag? And what about your sister?' he said, inquiring about Najma, who was in the back seat with Milat.

'She is translating for women,' said Wasiq.

'Then why do you have luggage?'

Wasiq smiled, conspiratorially. 'It's okay,' he said, bringing the conversation to an end.

As they drove, Najma called Bahar. 'We're moving towards the city,' she said. 'You should come as well, we have a good chance to get inside today.'

Bahar says she told Najma that only her father was going to the airport, that he wouldn't allow her to come too. 'She was upset,' says Bahar, 'but I told her, "This is my father's decision."'

Jamshid dropped Najma and the others in front of the Ministry of Interior Affairs compound at the western end of the airport. 'Najma gave me 500 Afghani and I returned 200,' says Jamshid. 'They opened the doors and said goodbye.'

Shahid was calling Wasiq regularly to check on the group's progress. Jamshid had dropped them several kilometres from Abbey Gate, and Nizam was growing impatient. 'I was being childish,' he says, 'complaining of a sore back from the bag I was carrying. I wanted to try again with the Americans, myself, but Shahid convinced me to wait.'

Just after 5 p.m., Wasiq called Shahid and told them they were close. But the crowd had grown even bigger in the time it had taken the three to travel to Abbey Gate. So they gripped one another by the hand and thrashed their way towards the canal.

At around 5.30 p.m., Shahid finally saw his cousins and Milat waving their hands above their heads as they continued shoving their way through the crowd. Five minutes later, they had made it to where Shahid and Nizam were standing on the concrete-topped stone wall on the edge of the canal. The crowd surged and swayed, and Shahid held Nizam's hand to prevent him from losing his balance and falling onto the people standing in the canal.

'The crowd was extreme,' says Nizam. 'Only a few people were being allowed into the airport. Some people were climbing over the walls, but the Americans on the other side would catch them, bring them to the entrance and put them in the water. Najma and Wasiq were pressed up against me. Shahid was trying to get into the water but the canal was full of people. None of us were able to get in.'

Among the crowd was Abdul Rahman Al-Logari, a former engineering student turned Islamic State Khorasan Province (ISKP) militant. Al-Logari had been arrested four years earlier in India, transferred to Afghanistan, jailed at the Parwan Detention Facility at Bagram Airfield, and was among the thousands of prisoners indiscriminately released by the Taliban on 15 August.[3] Carrying around 15 kilograms of explosives in a bag or vest packed with ball bearings, Al-Logari struggled through the crowd until he was opposite where the Marines from 1st platoon were spread along the pathway.

Around the same time, Nizam, Shahid and the others were desperately trying to attract the attention of the same Marines. 'We were watching them check others' documents,' says Nizam. 'I was trying to show them mine.'

< >

That same afternoon, I had ridden my motorcycle through the city to Darulaman, on the southern outskirts of Kabul, and more than 15 kilometres from the airport. I had gone in search of changes in the urban landscape to photograph. Away from the chaos unfolding at the airport, the city was undergoing an abrupt and unceremonious transition. The Taliban's intolerance of superficial expressions of heresy and the public's desperation to avoid their ire meant that many of the symbols that had come to typify the post-2001 Afghan capital were being stripped from its facades.

The Afghan flags tied to car aerials, attached to government buildings and vehicles, and hanging from light posts on the city's main roads, were being replaced by the Taliban's austere white banner; murals depicting valiant soldiers, female musicians and 'national heroes' of past eras were painted over in favour of Qur'anic script; with the war ostensibly over, some of the foreboding concrete blast walls on which many such murals were painted were removed with cranes, and the steel barriers preventing trucks carrying explosives from entering the centre of the city were cut down with blowtorches; the ubiquitous windscreen decals glorifying anti-Taliban martyrs disappeared almost overnight; and the depictions of heavily made-up brides adorning beauty parlours were hastily torn down or covered with spray-paint.

When I rode past a handmade Taliban flag attached to a bamboo pole at the entrance to the American University of Afghanistan (AUAF), at the end of Darulaman Road, I pulled over. The light from the setting sun was beginning to climb up the concrete perimeter wall. I introduced myself as a journalist to the lone Taliban guard and asked if I could photograph the entrance. The fighter asked me to come with him while he conferred with his commander.

In the two weeks since the Taliban had taken control of Kabul, being pulled in by fighters for questioning had become an almost daily routine. It was more of an inconvenience than anything else, and, aside from instances where tensions were high—outside airport gates and at protests where journalists were flailed with hosepipe, and punched and rammed with rifle butts, like everyone else—to me, the fighters were generally polite and apologetic.

The fighter drove me deeper inside the campus to speak with his superior. While I waited, messages started appearing on a WhatsApp group thread a fellow foreign journalist had initiated on 13 August for those planning to stay through the takeover. At 6.11 p.m., a message appeared from Marcus Yam, an American photographer: 'Did anyone hear about an explosion at the airport gate[?]' The threat of an attack at the airport had already been making the rounds among the journalists in Kabul. 'Just in case people are too busy to read news reports [at the moment],' Charlie Faulkner, a British journalist, had written on the same thread earlier that day, 'the threat of attack at the airport and processing centres today is very real.'

The night before, I had been at Abbey Gate for several hours, attempting to connect Afghans with Australian visas to Australian special forces members working the line with the Marines. I had dressed in local clothes and covered my head with a scarf in the hope I wouldn't stand out as a foreigner, and, with the help of a friend (the person who translated many of the interviews for this book), I waded into the crowd with one visa holder and left a family of six in a taxi a 20-minute walk further back. The three of us gripped one another's wrists, certain that if we let go we'd lose one another. I spoke to British soldiers on the line who told me the Australians were at the other end. They were not—they had packed up and were only hours from departing on the last Australian military aircraft. The crush of bodies, the noise, the adrenaline, the smell of sweat and faeces in the dark, was terrifying. I regretted bringing a bag with my camera; not for a second did I consider using it, and I was certain it would be torn from my shoulder as we pushed through the flow of the immovable crowd. We fell against mothers carrying babies, with the weight of hundreds of people behind us, and were flogged with electric cables by Taliban fighters. We looked into the canal, but it was so packed with people we couldn't see the water. At 10.30 p.m., diplomats who were trying to coordinate with the soldiers inside the airport told me I should leave immediately.

I was still waiting to be questioned by the Talib in charge of securing the AUAF as more details of the bombing started to trickle through on Twitter and the WhatsApp group.

'Explosion reported at East Gate.'

'I have someone at east gate and says there was no explosion.'

'It's been confirmed by DOD.'

'It's confirmed. Suicide attack at baron hotel gate. US soldiers injured.'

'ANYONE ON THIS GROUP NEAR AIRPORT LEAVE NOW. SECONDARY ATTACK POSSIBLE.'

'Turkish defence ministry has reported second explosion.'

'Updated reports indicated that at least 15 people were injured outside the Abbey Gate at Kabul Hamid Karzai International Airport (KBL/OAKB) when suspected Islamic State (IS) suicide bombers and gunmen attacked the Baron Hotel.'

At 6.30 p.m., half an hour after I was first pulled inside the AUAF, the Taliban fighters drove me back to the entrance in their commandeered police truck. They asked me to take their photo, then waved me off. Although there was still little understanding of the scale of human destruction caused by the bomb—there was only one—I tore through Kabul towards the nearest trauma hospital, arriving outside its main entrance 20 minutes later.

Scores of people were gathered at the entrance of Emergency Hospital, a trauma centre for the war-wounded run by the Italian NGO of the same name. Some had already been bandaged and discharged, walking with wrapped-up heads as they spoke into their phones. Families fought with hospital guards who were only allowing entry to the wounded. Bright coloured lights from the kebab restaurant across the road and floodlights on the hospital walls overpowered the dying daylight as, one after another, ambulances, police trucks and taxis pulled to a stop outside the entrance and offloaded the dead and wounded. Journalists and camera crews arrived. A woman with squiggles of dried blood down her face berated the foreigners among us for what we had brought to her country.

I had waited outside the hospital for casualties numerous times over the years, but I had never seen the number that were coming in this night. Another hospital, just a few kilometres away, was receiving patients at twice the rate.

< >

Corporals Russell and Christensen were a few hundred metres from Abbey Gate, driving their four-wheeler along the inside of the eastern perimeter of the airport, when they noticed people standing on top of walls outside the airport, craning their necks towards the canal. A group of Marines were running in their direction. They pulled the Gator up to speak to another Marine JTAC. 'The IED went off,' he said. No-one in the Gator had heard a thing. They continued on to Abbey Gate and found a group of Marines inside the outermost gate who Russell says were 'freaking out—like "Okay, what do we do? Do we go in? What are we supposed to do?" The squad leaders were trying to gather their guys and work out what they needed to do.'

Russell was waiting inside an inner gate, trying to work out what to do himself, when a Marine drove in from the outer gate on Casper, with two soldiers on the back. One was sitting up; he was bloody and had his face bandaged up. The other was lying face down. Russell and Christensen looked at one another. 'Fuck,' Russell said. 'This is real. This is happening.'

Russell lost track of Christensen and moved closer to the outer gate. He pulled out his mobile phone and messaged his mother to tell her he was okay—he expected their phones would soon be confiscated to prevent news leaking out. Russell saw a wounded woman lying on the ground, waiting to be tended to. The woman's daughter was beside her, covered in her mother's blood, and she was looking at Russell. 'I was about to go help them but was told, "No. Marines first! Marines first!"' A corpsman was working on two other casualties. Russell looked to his left and saw sergeant Nicole Gee. 'She was already dead,' he says. When Russell went to the casualty collection point and saw that each victim had at least two Marines working on them, he decided his job was to focus on security.

A Marine on top of a large Hesco barrier wedged into a corner between a shipping container and the perimeter was looking for others to help keep watch over the wall for follow-up attackers. Russell was helped onto the barrier and then joined two other Marines on the container. 'I looked in the canal,' says Russell, 'and there's just bodies ... everywhere. They're, like, piled on top of each other.'

Everyone in the canal looked suspicious. No-one listened to the Marines yelling at them to leave. Survivors stood and stared. One man, surrounded by dead bodies, laughed. Capsicum spray lingered in the air, leaking from punctured canisters on the tactical vests of wounded and dead soldiers. Scorch marks from the blast and scraps of flesh ran all the way to the top of the 7-metre-high fence on top of the Cohan Village wall.

A 10-year-old boy was pointing at Russell and the Marines on the shipping container while talking to somebody. 'I put the reticle of my rifle on his face,' says Russell. 'I put my rifle on this kid's face and he's looking at me and I'm thinking, "I'm about to shoot this kid in the head. I'm about to kill a kid because he might be trying to get me killed."'

The boy ran off, and Russell and the Marines on the container threw flashbangs into the canal to try to disperse the crowd wading among the bodies. When two machine gunners came up to replace them, Russell turned around and found that all the casualties inside Abbey Gate had been taken away. He jumped down and found Christensen, and the two knelt and trained their rifles on a guard tower on the Cohan Village perimeter, in case a shooter appeared. Beside Russell, a medical bag was on the ground, open, its contents spilling out and surrounded with wrapping from plastic wound dressings. A military boot was on its side nearby. 'That's when I realised I was terrified,' he says. 'I was shaking and huffing, like when you're about to start crying.' The two soldiers stayed for 10 minutes before being replaced by another company of Marines and returning to the gymnasium. At that point, there were four Marines, all from 1st platoon, confirmed dead.

< >

When Abdul Nizam came to, he was immersed in bodies on the service road beside the canal. His whole left side was scorched and torn by shrapnel. Shahid was lying beside him. They were still holding hands, but Shahid was dead. 'Najma was still breathing,' says Nizam, but barely alive. He didn't know about Wasiq or Milat.

Zara was at home with Bahar when breaking news of the bombing at the airport flashed up on TOLONews. 'A lot of time has passed,' she said to herself. 'Hopefully it's a good thing that we haven't received any bad news.'

A young man wearing the same tan-coloured *peran tunban* as Nizam pushed him several hundred metres in a wheelbarrow from the site of the attack to a taxi in Yakatoot. If it weren't for Nizam's torn, bloodied clothes, they might have been teammates in a novelty wheelbarrow race. The man with the wheelbarrow called Zara, telling her: 'Your husband is injured, but not critical, so don't be worried.'

‹ ›

Sometime around 5.30 p.m., Abdul Wasih arrived home, having tended to his friend. When he found that Najma, Wasiq and Milat were gone, he called Najma. When she failed to answer, he immediately left home and found a taxi. 'When I reached close to the airport,' he says, 'I heard about the blast. I tried calling them many times but got no response.'

Taliban fighters had closed off all roads leading to Abbey Gate. Wasih instead directed the taxi to the nearest and largest hospital in Wazir Akbar Khan and went straight to where staff were waiting to unload the ambulances they were expecting from Abbey Gate. Four dead bodies were carried from the first ambulance. In the second ambulance was Najma. Her eyes were closed, as though she was resting. At first, all Wasih could find was one single wound the size of a bullet or a ball bearing in Najma's abdomen. She couldn't possibly be dead, he thought. Then he rolled her on her side and saw an open wound the size of a saucer on her back. Another ambulance arrived. Shahid was inside. He was dead too.

Wasih continued looking for Wasiq. At around 7.30 p.m., Wasiq's phone was finally answered. 'I'm sorry,' the person on the other end said, 'he is no longer in this world.' Wasih found where the man on the phone was standing by the body of a young man who had been laid in a body bag. Half his head had been shorn off by the blast, and what remained of his face was covered in blood. Wasih removed the shoes on the body and examined the feet with the torch on his phone. He had treated Wasiq's big toe, which he had broken playing soccer, the night before. He saw a blackened toe with a broken nail.

By the end of the night, Wazir Akbar Khan hospital would receive a total of 142 dead bodies. Emergency Hospital, where I had watched casualties arrive, received 16. Staff from both hospitals and survivors from the attack claimed, without conclusive evidence, that many of the dead were victims of gunshots fired in the aftermath of the blast.

Milat had survived the attack and was recovering in hospital with severe concussion. He had no recollection of what had put him there and no-one had yet told him the fate of his friends.

The following morning, several hundred friends and family crowded into a small cemetery not far from the former Soviet Embassy. The bodies of Najma, Wasiq and Shahid were buried side by side. Najma's grave was distinguishable from the others by the perpendicular head- and foot-stones, as is customary for female dead. The neighbourhood's local mullah presided over the burial and was joined by another who was unfamiliar to the mourners. As Wasih sobbed over the graves of his two children and his nephew, the congregation listened, incredulous, as the stranger, who they presumed was with the Taliban, scolded him: 'Why would you allow your children to leave? This is an Islamic country now and you allowed them to leave to a country of infidels.'

'We felt as if blood was pouring from our hearts,' says Wasih. 'There was nothing we could do. We just remained silent.'

< >

'I've never been in a room full of Marines completely quiet,' says Russell. The soldiers were told to hand in their phones, and when they'd done so, most sat and stared at nothing. After two hours, the company commander and staff sergeant arrived to conduct a ceremonial roll call. After calling out the names and ranks of three Marines present in the room and receiving a response, the names of eight Marines from Ghost Company and Matt Soviac, the navy corpsman Russell and Christensen had driven to the hospital with a baby earlier that day, were called three times. A bell then chimed three times for each of the dead.

Another two servicemen were killed, and 39 servicemen and women wounded in the attack. Later, the company Russell's had been replaced by returned with weapons, coated in smears of sticky blood, optics shattered, belonging to the dead and wounded.

After the ceremony, during which the bodies of the dead soldiers, lying in American flag–draped coffins, were carried up a ramp and into the belly of a C-17, Russell and the rest of Ghost Company were put on security duty on the flight line. 'It was something for us to do,' says Russell. 'We never went back to Abbey Gate.'

13

Hamid Karzai
International Airport

A military transport plane with a small American flag printed on its tail landed as the sun rose on the morning of 16 August. Captain Arman Malik watched as he sat on the bonnet of one of his humvees as 100 or more Marines ran down the aircraft's cargo door towards the international military hub some 500 metres to the east. Within an hour, Malik saw the Marines reappear on the flight line outside the military terminal before separating into smaller groups and dispersing.

Malik hadn't seen lieutenant-generals Sami Sadat and Haibatullah Alizai or defence minister Bismillah Khan Mohammadi since the early hours of that morning. He suspected they'd left on one of the charter flights organised by Assadullah Khalid. In fact, while Mohammadi had departed, the two younger generals were still in the plush JSOC offices on the southern side of the runway. (After receiving treatment at the airport hospital, Sadat would take a C-17 to Dubai on 19 August, where he would transfer to another flight to Birmingham in the United Kingdom. Alizai would leave on 25 August for the United States.)

When a group of some 30 troops hurried along the flight line between Malik and where three Mi-17 helicopters were parked, Malik, still dressed in his jungle camouflage, approached them and asked in broken English whether they would take the vehicles and weapons he was minding off his hands. The Marines were uninterested and continued on.

There were still only a few hundred American servicemen and women, Turkish soldiers and members of the CIA Strike Units dedicated to securing the airport. On its civilian side, after two commercial planes had departed in the night, thousands of Afghans had remained inside the passenger terminals, on top of and inside aircraft, and sprawled along the apron where they were parked. The arrival of the American military transport stirred the crowd, large portions of which began moving, tentatively at first and then with purpose, towards the tarmac.

A second American C–17 now landed, deposited more troops, and departed. By this time, the crowds from the civilian side had crossed the runway and were converging on the military terminals, barracks and maintenance buildings. A group of 30–40 men came towards Malik. He called out for them not to come closer and fired in the air when they ignored his warning. Some of the men, undeterred by the warning shots, continued approaching Malik. When one moved towards a humvee, Malik fired a round from his M4 between the man's legs.

'You're killing civilians now?' the man cried.

'I warned you,' said Malik, 'but you didn't listen.'

When the rest of the men again moved forward, Malik switched his M4 to 'continuous', pointed it towards the ground behind him, and held the trigger for a full second, letting off a burst of rounds that ricocheted from the concrete into the distance.

'This guy is crazy,' one of the men said as they turned and left.

At 9 a.m., the American troops whom Malik had spoken with about the weapons returned. They said they had no vehicles of their own and asked if they could use any of his. Malik unloaded several M240 machine guns from one of the ARU humvees and helped the Americans couple them to the turret mounts. In total, Malik parted with 11 humvees. He also gave the troops four single-use rocket launchers. 'They were very grateful,' he says.

Soldiers from the same unit returned several times over the next hour and a half. Each time, Malik gladly handed over more vehicles, until his fleet had shrunk to about 10 from the 30 he'd started the day with.

At 10.40 a.m., a new American team in a small convoy stopped alongside Malik. The troops were suspicious, questioning Malik and loading his weapons and crates of ammunition into their own vehicles. They then ordered him into a vehicle, preventing him from returning to his Ranger to retrieve his personal belongings, and drove him to their camp, past a cordon separating the Afghan and international sectors on the military side of the airfield. One of the troops told Malik to keep walking to the military passenger terminal. When the Americans outside the terminal forbade him entry, he merged with the crowd, some in ANSF uniforms, that was waiting beyond a gate where a statue of a golden eagle ordinarily greeted arriving soldiers and military contractors. Some of the men Malik had fired warning shots near earlier in the morning were in the crowd outside the gate and jeered at him.

Malik saw the unit to whom he had given the vehicles and started talking to an Afghan interpreter who was working with them: 'I told him I'd helped the unit and that all I wanted was help to go back to get my keys and cash.' Also in his Ranger was a set of civilian clothes. Malik had no intention of joining the hordes trying to flee the country aboard an evacuation flight, even after having off-loaded the KKA and ARU arsenal to the Americans. But if he was to make it through the Taliban fighters guarding the airport's gates, he would have to shed his uniform and blend in with the civilians. However, the American troops were preoccupied and barely registered Malik's request.

By now, major Behzad Behnam had started responding to Malik's messages, but he had few contacts among the conventional American forces with whom he suspected Malik was dealing, and he could provide scant help from Islamabad, Pakistan, where he was now marooned. Complicating matters for Malik, bedlam was breaking out across the airfield, with thousands of Afghans invading the tarmac, clinging to a taxiing C-17, and duelling for several hours with thin lines of American and Turkish soldiers in what looked like some kind of modern-day infantry charge.

By late that evening, several hundred more American troops had arrived in-between intermittent runway invasions, and aircraft were once again coming and going without interruption. Malik climbed into the cabin of one of three damaged Mi-17 helicopters that had sat discarded by the flight line for as long as he had been coming to the airfield. He lay on the dusty floor and slept fitfully for two or three hours amid the clatter of gunfire. It was the first time he'd rested since the night before the Afghan Government had collapsed.

'I hadn't eaten or drunk anything since it all began,' says Malik of the morning of 17 August. 'I tried many times to get to my clothes, but the Americans wouldn't allow me in.' He decided to forget his attire and the keys and cash he'd left in his Ranger. It had probably been looted by the crowds the previous day, anyway, he reasoned. Inside a maintenance workshop he found a pair of oversized jeans covered in motor oil. He pulled them on, tightened the waist with his army belt, and then slipped into a pair of rubber sandals he found outside the workshop's bathroom door. On top, he would make do with his threadbare undershirt.

When a few hundred Afghans broke free of the American lines on the commercial side of the airport and rushed to the idling transport planes on the military side, Malik ran to join them and was eventually herded across the runway to the civilian terminal buildings. Others who were trying to leave said the Taliban fighters at the main gate knew there were government soldiers inside and were checking the phones of anyone trying to leave, so Malik combed his phone for anything that might reveal details of his past life and deleted it all. But the Taliban fighters guarding the airport entrance were more focused on controlling the masses outside, and

Malik made his way out of the gate and into Airport Circle without incident. He began walking along the same road the KKA and ARU convoy had driven three days earlier, past the JSOC entrance halfway along the airport perimeter and towards Martyr's Square at the south-western corner of the airfield.

Malik tried to call his brother, but his phone wasn't allowing him to dial out. A wave of exhaustion suddenly overcame him. He was weak from hunger, his head pounded from dehydration, and his throat was as dry as the road. He had no cash for a taxi to reach his family in Emirate City. Each step became an ordeal. When a friend called, Malik asked him to rendezvous at Martyr's Square with some clothes and money.

'I was so hungry,' says Malik. 'I couldn't take another step.' So he sat on the median strip to rest. An ANA pick-up driven by a grizzled Taliban fighter rolled past. Six or eight young fighters, some wearing plundered ANA jackets in spite of the heat, stared out from the vehicle at the crowds. The crowds stared back.

A boy of four or five walked up to Malik. 'Uncle, if I ask you something will you grant my wish?'

'Okay, yes.'

The boy twice more asked Malik to confirm the request, and each time he agreed.

'Will you give me 10 rupees so I can eat something?'

'He didn't know I hadn't eaten myself for three days,' says Malik. 'He was just a little boy. He was in need and I couldn't help him.'

Epilogue

I had been thinking about a book set in Afghanistan since late 2020. The Doha Agreement, signed that February, was already working to the Taliban's advantage. Thousands of their prisoners had been released, and battlefield commanders were capitalising on the 'active defence' posture the Americans had pushed Kabul into adopting while being careful not to overextend and cause the Americans to stall their withdrawal. I saw the Doha Agreement as a death knell for the Afghan Government, but I never anticipated it would come so quickly.

The book I wanted to write would follow the theme I'd been following for several years. I would chart how the United States' refusal to reconcile with the ousted Taliban regime, and the ensuing occupation, ignited the insurgency, just as it had in Iraq. I would follow the lives of rural Afghans whose experience of the war, unlike those in Kabul who, while also encountering horrific violence, were given an array of new opportunities, was one of deprivation and disaffection—a story less often told.

Admittedly, the fascination with those living behind Taliban lines was amplified because their lives were virtually off-limits to journalists. An unspoken race for access among writers, photographers and filmmakers began, intensifying in recent years as the prospect of a Taliban return to power became increasingly likely.

After the signing of the Doha Agreement, with US air support curtailed and the Taliban enjoying a wave of international recognition, some commanders began to open the doors to their districts. I had already been reporting on the ruthless exploits of the CIA's Afghan proxies from the 01 National Strike Unit in Maidan Wardak—albeit from the relative safety of Kabul and the provincial capital, Maidan Shahr—when opportunities to visit the villages where they occurred began to arise from the middle of that year. Those trips, which, for security reasons, lasted one night at most, were indeed as fascinating as I had expected. They also vindicated the hypothesis that the punitive neglect of the rural class— particularly those in predominantly Pashtun districts—and the violent ordeals they'd endured living among—and, often in cahoots with—the Taliban, were creating an increasingly unbridgeable gap between rural Afghanistan and the central government. The lack of accountability for their suffering was self-defeating for the aggressors, and, for journalists, I believed, the war's essential theme.

It must be said that the Taliban's military victory would never have come without the ineptitude and malfeasance of successive administrations in Kabul and their armed forces, and the hubris of the American-led international military coalition. The Taliban's readiness to seize the advantage after the signing of the Doha Agreement did, however, expedite the eventual collapse that the agreement ensured. The realisation that the Americans were leaving, along with the military support and air power that had given Kabul a lifeline since 2015, was the final straw.

Aside from the almost daily guerrilla-style attacks by the Taliban and other anti-government groups in Kabul—'The years-long fears of the vehicle in front of you blowing up or the guy on the motorbike opening fire,' as a friend who read an early version of this book reminded me—the war in Afghanistan had been fought largely in remote districts since the early 2000s. As I wrote in the prologue to this book, once the momentum swung decisively in the

Taliban's favour in the spring of 2020, and areas under government control started shrinking to virtual islands accessible only by air, many rural battlegrounds fell silent. The lives of those who had gained the most since the Taliban's fall in 2001—lives that had overcome hardship and flourished, which I'd rarely been compelled to write about—were all of a sudden under threat. While their physical safety may not necessarily have been at risk, their personal liberty, the simple freedom to choose the trajectory of one's own life, certainly was. For them, life without choice was no life at all.

If the threat of such loss had instigated a change in what I felt was pertinent to write about, 15 August completed the about-face. With the Taliban's victory came a level of scrutiny and critique that no insurgency warrants, no matter the wrongs of the government it was trying to overthrow nor the infringements on human rights it would institute once in power.

Amid the chaos of that day, I hugged farewell a tearful Aziz Tassal, a journalist with whom I'd worked for years and grown to love for his gentle company and care for his wife, three cheeky young daughters and everyone with whom he'd worked. I'd spent a week sharing a room with him in Uruzgan earlier in the year, reporting for an article published by *The Monthly* where we traded stories about our mutual friend Aliyas Dayee, a journalist from Helmand who had been assassinated three months earlier (the article won the 2021 Walkley Award for long-form feature writing). He'd calmly taken control when the car he was travelling in with Nanna Muus Steffensen, a journalist and my housemate, came under fire during a Taliban ambush in Maidan Wardak some months before. But on 15 August, he was inconsolable. 'They betrayed us,' he sobbed, before undertaking his own harrowing journey to the United States with his family.

The next day I photographed Noorullah Shirzada, a photographer with Agence France-Presse, carrying his baby into the French Embassy. The photo was published the day after by the French newspaper *Le monde*. Farshad Usyan, a friend who I also consider Afghanistan's best photojournalist, was also there. His passport was inside the embassy awaiting a visa, but the Taliban weren't allowing him in. Phone calls were made and eventually someone called his name. He disappeared behind the gate before we got a chance to say goodbye.

That day, 16 August, was also when BBC correspondent Kate Clark was flown out of Kabul.

On 17 August, I was detained along with Victor Blue, the American photographer staying at my house, for ten hours inside a house in Wazir Akbar Khan that a senior Taliban commander had commandeered. Also in the house were its residents, a family whose patriarch was a senior government official from western Afghanistan. As foreigners, Blue and I never feared disappearing indefinitely into a Taliban prison, and we spent as much time calming worried friends and relatives on the phones we'd been allowed to keep as we did making efforts to secure our release. The most confronting aspect of that day was witnessing the fear roiling the family members, prisoners in their own home. I asked about the amnesty the Taliban had announced for members of the former government and security forces. Weren't they reassured? But no-one trusted the Taliban to keep to their word. 'As soon as they form their government,' one of the family members told us, 'they'll go after their enemies one by one.'

Esmat and Sebghat, Hamdullah Mohib's nephews, didn't depart as planned on 15 August, but they managed to board an evacuation flight, with the bag containing their uncle's personal effects, in the chaotic days that followed. 'They went through great hardship,' says Mohib, but 'they made sure they had that bag with them, even if it meant they had to leave their own belongings behind.'

Before dawn on 22 August, I rode on one of four buses transporting to the airport a total of around 140 Afghans who had been included in evacuation flight manifests. Among them were several journalists and Wahid, the long-time manager of the house whose lease I had taken over three years earlier (Mushu, the house dog, also survived the takeover). The irony that foreigners might help locals get through the Taliban checkpoints between the Serena

Hotel, where the buses were staged, and the airport was absurd and cruel. Once the convoys had passed through crowds of desperate Afghans also trying to enter, the incessant gunfire from the CIA proxy unit guarding the entrance, and inside the gate, an initial wave of relief was swamped by a deluge of grief as those on board, who for days could think only of getting inside the airport for an evacuation flight, now realised it was time to say farewell to their country.

Rateb Noori, Radio Free Europe's Dari Language Service's editor-in-chief, stared glassy-eyed towards where American military aircraft engines roared at an idle. Once we'd parked on the edge of the flight line on the military side of the airport, with the dawn painting the airfield in soft blue, I photographed Omaid Khalil Rahman, a journalist with whom I'd worked over the years, and the brother of Aziz Tassal, with his young daughter and infant son, standing before the giant tail of an American C-130. Bilal Sarwari, perhaps the Afghan voice on his generation's conflict best known to international radio listeners, was among the crowd waiting for an evacuation flight. Ghulam Reza Mohammadi, a UNESCO field worker who had given me a tour of the remains of the Buddhas of Bamiyan that July, was also there with his family.

What made watching them leave even harder to accept was that they were the lucky ones. Outside the airport were tens of thousands more without the requisite connections to get them in, many of whom had just as much reason to fear the future. Selfishly, the outflow of friends and colleagues also meant there was now a dearth of local journalists and translators to work alongside, and raised the question of whether working with those remaining would put them at greater risk.

Before the evacuation came to a close on 31 August, like most of Kabul's resident foreign journalists, for me the sleepless days were divided between documenting the disaster unfolding around the airport and trying to get Afghan friends, colleagues and others inside its walls. On 25 August, as described earlier, I needed help finding my way through the backstreets of Yakatoot to Abbey Gate, where Australian diplomats had told me that Australian special forces would be waiting to receive an Afghan journalist who had been issued an Australian visa. Anthony Loyd, a British journalist who was also in Kabul, had introduced me to Elias Baheer, a 27-year-old university lecturer from Kunar province who had helped him get to Abbey Gate, the night before for reporting purposes. Baheer endured the night battling the crowd, hose-wielding Talibs, and the threat of a suicide bomber that eventually saw us leave Abbey Gate, without complaint. He was as disappointed to have failed as the journalist and I were. He offered to help us try another time, but the Australians left Abbey Gate that night, never to return—they flew out with the remaining Australian military and diplomatic personnel the following day. The journalist was unable to leave Afghanistan before his visa expired after three months. The Australian Government never renewed it and, at the time of writing, he remains in hiding.

Baheer was trying to leave, too. His wife, who was pregnant, and his children were already living in the United States. The American University of Afghanistan where he worked had closed, and he feared the affiliation would attract the Taliban's ire once they had combed through the university's records. He applied for a Pakistani visa through an agent who charged six times the usual price. The visa was issued, but Baheer would need a US visa before he could be reunited with his wife and children. While he planned an escape, Baheer accompanied me on more than 50 interviews as a translator for specific aspects of this book, wearing sunglasses and a headscarf while on the back of my motorcycle to avoid being recognised if, as he feared—and as I initially doubted—the Taliban were looking for him. Surely the Taliban, I reasoned, had bigger fish to fry than a university lecturer.

After the night Baheer and I spent at Abbey Gate, the fallout from the ISKP suicide bombing that occurred there the following night would consume much of the time he and I spent together.

Three days later, at the opposite end of the airport, an American drone pilot launched a Hellfire missile at a Corolla station wagon moments after it pulled into a residential driveway. The bombing at the airport had put the US military on high alert for a second attack. Several drones had been surveilling the white Corolla for hours that day, and it was suspected that its driver was an ISKP fighter and his vehicle was carrying a bomb.

'U.S. military forces conducted a self-defense unmanned over-the-horizon airstrike today on a vehicle in Kabul, eliminating an imminent ISIS-K threat to Hamad [sic] Karzai International Airport,' said a US military spokesman in a statement that day. 'We are confident we successfully hit the target. Significant secondary explosions from the vehicle indicated the presence of a substantial amount of explosive material.'[1]

The driver, Zamarai Ahmadi, a father and long-time electrical engineer for a US-based aid organisation, was killed instantly along with nine others from his extended family, including seven children, some of whom had clambered inside the car to welcome Ahmadi when he arrived home.[2] Had the strike occurred in a less accessible location, like countless others in remote areas in Afghanistan— not to mention Yemen, Pakistan, Somalia and beyond—the true identity of the victims may never have been known.

A US military investigation concluded that the errant strike amounted to a 'tragic mistake'.[3]

In the months after the blast at Abbey Gate, allegations began to emerge against the American Marines and British soldiers who had survived the blast and tried to bring the area under control. A number of casualties from the blast were, according to staff from both Wazir Akbar Khan Hospital and Emergency Hospital, victims of gunshot wounds. Several international media outlets have since reported on the allegations and concluded the Marines, who they claim fired at survivors of the blast in and around the canal, were likely responsible for many of the deaths.[4] Based on the interviews Baheer and I conducted, however, and on other information that has since come to light, I wasn't prepared to reach a definitive conclusion, and for that reason I made only a minor reference to it in this book. I refer to it in more detail here because it warrants an explanation.

Of the 62 patients Emergency admitted, 10 were registered as having suffered gunshot wounds. I personally saw one body at Wazir Akbar Khan Hospital on 27 August with a single small head wound which the man's family believed was the result of a bullet. I saw another man in the hospital's ICU ward who later succumbed to a similar head wound, which his sister, who had survived the attack, also said was caused by a bullet. Staff from neither of the two hospitals, however, retrieved bullets from patients said to have been killed or injured by gunshot wounds, nor did they possess X-rays that depicted them.

Military investigators in the US—with whose findings I've rarely been satisfied, and who didn't interview a single Afghan in this case—stated that wounds caused by the 5-millimetre ball bearings packed around the explosive device—photographs of which, purportedly removed from dead and wounded servicemen and women, they provided to the media—killed all 13 US service members and could have been mistaken for gunshot wounds in other victims.

We spoke with five other survivors and witnesses of the blast who said they hadn't seen any gunmen other than the foreign forces on the airport side of the canal and along the wall behind. They claimed the foreign forces had opened fire on civilians in the aftermath of the blast, but their accounts didn't corroborate one another, varied dramatically, and were often inconsistent or changed over time. Some said the firing began immediately after the blast, as the troops tried to stop a rush on the gate, while others claimed it was two or three minutes after. One witness said the foreigners started firing only after most of the walking wounded had moved away from the blast site.

Regardless of the physical cause of death, the dead and wounded from the 26 August bombing at Abbey Gate, including Najma, Wasiq and Shahid, all died running from a future under the Taliban.

I had already met Nadia when the bomb was detonated at Abbey Gate, but I wouldn't ask whether she would consider contributing her story to this book for another six weeks. By then I'd conducted close to 100 interviews and could see that the book was taking a vastly different form to the one I'd expected to write just a couple of months earlier—and necessarily so. The overnight turmoil gripping those in Kabul who had once built lives and hopes out from under the shadow of the previous Taliban regime, made the themes I'd followed in Afghanistan over the preceding six years all of a sudden seem less urgent.

Nadia lived in a safe house and began helping Penelope with the growing case load of women and families with specific and verified fears of the Taliban. The work wasn't without risks, but Nadia is impetuous, detests the idea of putting her life on hold while she waited for a way out, and loves to help others. While being driven in a taxi with a male colleague also working with Penelope one day, Nadia was stopped by Taliban fighters—now police—manning a roadblock. The fighters disapproved of Nadia being in a car with a man who was neither a relative nor her husband. The two were taken into a police station, questioned and released after an hour. She now carries a razor blade in her bag. 'The next time that I am captured by the Taliban,' she wrote to me, 'I can defend myself, kill myself.'

The day after Nadia fled her home in September 2022, Amin, her father, told the Taliban fighter to whom he had promised his daughter that he had changed his mind about the marriage. The next day, a group of armed men arrived at the Aminis' house, tied and blindfolded Amin and took him away. He was held with other prisoners in a darkened room and fed only bread and water. Nadia was unaware. Those who knew kept her in the dark, fearing she would turn herself in to secure her father's release. When she asked her mother about him, Shukria changed the subject. Nadia believed he was avoiding her out of shame.

Nadia kept a diary, wrote poems and thought about her family constantly. Of the days before her escape she wrote:

Tears welled up in my eyes many nights.
Every night I ask a question of God.
When? And how will all the difficulties and hardships end.
The night that I could not sleep and was moaning under the
  duvet.
But there was no sympathy and there was no one to hear my cries.
I was hiding the sound of my cries under the pillow and
  waiting for the end of my problems to come.
And at the same time thinking of putting a deadline to my life
  and story.

But amid her dark days, Nadia has glimpses of hope as well. She has adopted a cat, which she has named Noor Pour, and threw herself a faux graduation party for the degree in Islamic Studies at Abu Hanifa she will never finish.

Four months after his capture, in January 2022, a rival group— who Amin believed were also Taliban—broke into the building where he was being held to release some of his fellow captives. Amin, bearing scars and bruises from beatings, was freed as well.

In early April 2022, under Penelope's watch, Nadia faced her father for the first time since she fled home. When she saw him, she offered forgiveness. 'The Taliban made hate inside each member of our family,' she told him. 'You weren't thinking when you made your decision.'

The reunion was also a goodbye. The next day, 6 April, after months of efforts initiated by Penelope to secure her safe passage out of Afghanistan, Nadia boarded a flight out of Kabul.

Captain Arman Malik lives in fear. As he was doing throughout our numerous interview sessions in Kabul, he continues to move from house to house to evade capture. Like many veterans of the former armed forces, Malik has grown his beard and taken to wearing traditional Afghan dress. His extended family have been visited by Taliban fighters who demand they hand him over. Although not even they know where Malik is, they tell the fighters they haven't spoken to him in years.

Malik sends me videos of former commandos and special forces soldiers being arrested and thrown into car boots, being beaten and humiliated in captivity and having their throats cut. He feels abandoned by his KKA superiors who got out before 31 August, and by the Americans with whom he fought for nearly a decade. Lieutenant-general Haibatullah Alizai and major Behzad Behnam maintain efforts are being made to exfiltrate soldiers like captain Malik, but when the doors to a life outside Afghanistan swung shut after the two-week-long asylum aberration at the end of August, the chances of evacuation for anyone other than dual nationals or existing visa holders dropped to almost zero.

Further frustration came with the news that a reported 20 000 members of the Zero Units—with whom Malik and the ARU, along with American Delta Force soldiers, were initially supposed to collaborate in securing Kabul during the evacuation—and their families have been, or are in the process of being, resettled in the United States or elsewhere outside Afghanistan.[5] Among them are almost certainly those responsible for the summary executions of prison escapees described in this book, not to mention those involved in the campaign of vicious night raids in Maidan Wardak in 2019.

Hamed Safi and his family first landed in Doha, Qatar, where they spent two nights before boarding a chartered commercial flight to Dulles Airport in Washington, DC. They were then driven by bus to a camp complex in nearby Virginia. When Hamed and his family alighted the bus, the camp staff, mostly Afghan Americans, were standing and applauding. 'Welcome, welcome,' they said in Dari.

'Believe me Andrew,' says Hamed, 'when I saw them I became so emotional. Tears came, but I controlled myself. I said to myself, "Look at the humanity here."'

Hamed and the other new arrivals were offered food and drink, and clean clothes from a great pile of second-hand garments. 'I saw my wife taking clothes for my kids,' he says. 'I remember when I myself was buying the best clothes for my kids. Now my wife was collecting them from a pile of donations. I'll never forget it.'

Next, the family were flown to Fort Bliss, an army base in New Mexico, where they shared a dormitory room with another family while their applications for asylum were fast-tracked. Hamed's sister Samira adopted her nephew Massoud and, on their youngest son Yasin's third birthday, after 47 days inside Fort Bliss, the Safis were flown to Sacramento, California, where they were collected from the airport by Hamed and Samira's brother and driven to their new home. A month later, on 9 October, Zarifa gave birth to a baby boy, Younis. Heela, their daughter, is at school in a class with four other Afghan students.

Hamed's aunt Shahla, who was a surrogate to Hamed and his brother Mahmoud after their mother emigrated to the US, hasn't spoken to him or his mother—her sister—since they left Kabul. 'She thinks I should have called them and told them to come to the airport,' he says. 'But I didn't even know whether my family or I would be allowed in. All I knew was that I wouldn't leave my family.'

On 1 November, a couple of days before I left Kabul, Baheer left his apartment in Shahr-e Naw and was looking at his phone while walking to a nearby grocery store. When he felt a hard slap across his cheek, he thought it must have been a friend, but when he turned around he saw two men he'd never seen before. As one tied his hands behind his back with a scarf, Baheer protested: 'Wait. Who are you looking for?'

'Elias,' one of the men said. 'We know everything about you.'

They were Talibs. When a police pick-up pulled up, the two men wrestled Baheer inside, clubbing him with the stock of a Kalashnikov when he resisted. They drove him to a nearby compound and threw him inside a shipping container. 'We've been searching for you,' they said. 'You've been hiding from us.'

Baheer ended up on his hands and knees. 'They were kicking me like a football,' he says. When the Talibs accused him of being a spy, Baheer told them he was a lecturer at the American University and that he also worked at another private education centre. But his interrogators knew that already. They named his boss and accused him of being a spy as well.

They emptied his pockets and took his identity cards and several hundred US dollars I'd given him the day before for his work. 'You can't hide from us anymore,' one of the Talibs said as they ushered Baheer from the compound. 'And soon you'll be sent to the afterlife.'

Baheer spent the next three nights recovering at a friend's house. Before I flew out on 3 November, we drove to a travel agent and purchased a ticket for Baheer to Islamabad, for 10 times the pre-Taliban takeover price. He left Kabul four days later with a single carry-on suitcase. After three and a half months spent hiding in a cheap Islamabad hotel with an expired Pakistani visa, in February 2022, the US Embassy granted his visa. On arriving at John F. Kennedy International Airport in New York, he collected his suitcase and left to see his wife for the first time since before the Taliban returned to power, and his newborn son for the first time.

Notes

Prologue

1 Asma Saayin, 'Afghan passports up for grabs in black market', *Pajhwok Afghan News*, 17 September 2021.

1 Antenna Post, Chak District, Maidan Wardak Province

1 Joshua Young, 'Last Marines exit Sangin, Afghanistan', *Defence Visual Information Distribution Service*, 5 June 2014.

2 Andrew Quilty, 'Static war: Helmand after the US Marines' return', *Afghanistan Analysts Network*, 23 April 2020.

3 JP Lawrence, 'US forces leave Kandahar Airfield as drawdown continues in Afghanistan', *Stars and Stripes*, 13 May 2021.

4 RFE/RL's Radio Azadi, 'District in Afghanistan's Maidan Wardak Province falls to Taliban', *Gandhara*, 21 May 2021.

5 International Crisis Group, 'Taliban propaganda: Winning the war of words?', *Asia Report No. 158*, 24 July 2008.

6 Andrew Quilty, 'When the raids came', *Harper's Magazine*, September 2021.

7 Ed Darack, 'The final flight of Extortion 17', *Smithsonian Magazine*, March 2015.

8 Kate Clark, 'The trouble with torture: NDS, Special Forces and the CIA', *Afghanistan Analysts Network*, 29 March 2012.

9 Ibid.

10 'Remarks by President Trump on the strategy in Afghanistan and South Asia', *trumpwhitehouse.archives.gov*, 21 August 2017.

11 Andrew Quilty, 'The CIA's Afghan death squads', *The Intercept*, 18 December 2020.

12 Thomas Gibbons-Neff, Eric Schmitt and Adam Goldman, 'A newly assertive CIA expands its Taliban hunt in Afghanistan', *The New York Times*, 20 October 2017.

13 Quilty, 'The CIA's Afghan death squads'.

14 Quilty, 'When the raids came'.

15 US Department of State, 'Agreement for bringing peace to Afghanistan', 29 February 2020.

16   Gulabudin Ghubar, 'Mohib says ANDSF will "break Taliban's backbone in four months"', 10 June 2019.

17   Lyse Doucet, twitter.com/bbclysedoucet/status/1319654623473504256.

2   Presidential Palace, Kabul

1   Bill Roggio, 'Mapping Taliban control in Afghanistan', *FDD's Long War Journal*, 2021.

2   Yaroslav Trofimov and Margherita Stancati, 'Taliban covert operatives seized Kabul, other Afghan cities from within', *The Wall Street Journal*, 28 November 2021.

3   'Afghanistan: Dawa Khan Menapal assassinated in Kabul', *BBC News*, 6 August 2021.

4   'Taliban kill Afghan radio station manager, kidnap journalist—officials', *Reuters*, 9 August 2021.

5   The White House, 'Remarks by President Biden on Afghanistan', 16 August 2021.

6   Joydeep Bose, 'Why did Biden choose August 31 as deadline for US withdrawal? Here's a timeline', *Hindustan Times*, 30 March 2022.

7   The White House, 'Remarks by President Biden on the way forward in Afghanistan', 14 April 2021.

8   Susanne Koelbl, interview with Afghanistan President Ashraf Ghani, 'I know I am only one bullet away from death', *Spiegel International*, 14 May 2021.

9   The White House, 'Remarks by President Biden on the drawdown of US Forces in Afghanistan', 8 July 2021.

10   Steve Coll and Adam Entous, 'The secret history of the US diplomatic failure in Afghanistan', 10 December 2021.

11   Syed Salahuddin, 'UAE builds $190m township in Kabul', *Arab News*, 24 April 2018.

12   Amrullah Saleh, twitter.com/AmrullahSaleh2/status/1426150020349 374468?s=20. The ANSF was also referred to as the Afghan National Defense and Security Forces, or ANDSF.

13   Mohamed Madi, Ahmad Khalid and Sayed Abdullah Nizami, 'Chaos and confusion: The frenzied final hours of the Afghan government', *BBC News*, 8 September 2021; Yaroslav Trofimov, Vivian Salama and Dion Nissenbaum, '"The Taliban are here": The final days before Kabul's collapse', *The Wall Street Journal*, 20 August 2021.

14   US Department of State, 'US Refugee Admissions Program Priority 2 Designation for Afghan nationals', 2 August 2021.

3 Shah Shahid, Kabul – I

1 Shadi Khan Saif, 'Taliban urged to respect teachings of Imam Hanifa', *Anadolu Agency*, 20 June 2019.

2 Zahra Rahimi, 'Govt plans to bring madrassas under state control', *Tolo News*, 8 January 2021.

3 James Meek, 'Scorched earth legacy of vanished regime', *The Guardian*, 17 November 2001.

4 Ahmad Shakib and Rod Nordland, 'Waves of suicide attacks shake Kabul on its deadliest day of 2015', *The New York Times*, 7 August 2015.

5 David Tarrant, 'Extortion 17: What really happened on America's deadliest day in Afghanistan', *Task & Purpose*, 3 August 2021.

6 Humanitarian Response, 'Kapisa Province—Reference map', United Nations Office for the Coordination of Humanitarian Affairs, 9 February 2014, https://www.humanitarianresponse.info/en/operations/afghanistan/infographic/afg-kapisa-province-reference-map.

7 United Nations International Organization for Migration, 'Irregular migrant, refugee arrivals in Europe top one million in 2015: IOM', *International Organization for Migration*, 22 December 2015.

8 'Number of refugees to Europe surges to record 1.3 million in 2015', *Pew Research Centre*, 2 August 2016.

9 Ibid.

10 Rights in Exile Programme, 'Family reunification: Refugees United International Family Reunification', Refugee Legal Aid Information for Lawyers Representing Refugees Globally, https://www.refugeelegalaidinformation.org/family-reunification.

11 Afghanistan Energy Survey—location profiles, 'Karte Naw: Kabul District, Kabul Province'.

12 Thomas Gibbons-Neff and Yaqoob Akbary, 'In Afghanistan, "who has the guns gets the land"', *The New York Times*, 3 December 2021.

13 Laiq Zirack, 'Afghanistan's higher education system has a stark geographic divide', *The Diplomat*, 24 July 2020.

4 Emirate City, Kabul – I

1 The White House, 'Remarks by President Biden on the drawdown of US Forces in Afghanistan', 8 July 2021.

2 Robbie Gramer and Jack Detsch, 'Evacuating Afghanistan was "like pulling teeth"', *Foreign Policy*, 10 February 2022.

3 Vivian Salama, 'Internal State Department cable warned of Kabul collapse', *The Wall Street Journal*, 19 August 2021.

4 George Packer, 'The betrayal', *The Atlantic*, 31 January 2022.

5 Presidential handout, 'Afghan president holds security call before reports of leaving country, say reports—video', *The Guardian*, 16 August 2021.

6 Zabihullah, twitter.com/zabehulah_m33/status/14268153757070991 36?lang=en.

7 The US State Department did not respond to my requests to speak with West for this book.

8 'Ashraf Ghani: Ex-Afghan president describes moment he fled the Taliban', *BBC News*, 30 December 2021.

9 Emma Graham-Harrison, 'Ashraf Ghani blames international allies over Afghanistan's fall to Taliban', *The Guardian*, 31 December 2021.

5 Resolute Support Mission Headquarters, Wazir Akbar Khan, Kabul

1 Sulaiman, 'Afghan forces retake districts in north after Taliban "publicity victories"', *Salaam Times*, 28 June 2021.

2 The Pentagon did not respond to questions addressed to Admiral Vasely about this conversation.

8 Fort Myer, Virginia, USA

1 'Full transcript and video: Trump's speech on Afghanistan', *The New York Times*, 21 August 2017.

2 Jacob Pramuk, 'What Trump said about Afghanistan before he became president', *CNBC*, 21 August 2017.

3 Alissa J Rubin, 'Did the war in Afghanistan have to happen?', *The New York Times*, 23 August 2021.

4 Mark Oliver, 'The new Afghan administration', *The Guardian*, 6 December 2001; staff and agencies, 'Taliban surrender in Kandahar', *The Guardian*, 7 December 2001.

5 Lyse Doucet, *A Wish for Afghanistan* (podcast), episode 1, 'The envoy', *BBC News*.

6 David Kilcullen, interview with the author, 19 September 2021.

7 Ray Suarez, 'Background: Surrender terms—Would an arrangement with Omar', *PBS News Hour*, 6 December 2001.

8 eMediaMillWorks, 'Text: Pentagon briefing with Secretary Rumsfeld', *The Washington Post*, 19 November 2001.

9   Staff and agencies, 'Taliban surrender in Kandahar'.

10 Barnett Rubin, 'An open letter to the Taliban', *The New Yorker*, 27 February 2018.

11 World Peace Foundation, 'Afghanistan: Soviet invasion and civil war', *Mass Atrocity Endings*, Tufts, 7 August 2015.

12 'Afghanistan's refugees: Forty years of dispossession', *Amnesty International*, 20 June 2019.

13 Lyse Doucet, *A Wish for Afghanistan* (podcast), episode 3, 'The president', *BBC News*.

14 Elias Groll, 'The United States has outspent the Marshall Plan to rebuild Afghanistan', *FP Insider*, 30 July 2014.

15 NATO Secretary General Jens Stoltenberg, 'Closing press conference following the meetings of NATO Foreign Ministers in Riga, Latvia', *NATO*, 2 December 2021.

16 'ISAF's mission in Afghanistan (2001–2014) (archived)', *NATO*, 19 August 2021.

17 Lorne Cook and David Keyton, 'NATO chief says mission creep, corruption hurt Afghan effort', *AP News*, 2 December 2021.

18 'Mapping CIA black sites', *Amnesty International*, 5 April 2010.

19 World Bank staff, 'Rural population (% of total population)—Afghanistan', estimates based on the United Nations Population Division's World Urbanization Prospects: 2018 Revision, *The World Bank*, 2018.

20 'Afghan civilians', *Costs of War*, Watson Institute for International and Public Affairs, Brown University, April 2021.

21 Luke Harding, 'No US apology over wedding bombing', *The Guardian*, 3 July 2002.

22 Barack Obama, 'New Hampshire Primary speech', *The New York Times*, 8 January 2008.

23 Mark Landler, 'The Afghan War and the evolution of Obama', *The New York Times*, 1 January 2017.

24 Ibid.

25 David Kilcullen, interview with the author, 19 September 2021.

26 Human Rights Unit of the United Nations Assistance Mission in Afghanistan, Annual Report 2011, *Afghanistan: Protection of Civilians in Armed Conflict*, February 2012.

27 'Karzai issues "last warning" to US military on civilian deaths', *France 24*, 29 May 2011.

28 Eric Gaston, 'Karzai's civilian casualties ultimatum', *FP Insider*, 2 June 2011.
29 Associated Press in Kabul, 'Obama heralds formal end of war in Afghanistan after 13 years', *The Guardian*, 29 December 2014.
30 Jon Lee Anderson, 'The fall of Kunduz', *The New Yorker*, 6 October 2015.
31 'Number of fatalities among Western coalition soldiers involved in the execution of Operation Enduring Freedom from 2001 to 2021', *Statista*, October 2021.
32 'Remarks by President Trump on the strategy in Afghanistan and South Asia', *trumpwhitehouse.archives.gov*, 21 August 2017.
33 Ibid.
34 Ibid.

9   Deh Sabz District, Kabul

1 Matthieu Aikins, 'Inside the fall of Kabul: An on-the-ground account', *The New York Times Magazine*, 28 December 2021.

11   Shah Shahid, Kabul – III

1 Nelson asked to be identified by a pseudonym as he remains in the military and was not given permission by his command to speak.
2 According to a senior Afghan intelligence official who was among those evacuated with the French.
3 Lynsea Garrison and Stella Tan with Soraya Shockley (producers), 'The decision of my life', *The Daily* (podcast), *The New York Times*, 13 October 2021.

12   Hamid Karzai International Airport, Abbey Gate

1 'Najma Sadeqi: Goodbye media', *Afghan Insider*, 19 August 2021, https://www.youtube.com/watch?v=IHsUBe3onzM.
2 Helene Cooper, Eric Schmitt and Thomas Gibbons-Neff, 'As US troops searched Afghans, a bomber in the crowd moved in', *The New York Times*, 27 August 2021.
3 Eric Schmitt, 'US military focusing on ISIS cell behind attack at Kabul Airport', *The New York Times*, 1 January 2022.

Epilogue

1   US Central Command Public Affairs, 'US Central Command statement on defensive strike in Kabul', *US Central Command*, 29 August 2021.

2   Christoph Koettl, Evan Hill, Matthieu Aikins, et al., 'How a US drone strike killed the wrong person', *The New York Times* (video), 10 September 2021.

3   Transcript, 'General Kenneth F McKenzie Jr, Commander of US Central Command and Pentagon Press Secretary John F Kirby hold a press briefing', *US Central Command*, 17 September 2021.

4   Nick Paton Walsh, Sandi Sidhu, Julia Hollingsworth, et al., 'Testimony from US Marines casts doubt on Pentagon's account of Kabul airport attack aftermath', *CNN*, 12 February 2022; Brian J Conley, Mohammad J Alizada, Samira Nuhzat, et al., 'Suicide bomber who killed US troops and Afghans "likely" used unguarded route to Kabul Airport gate', *ProPublica*, 4 February 2022.

5   David Ignatius, 'Opinion: Inside the CIA's desperate effort to rescue its Afghan allies', *The Washington Post*, 30 September 2021.

Acknowledgements

This book is dedicated to the Afghan journalists and storytellers who escaped their country in the days following the Taliban takeover.

Although the stories in the preceding pages were mostly taken from a narrow window over summer in 2021, *August in Kabul* is the culmination of the eight years I lived in Afghanistan beginning in December 2013. There are too many people who have helped, inspired and supported my work in that time to mention here, but I hope they will recognise their contribution in these pages nonetheless.

The book wouldn't have ever come to be had it not been for its editor, Minh Bui Jones, who first suggested working on a book set in Afghanistan in late 2020 and ultimately narrowed the focus to the fall of the Afghan Government, the departure of the Americans, and the return of the Taliban as it became inevitable in July 2021. His calm, methodical approach to what was at times an overwhelming process for this first-time author was invaluable.

Those whose stories are described herein—and many whose stories are not—were more than generous with the time, thought and pain they shared.

There are several people I can't name, for their own safety and wellbeing, but whose support while reporting before, during and after the Taliban's return to Kabul, in enduring that turbulent time, and in reading early versions of this book's manuscript, cannot be overstated. Among those I can name are Victor Blue, Ravi Candadai, Mikel Drnec, Thomas Gibbons-Neff, Sune Engel-Rasmussen, Alexandra Williams, Payvand Seyedali, and the friend I refer to in the epilogue as Elias Baheer.

At home in New South Wales, Kate, John and Jenny Hodges, Mark Callanan, Wendy Dunn, Neil and Geordie Kennedy, Chris Hilton, James Alcock and Jess Good provided beautiful places to live and write. Matt and Emma Siegel both housed and fed me while I wrote through a bout of COVID-19.

Nathan Hollier from Melbourne University Publishing had faith in taking on an unpublished author.

And finally, my father, Brian Quilty, who helped spark my own late interest in books at the ripe age of 28 when he suggested I pull John Steinbeck's *The Grapes of Wrath*—coincidentally or not, a story of great injustice and flight—from the bookshelf in the room where he was dying at the time. And my mother, Anne Quilty, whose support has been emphatic and forever.

Index